ROYAL TRAVEL

ROYAL TRAVEL

Richard Garrett

BLANDFORD PRESS

Poole   Dorset

First published in the U.K. 1982 by Blandford Press,
Link House, West Street, Poole, Dorset, BH15 1LL.

Distributed in the United States by
Sterling Publishing Co., Inc.,
2 Park Avenue, New York, N.Y. 10016.

British Library Cataloguing in Publication Data

Garrett, Richard
  Royal travel.
  1. Visits of state—History
  2. Great Britain—Kings and rulers
  I. Title
  910'.8   G242

ISBN 0 7137 1182 5

Phototypeset by Oliver Burridge and Co. Ltd., Crawley, Sussex
Printed in Singapore by Toppan Printing Co. (S) Pte. Ltd.

CONTENTS

ACKNOWLEDGEMENTS

Many people helped me with the preparation of this book, and I am especially grateful to Mrs Michael Wall DCVO—recently Assistant Press Secretary to The Queen, to officers of HM Yacht *Britannia*, to officials of the National Railway Museum, to the Queen's Flight, the Air Historical Branch of the Ministry of Defence, British Railways Board, the National Motor Museum, and to the librarians of the London Library and the National Maritime Museum's library.

Some of the books I consulted are listed in the select bibliography. I also studied a number of newspapers and magazines—in particular *The Times*, *Illustrated London News* and *Flight International*.

In instances where I have quoted extracts from the diaries and correspondence of previous kings and queens, I am grateful for the gracious permission of Her Majesty The Queen to republish the passages concerned. They were originally made public in *Victoria R.I.* by Elizabeth Longford, *Edward VII* by Philip Magnus, *King George V* by Harold Nicolson and *King George VI* by John Wheeler-Bennett.

Finally, I am grateful to my cousin, Lieutenant Colonel P C Garrett, who assisted me with some of the research; to Roy Gasson of my publishers who made the whole thing possible; to Jonathan Grimwood who edited the text with such skill and understanding; to my wife for checking the manuscript, to Susan Reid who typed it, and to Scilla Greenfield who prepared the index.

Photographs and illustrations are supplied or are reproduced by kind permission of the following: Aviation Photographs International: 162, 163 t & b, 167 t & b, 168. BBC Hulton Picture Library: 14, 16, 17, 28, 29, 31, 33, 34, 36, 37, 40, 41 t & b, 66 t & b, 67, 69, 71, 77 t & b, 104, 204, 205 t, 207 t & b, 216, 220. Fox Photos: 87 t/bl/br, 111 b, 138, 142, 147 b. Halcyon Photographic Library: 139, 175 b, 179. London Transport Executive: 106, 113, 175 t. Mary Evans Picture Library: 8 t & c, 19 tr & b, 46, 47, 50, 51, 53, 62, 123, 147 t, 192 t & c, 195, 196 r. National Motor Museum: 117, 118, 120, 124, 130. Popperfoto: 8 b, 9 l & r, 13, 19 tl, 55, 56, 70, 81, 83 t & b, 91 t & b, 95, 96, 102, 105, 109, 111 t, 116, 136 b, 151 tl/tr/b, 157, 159 t & b, 169, 173, 177 t & b, 181, 186, 196 l, 199, 202, 205 b, 208, 211, 212 t & b, 214 tl/tr/b, 215, 217, 219 l & r, 223, 227 tl/tr/b, 229, 231, 234. Rex Features: 134.

INTRODUCTION

When Prince Albert died, in 1861, Queen Victoria withdrew from public life. Her subjects agreed that a period of mourning was appropriate, provided it did not last for too long: but the Queen, unable to come to terms with her bereavement, remained in seclusion. Although she was only 42, she wrote that, 'My *life* as a *happy* one is ended', and unfortunately it seemed that her life as a public figure had also reached its conclusion. It was not until 1866, five years after Albert's death, that she could summon up the resolution to make again the brief journey from Buckingham Palace to Westminster for the state opening of Parliament.

This was not good enough for the public. In March 1864, when she was still immersed in her grief at Windsor, some wag put up a poster outside Buckingham Palace. It read: 'These commanding premises to be let or sold in consequence of the late occupant's declining business.'

The Queen, obviously aware of the growing discontent, took the unprecedented step of writing an anonymous letter to *The Times*. It was at once a protest that she was performing her duties and a plea for understanding. She promised that, 'The Queen will do what she can—in the manner least trying to her health, strength and spirits—to meet the loyal wishes of her subjects, to afford the support and countenance to society, and to give the encouragement to trade which is desired of her. More the Queen cannot do; and more the kindness and good feeling of her people will surely not exact from her.'

Her subjects were not so sure. Grief can reach a point when it becomes indulgent, and to many people the Queen's had long passed this point. If she were to win back the affection of the public, she must be seen —and frequently. *Be seen* is a rule sovereigns neglect to their peril.

Normally, to be seen involves some sort of journey, no matter how short. There are rare occasions when an appearance on a palace balcony will suffice. But these are exceptions that can only be justified by something very special, such as the end of a war, a coronation, a royal wedding

On 22 August, 1885, the Prince of Wales (later Edward VII) sailed from Aberdeen in the steam yacht Osborne for a nine-week holiday in Europe. Before setting off overland across the Continent, he spent several days cruising in the Norwegian fjords with a party of friends. He came ashore at Frognersaeter near Christiana. (Top left and right.)

Returning from India in 1876, the Prince of Wales broke his journey at Cairo, where the Khedive loaned him his palace. He attended a concert featuring the works of Offenbach at the newly built opera house; shot innumerable quail; and went to see the pyramids. (Centre.)

When, in 1922, another Prince of Wales (later Edward VIII; later still, Duke of Windsor) landed at Hong Kong, he was transported through the streets by Chinese coolies. (Bottom.)

or birth, or a silver jubilee. At other times, the monarch must go to the people, and this necessitates travel.

In this book I have outlined the history of royal travel from its early days to the present. Queen Elizabeth II has made more such journeys than any of her predecessors; not least because the ratio of time to space has been greatly affected by the development of air travel. Consequently, she has been able to journey to the uttermost ends of the Commonwealth without being cut off from affairs of state at home. Such ventures would have been impossible in the past—even to her father, King George VI. The King admittedly made two fairly long-distance flights in an aeroplane during World War 2, but these were occasioned by the hazards of war. When he made his last overseas visit (to South Africa in the winter of 1946-1947), he travelled with his family in a battleship.

The turning point was—significantly, some might say—in 1952, when the present Queen (then Princess Elizabeth) and her husband departed on a tour that should have taken them to East Africa and Australasia. Instead of embarking in a ship, they boarded an aircraft at London airport. It was while they were in Kenya that the King died, and the new era of royal air travel began.

Another, though less pertinent, explanation of the Queen's considerable tally of journeys at home and abroad is the length of her reign. At the time of writing, she has occupied the throne of Great Britain and those of several Commonwealth countries for 29 years. During the past 250 years, only two other sovereigns (George III and Queen Victoria) have reigned for longer.

In Japan, HRH decided to demonstrate that he could haul a rickshaw. He set off at a brisk pace with Admiral Halsey on board. Then something went wrong and one of the wheels buckled. (Top left.)

The Duke of Edinburgh took up competitive driving after trouble from a wrist injury compelled him to give up polo. On this occasion, at the Windsor horse trials, he negotiated the obstacle course in torrential rain. (Top right.)

The transportation, arrangements and occurrences of royal travel are all interesting to the layman, who makes his trips with less ado and, come to that, in less comfort. But there is another aspect of these journeys that is more intriguing and more important. They demonstrate the style of the sovereign and the sovereign's attitude to the job and to the people. As such, they reveal as much as anyone outside royal circles can hope to learn about the person who occupies the throne.

For many centuries the attitude of the sovereign to the people was rapacious. In more recent times it became very much more kindly, and yet still aloof. It was Edward VIII, when Prince of Wales, who introduced a vastly more informal approach and tried to dispense with many of the conventions (such as horse-drawn carriages) that had been previously considered indispensable to such occasions. He preferred to be in amongst his people; shaking them by the hand.

King George VI—that shy and, in some opinions, saintly, monarch— was more reserved, though Queen Elizabeth (now the Queen Mother) took the new style of monarchy several stages further by mingling and talking with the people. This obviously influenced her daughter, who has always been impatient of attempts to keep her subjects at too great a distance.

It might seem that the logical development of all this would be a completely informal style of monarchy. However, having worked on this book, it seems to me extremely unlikely that this will ever happen. The Queen is prepared to meet her people halfway, but there is an invisible barrier beyond which she will not go. Her private and her public life are two very different matters, and she has a kind of genius for keeping them apart. As Harold MacMillan once remarked: 'She means to be a Queen and not a puppet'. Her's is the face of majesty; despite her sometimes informal approach, this should never be forgotten.

Nor, one suspects, would the public welcome it any other way. There can be no glamour without an element of mystery; a sovereign who was accessible might easily become ordinary, and that would never do. Although the question 'Is she the same at home?' may be fascinating; a complete answer (and there have been many attempts to supply it, but nothing definitive) could be disappointing.

Many people have helped me with this book, even, in some instances, to the extent of checking the various chapters for accuracy. A list of their names appears at the beginning. However, I can only confess that, if there are any mistakes, they are nobody's fault but mine.

Richard Garrett
Tunbridge Wells, 1982

1
LIVERY AND LODGINGS

On 29 July, 1981, Britain burst into a blaze of pageantry, further ornamented the previous night by a stupendous firework display, said to be the most magnificent since the late eighteenth century. The occasion was the marriage of the heir to the throne to Lady Diana Spencer. As most newspapers informed their readers, the popularity of the Royal Family had never been greater.

No doubt this was true, and, equally certainly, the occasion—coincidence though it may have been—could hardly have been better timed. For a few blessed days, the public mind was diverted from such matters as unemployment, urban violence, the chronically sick state of the economy, and the no less chronic anxiety about the ability of governments to control their use of nuclear weapons. For once anxiety was balanced by promise, fear by joy.

The aftermath of a marriage ceremony is a honeymoon. The Prince and the girl who was now the Princess of Wales, spent theirs in the Mediterranean, cruising in the royal yacht *Britannia*. The yacht would have been on passage through those waters in any case, as she was on her way to Australia—to await the Queen, who was due to attend a September meeting with the heads of Commonwealth countries.

Every newshawk in the free world (plus many a said world's citizen) was eager to glimpse and to photograph the royal lovers—who, nevertheless managed to elude the waiting lenses. The vanishing act of *Britannia*, which began after she had left Gibraltar and lasted until she reappeared at Port Said, was not really such a difficult feat of evasion. The Mediterranean, after all, is a relatively large sea in which the royal yacht (to quote a Buckingham Palace spokesman) would 'seldom have been more than a speck on the horizon—if that. One has only to think of the difficulties experienced by the RAF when, with every facility and in a relatively small area, they are looking for a ship in distress.' Moreover, there are something like two thousand Greek islands, many with beaches that are accessible only by sea.

It would have been a dubious achievement to have found the royal honeymooners. For them to avoid detection required less skill.

The aircraft in which the royal couple set off from Eastleigh airport, near Southampton, to Gibraltar, where their cruise was to begin, was an Andover of the Queen's Flight. This aircraft is the military version of the HS748, a turbo-prop aeroplane of by no means recent vintage. Anyone given to anxiety may well have been alarmed when, not long before the honeymoon, a commercial HS748, which had been relegated to the transport of freight, crashed on its approach to East Midlands Airport. The cause of the disaster was a rear cargo door that had become detached. It lodged on the port tailplane for long enough to throw the aircraft out of control. Seconds afterwards, the wings were torn off.

At the time, the cause of the crash was unknown—though people were vaguely reassured by the announcement that, due to the exceptionally high standards of maintenance, no such accident was likely to occur to an HS748 of the Queen's Flight. (Similarly when, in August of that year, a Wessex helicopter plummeted from the sky, killing all thirteen passengers on board, we were informed that there were no plans to ground the Flight's two Wessex machines. It must have been a bold decision: the journey that had such tragic consequences was from a gas rig in the North Sea to Bacton in Norfolk. The route had been flown on occasions too numerous to count, the weather was fine, the sea unusually placid. The reason had to be a mechanical fault of awesome proportions).

The only one to benefit from the use of an Andover on the outward stage of the honeymoon was the Prince—who enjoys flying these aeroplanes. Certainly, his immaculate landing at Gibraltar won applause. The Andover's journey from Eastleigh took seven hours, which included a refuelling stop in Portugal. One could not have blamed the Princess, had she reflected that, by travelling on an ordinary scheduled commercial flight, the trip would have been non-stop and would have lasted a mere three hours. Furthermore, had there been any great turbulence along the route, the commercial jet would have flown over it, whilst the Andover, with a cruising altitude of 15,000 feet (4,580m), would have been compelled to go through it.

But royal travel is not affected only by the aeroplanes, ships and other methods available for getting from A to B. Other factors count and people are by no means the least of the matters that must be taken into consideration. On a visit to the USA, a month or two before the royal wedding, both the Prince of Wales and his aunt, Princess Margaret, were greeted less than enthusiastically by American IRA supporters. Indeed, the behaviour of the mob was such that members of the royal family were advised to stay away from a land with which, we are continually told by various politicians, Britain has a special relationship.

The King of Spain's absence from the Prince of Wales's wedding was a deliberate political gesture, enforced upon him by a combination of British and Spanish diplomatic ineptitude: he is known to be on friendly terms with the British royal family. However, when in the autumn of 1980, the Queen visited Morocco, the behaviour of her host, King Hassan II, was not beyond reproach—though we were assured that no disrespect was intended. Even so, and whatever was going on in the mind of the Moroccan ruler, its results seemed to be strangely discourteous.

He was apt to keep his guests waiting and to make sudden changes of plan that threw the programme into confusion. Writing in the *Daily Telegraph*, Ann Morrow remarked that, 'The Queen's unflappability was being severely tested', and that her 'patience wore a little thin.' Nevertheless, a Buckingham Palace spokesman was quick to protest that, in fact, Her Majesty and Prince Philip were 'perfectly content' with their treatment. The Palace, as ever, was being tactful.

The excuse given for King Hassan's conduct was fear of assassination

When the present Queen visited Morocco in 1980 as the guest of King Hassan (seen waving at the crowds), her royal patience was put to a severe test by her host's erratic conduct: Hassan's fear of assassination was said to be the reason.

—a condition that, if reports are to be believed, amounts almost to paranoia. Whether the Queen took this into account is not recorded. It certainly seems doubtful that previous sovereigns would have been content with such unpredictable comings and goings, and they would probably have been surprised by their descendant's royal patience—thin though it may occasionally have worn.

Such ideas as royal expedience, diplomacy and sensitivity to the prevailing winds of opinion were things of no account. When sovereigns toured their realms or, occasionally, the realms of other sovereigns they were demanding to a fault. Despite the fact that a visit from the ambulant court was the occasion for a fair and merrymaking on a considerable scale, the memory that lingered afterwards was of a hangover.

Since most royal travel was confined to places within the realm, there was—with a few exceptions, such as Henry VIII's Field of the Cloth of Gold—no question of making a good impression on foreigners. The journeys were, perhaps, more in the nature of a landowner inspecting his estate, trying, occasionally, to right a wrong and always alert to any devilment that might be afoot. Each monarch had his likes and dislikes, and—more often that not—his eccentricities.

William Rufus, son of William the Conqueror, saw nothing strange in the fact that his male entourage, released from the restraints of the court in London, should suddenly change into female dress. This tendency

When Henry VIII set out with his fleet from Dover in 1520 to meet Francis I at the Field of the Cloth of Gold, he was determined to out-dazzle and politically out-manoeuvre the French monarch. (From the original at Hampton Court, by Volpe.)

towards transvestism misled any common country dwellers at their peril. There was nothing feminine in his courtiers' taste for rape and pillage.

Henry I insisted that, at the end of a hard day's travel, the feet of his horses be bathed with his host's wine, while his grandson, Henry II, was so continually on the move, that he inspired the historian E S Turner to refer to his household as 'the Saddle-Sore court'. Even at the end of a particularly long day's journey, his energy was such that he worked on documents of state until far into the night. Indeed, even as he rode, a scribe was compelled to keep pace with him, as he dictated.

The fact that Henry II was able to remain vigorous, while his attendants suffered the extremes of exhaustion, was probably due—in some part at any rate—to the difference in accommodation at their disposal. The Sovereign was always entertained at the finest house in the neighbourhood: his courtiers were less fortunate. The King's marshalls were supposed to find lodgings for them. Frequently, however, they would rather accept bribes from householders who did not relish the idea of these unwanted guests. On at least one occasion the knights fought among themselves—with the prospect of a roof for the night as the winner's prize.

Edward I, as a young man, did little to increase the popularity of royal tourism. Accompanied by a band of two hundred lusty supporters— many of them from his lands in Europe—he rode across England, taking whatever he pleased. On one occasion, he occupied a monastery, expelled the monks, removed all the food and flogged the servants.

On another royal journey, a young man, who unwittingly obstructed the King's progress, suffered the removal of an eye and an ear for his presumption. It is small wonder that when, some years later, Edward made a trip by river from Boston to Lincolnshire, his barge was fitted with armoured latticework to protect its occupants from stones, bricks and other missiles.

In his role as a husband, Edward I was more considerate. The women who accompanied him on his journeys were required to keep up with him on horseback, however when the Queen was pregnant, she was allowed to travel in a litter. At various stages of the journey, apples, nuts, pomegranates, and other fruits were procured to satisfy her sudden and quite unpredictable appetites for such delicacies.

Until the reign of Queen Victoria, the only example of a state visit by an English monarch to an overseas country, as opposed to a war-like visit, or a trip home to Hanover, was Henry VIII's meeting with Francis the king of France at the Field of the Cloth of Gold. Five thousand workmen—two thousand of them from England and Flanders—were

Henry's residence for this sumptuous fortnight was the castle at Guines, which was embellished until it looked like something from a fairy tale. With five thousand followers attending him, the English King's arrival was extremely impressive—which was just what Henry VIII and Wolsey intended it to be.

employed on building the setting for this tremendous spectacle. The Castle of Guines underwent alterations to suit its role as Henry's headquarters; a summer palace, such as a fairy tale might have inspired, was erected beside it. It was to be used for the main entertainments during this extravagant fortnight.

Almost exactly halfway between the Castle of Guines and Francis's base at Ardres, there was a shallow depression known as the Val d'Or, which may have prompted the name of the occasion. The edges on either side were reshaped by armies of workmen, a pavilion was erected, and lists prepared for tournaments and other royal sports. At a point precisely midway across the valley, a spear marked the place where, on their first encounter, the two kings would meet.

Under Wolsey's capable direction, the labourers, craftsmen and artists toiled away. Lengths of timber from Holland, too long to be transported aboard ship, were lashed together in rafts and floated down the coast. When Henry and his Queen (Katherine of Aragon) set off on 5 June, 1520 they were attended by five thousand followers. Wolsey's suite was scarcely less impressive.

The public was not admitted to the Field of the Cloth of Gold. With so many in the royal entourage, there would hardly have been room for any more spectators. But there was free wine to be had in Calais, and nobody was in the mood to complain.

On one evening, the two monarchs came as near as they could manage to expressing trust in each other. Francis presented himself at Guines to be entertained by Katherine; Henry repaired to Ardres, where the Queen of France presided over the banquet. But, underneath all this there was a perpetual spirit of rivalry. At some point, Henry, accompanied by seven knights, took on Francis (also attended by seven knights) in the lists. The outcome is not recorded, though Henry must have been accounted the favourite. His skill at jousting was considerable. Once, in a tournament at Greenwich, he and the Marquis of Dorset challenged all comers. In the combat, Henry broke twenty-three spears and toppled one rider—horse and all.

However, on the one occasion when it rained, Francis had his revenge. He threw Henry in a wrestling bout, which somewhat spoilt the English sovereign's enjoyment of the day's sport.

◆

It cannot have been a coincidence that Shakespeare was born during the reign of Elizabeth I. It was an age intoxicated by poetry which, during a royal progress, gushed out in torrents. Some of it was in English, some in Latin. Most of it was sycophantic to a degree not very far from nauseous. You could, it appeared, say anything—as long as you praised the Queen, and made it rhyme.

Arrangements for Elizabeth I's coronation on 15 January, 1559, were carefully worked out; even to the extent of producing a volume of diagrams showing who and what should be where.

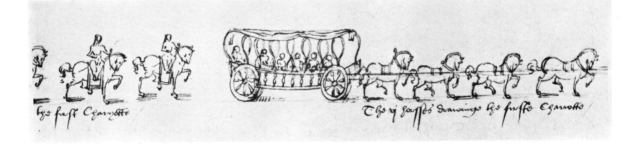

Elizabeth was never one to say, 'do not go to all this trouble on our account.' She gleefully calculated the cost to her host, reflecting that, in many cases, such extortion was his just forfeit for some minor misdeed too small to merit a spell in the Tower. In others, as she no doubt calculated with her customary shrewdness, it was payment in advance for a favour yet to be asked. Whichever the case, the price was considerable. Three days spent at Kenilworth as the guest of the Earl of Leicester set her host back £1,000 a day. Admittedly, the festivities included a musical extravaganza that would not disgrace a present day London West End stage. A six-day visit to a lesser stately house worked out at £600, and the bills for a more lavish seven-day sojourn, though not quite on the Earl of Leicester's scale, added up to £2,000.

Nevertheless, Elizabeth found no lack of prospective hosts. Each tried to out-perform the others, even in such trivial matters as dress. For instance, Sir John Harrington, who lived at Cowdrie, once remarked that, 'The Queen loved to see me in my last frize jerkin and saith, "'tis well enough cut". I will have another made like it. I do remember she spit upon Sir Matthew's [a rival host—Sir Matthew Arundel] and said "The fool's wit was gone to rags". Heaven spare me from such jibing.'

Every road the Queen's horse trod had to be swept beforehand. If she obviously enjoyed these trips, her household was less enthusiastic. On one of them, a courtier named Gilbert Talbot informed his father; 'Late yesternight this purpose altered, and now at this moment Her Majesty thinks to go no further than Grafton: however, there is no certainty, for these three or four days it [Elizabeth's mind] has changed every five minutes.'

Although the cavalcade of a royal progress by Elizabeth was long and impressive, it gave little indication of the fact that it involved participation of the military. A thousand or so troops were nearly always somewhere in the vicinity. Anyone who wished for an audience with the Queen had to satisfy the scrutiny of the Secretary of State, Sir Francis Walsingham, who was, to all intents and purposes, head of her secret police. Nevertheless, despite all the precautions, security was a problem. One particularly tricky custom was for men, decked out in green, to emerge from the woods, either to make a presentation to the Queen or else to regale her with yet another ode. The difficulty for Walsingham's men was to decide who was engaged in suitably loyal entertainment and therefore to be applauded, and who was a would be assassin.

Such a potentially dangerous decision must have been particularly difficult on one progress, when a nymph appeared out of a copse carrying a crossbow—which she gave to the Queen. However, the gift was well received, as there were about thirty deer in the vicinity. Elizabeth immediately put it to use by killing four of them. That evening, she was able to enjoy the bloody spectacle of sixteen bucks being mauled to death by greyhounds.

English royalty has always been fond of hunting. Elizabeth was no exception. A royal progress might, or might not, be a happy occasion for those who hoped to win her approval; for any wildlife unfortunate

When reporting royal tours, the Victorian press allowed its imagination considerable freedom. This artist's impression of a royal party being chased by a rogue elephant in Nepaul Terai (Nepal) was something of an overstatement. (Top left.)

Touring India in 1875, the Prince of Wales was evidence of his mother's 'dominion over palm and pine'. While in Poona, he took the opportunity of riding on an elephant for the first time. (Top right.)

Like the sovereigns before him, George V liked to hunt. At Sandringham, he shot pheasants; at Balmoral, stags; in Nepal in 1912, he turned his attention to bigger game, such as tigers. (Bottom left.)

enough to be in her vicinity, it was a disaster. On one occasion, when she happened across a hart that had misguidedly strayed in her direction, she spared the creature's life, first taking the young animal's ears, as, she smilingly remarked, 'a ransom'.

———————————◆———————————

In early January, 1603, Dr Dee, Queen Elizabeth's physician, warned her that the air of Whitehall did not seem to suit her, and that she had best remove herself to the palace at Richmond. His advice came too late. On the 14th of that month, she fell ill with a cold. By 15 March she was very ill indeed and, at 3.00 am on the 24th, she died.

A courtier named Sir Robert Carey afterwards recalled her final hours. 'The Queen grew worse and worse,' he wrote, 'because she would be so, none about her being able to go to bed. My Lord Admiral was sent for . . . what by fair means, what by force, he got her to bed. There was no hope for her recovery, because she refused all remedies.

'On Wednesday the 23rd March she grew speechless. That afternoon, by signs, she called for her Council, and by putting her hand to her head, when the King of Scots was named to succeed her, they all knew he was the man she desired should reign after her.'

Upon this somewhat slender evidence of Elizabeth's wishes, James VI of Scotland became James I of England. Her father, Henry VIII, had made it plain that he would never tolerate the idea of a Stuart sitting on the English throne and the situation was, without exaggeration, explosive. Indeed, as the historian John Nichols, writing in 1823 has pointed out; 'It still remains a doubt whether the Queen intended it for a sign or not.' In Carey's mind, however, the royal gesture was conclusive, and the news must be conveyed at once to James in his palace at Holyrood. Helped by his brother, he managed to get out of the palace of Whitehall in defiance of a ban forbidding anyone to leave the court. His sister, Lady Scrope, handed him a ring that the Scottish King had once given the English Queen; this, they agreed, would provide evidence that Elizabeth was indeed dead. He then climbed into the saddle and set off on the 400 miles between Richmond and Edinburgh.

On the first night, he rested at Doncaster—160 miles away. The second night found him in his own house at Widdrington with 300 miles behind him. As he was crossing the border early on the following morning, he was thrown and fell heavily to the ground. His horse kicked him in the head, and Carey was severely bruised and lost much blood.

Despite his injuries, the single-minded Sir Robert soldiered on. From this point, inevitably, his progress was slower. When, at last, he reached Holyrood, it was late at night and James had gone to bed.

Nevertheless, the King of Scotland, who was now also King of England, rose to greet him. To mark his appreciation of Carey's epic ride, he immediately (and, perhaps, appropriately) appointed his visitor a gentleman of the bedchamber.

Back in London the authorities proclaimed James as King on 31 March. Despite this James decided that the sooner he showed himself in his new realm the better it would be. His Queen and their children could follow later. On Tuesday, 5 April, ten days after the death of Elizabeth, James set off for London. The progress turned out to be remarkably leisurely, not least because his subjects took great pains to entertain him; in a manner befitting their new king and by whatever means would secure them the greatest advantage. Few were disappointed. As E S Turner writes in *The Court of St. James*, 'on his . . . way from Holyrood to London James hunted everything that ran and knighted everything that crawled.'

The Bishop of Holyrood had been sent in advance to Berwick-upon-Tweed to satisfy himself that the first town on the English side of the border would be suitably prepared for the royal arrival. As the King approached the gates, Berwick erupted; one observer later said that, 'a better peal of ordinance was never in any soldier's memory.' It was, this diligent reporter wrote, 'sometimes more dreadful than thunder, that all the ground thereabout trembled as if in an earthquake, the houses and towers staggering, wrapping the whole town in a mantle of smoke.'

But the smoke quickly cleared, and presently the Gentleman Porter of Berwick was presenting James with the keys of the town. For this small service, he was knighted on the spot.

Thereafter, the new King of England handed out knighthoods with an abandon that did much to cheapen their prestige. At York, for example, he dubbed 33 local worthies; whilst at Belvoir Castle in Rutland he dubbed 48. But the record was reached in the city of London when, with unparalleled industry, he, 'thrice imposed the knightly slap' 133 times. By this time, however, his memory for names was becoming less than reliable. If one report is to be believed, he began to mumble, 'Arise Sir What-You-Will'. (The Duke of Edinburgh made a similar gaffe in more recent times. When opening a new annex to Vancouver City Hall in 1969, he announced, 'I declare this thing open—whatever it is'. Since it was a wet day and the total audience amounted to about fifteen shoppers sheltering beneath their umbrellas, it did not seem to be very important. However, ever since, the annex has been known as 'the East Thing'.)

King James drew the line at conferring knighthoods on tradesmen, sometimes to their advantage. At Doncaster, he stayed at an inn named The Bear. Since the landlord could not be regarded as promising material for the nobility, he was presented with the lease of a manor house 'of good value', which was probably far more rewarding in the long run.

As if to show that he could be merciful as well as generous, James released the inmates of several prisons along the route, except those who were guilty of those three deadly sins: treason, murder or popery. This apparent amnesty cost one thief his life—which may well have taught others a harsh but salutary lesson about the dangers of depending on royal whim.

The thief had been following in James's wake ever since he crossed the border at Berwick. At Newark, he decided to enrich himself by dipping into the courtiers' purses. When he was caught, his arrest was reported to the King, who, without giving the wretched fellow the benefit of a trial, immediately ordered the town's recorder to prepare a warrant for his execution. He was hanged a few hours later, at the very moment when the inhabitants of the Newark jail were unexpectedly being given their freedom.

James I was by no means one of nature's horsemen. A servant hoisted him into the saddle and he remained there in a virtually supine position until the time came for him to dismount. But his determination to travel by this method was inflexible. As he said at York, when somebody suggested that he might be more comfortable in a carriage, 'I will have no coach, for the people are desirous to see a King, and so they shall, for they shall as well see his body as his face.'

Even after he had fallen off, during the stage between Lincoln and Cambridge, and badly bruised one of his arms, he refused to give up.

Now and then there was a diversion. When he was taking a meal by the roadside in Sherwood Forest, a party of huntsmen emerged from behind the trees—each clad in Lincoln green. Their message was clear and James needed no persuasion. Without waiting to finish his food, he joined them and proceeded to diminish the local population of wildlife.

As he crossed the Fens, one hundred giants, each twelve or fourteen foot tall, were observed striding towards him. Somebody explained, with great geographical inexactitude, that these beings lived 'on the maine of Brazil, near to the Straits of Megellen'. In fact, they were local farmers on stilts intent on catching the royal eye before presenting a petition. The King said that it would have to wait until he was established in London.

The nearer the Sovereign and his suite were to the capital, the greater the crowds became, until, 'the multitude of people in the highways, fields, meadows, closes and on trees, were such that they covered the beauty of the fields, and so greedy were they to behold the countenance of the King, that with much unruliness they injured and hurt one another, some even hazarded to the danger of death.'

Throughout the journey, which took five weeks, James was not too preoccupied to attend to business. He made arrangements for members of his Scottish entourage to receive appointments at the English court. At Newcastle, he wrote a letter containing instructions about a new coinage. At Berwick he had assured the Lord Chamberlain that, as the Queen and his two eldest children would not be long in joining him, the best of the late Queen Elizabeth's jewels and furniture should be put into safekeeping for them.

When, at last, the new King and his followers reached Whitehall, James embarked in a barge for the final stage of the journey to the Tower. As the craft approached, 230 pieces of ordnance fired a salute, producing a thunder beside which the display at Berwick must have seemed no more than a squib.

◆

As Prince of Wales and, later, as King, Charles II made two journeys abroad that are better listed as 'royal escapes', rather than as 'royal progresses'. The first occasion was in 1646 after his father's defeat at Oxford. He was in Cornwall at the time, and his flight to France, by way of the Scilly Isles and a protracted stay in Jersey, was by no means uncomfortable, and was not even particularly dangerous.

The second departure followed the Battle of Worcester in 1651, two years after the execution of Charles I. Since he had been crowned at Scone in Scotland on new year's day, Charles now considered himself the lawful monarch, albeit, for the next eight and a half years, a sovereign in exile.

During the long journey that took him from the field at Worcester to the Sussex coast, he made masterly use of his talents as a mimic (when assuming a disguise), as a strong swimmer (when negotiating rivers), and as a man with a good eye for an oak tree. The tree in question was a large, bushy pollard oak situated in the grounds of Boscobel—a former hunting lodge in the Forest of Brewood not far from the River Severn in Shropshire.

Charles chose this particular oak for the very sensible reason that there was plenty of space around it. As he told his companion, a courageous Royalist major named Carlis, it would be impossible for anyone to creep up and take them by surprise. It was just as well. Many years later, when talking to Samuel Pepys, Charles recalled, 'We see the soldiers going up and down, in the thicket of the wood, searching for prisoners escaped, we seeing them now and then peeping out of the wood.' Since there was a prize of £1,000 on the fugitive monarch's head, they might have done better to peep more closely.

At last Charles reached sanctuary of a kind in a house at Hinton Daubnay in Hampshire. A colonel who lived nearby, and who had fought with the Royalist forces, was instructed to find a ship's captain who was prepared to take the royal fugitive across the Channel to Fécamp in Normandy. Eventually Nicholas Tettersell, who owned and skippered the 34-ton coal brig *Surprise*, agreed to undertake the assignment in return for £50. The departure would be from the Sussex coast near Brighton.

His passengers were described as, 'two special friends of mine who have been engaged in a duel, and there is mischief done.'

On the journey from Hinton Daubnay to Brighton, the King and the two companions that accompanied him were nearly arrested by a cavalry unit. But the soldiers were in a hurry, and nobody thought to examine the strangers with proper thoroughness. Which was just as well; Charles was six foot two inches tall, his bearing was princely, and his features were unmistakeable. The landlord of the inn where he was introduced to Tettersell recognised him immediately, as did the master mariner, who promptly increased his fee for the journey to France.

Eventually, after some hard bargaining, the matter was settled, but now there was another difficulty: the tide was low, the *Surprise* was grounded in a creek a mile or so away, and it would be impossible to sail that night. Deciding that the cabin of a small ship tucked away in obscurity would be safer than a tavern, Charles decided to go aboard at once. Tettersell, in the meanwhile, should round up his crew.

Next morning, at seven o'clock, *Surprise* floated off the mud, and, her sails filling with a favourable wind, the little ship set course towards the Isle of Wight. She had not made her departure a moment too soon. Within an hour, a squadron of horsemen arrived at the creek, tipped off, presumably, by an informer in Brighton.

As Tettersell explained, he was due at Poole in Dorset to pick up a cargo. If he were to make a diversion to Fécamp, he would need an alibi. Quite apart from the question of his personal survival, he had to make a living under the Commonwealth regime.

Charles and his aide, John Wilmot (later the first Earl of Rochester), must approach his deck hands, posing as merchants who were on their way to collect debts in Rouen. They were to offer the sailors bribes, in return for which they should *compel* their captain to change course. When Wilmot suggested that this was more or less inciting a mutiny, Tettersell agreed. Yes, he said, that was what he had in mind.

The wind remained fair; the sea was moderately calm. Charles impressed Tettersell with his knowledge of navigation, and the crew seemed to accept the story of the debt-collecting expedition. At all events, they accepted the money and went through the charade of dictating their captain's route.

Off the French coast, there was an unpleasant moment or two, when a privateer from Ostend appeared on the horizon, and another when the wind backed to the north-east and began to blow hard. Nevertheless, Charles and Wilmot were rowed safely ashore by the mate of *Surprise*, a Quaker named Richard Carver. Then, his task completed, Tettersell headed back for England.

The change in the wind's direction suited him. He made the passage to Poole in such good time, that nobody remarked on his unpunctuality.

◆

Charles II's return to England from Holland on 25 May, 1660, was a very different matter. A ship of the line called *Naseby* after the battle was hastily, and not without tact, renamed HMS *Royal Charles*. On 23 May, she arrived to collect him. On board there were 100 lb of roast beef, a wealth of silver plate and a young man, soon to be appointed clerk of the King's ships, named Samuel Pepys.

As the royal party embarked, Dutch soldiers tapped out a carefully measured drum beat as became a sovereign. Mary, Princess of Orange wept, Charles, himself, was seen to shed a kingly tear and 50,000 enthusiastic spectators yelled their approval.

For much of the voyage, the King walked the warship's deck, accompanied by his dogs (which inconsiderately relieved themselves on deck) and by Pepys. He talked about his adventures after the Battle of Worcester and Pepys, good reporter that he was, took notes. Even when the monarch was rowed ashore at Dover in an Admiral's barge, Mr Pepys, in company with one of the dogs and a footman, followed close behind in a rather more modest craft.

As Charles stepped ashore, he knelt and murmured a prayer of thanks. The Mayor of Dover presented him with a bible, and, from the castle, the roar of guns saluted the restored sovereign. The monarchy was back.

◆

The royal journeys of the early Hanoverians had little of the spectacle or, indeed, the drama that coloured those of the Tudors or the Stuarts. Most of George I's trip to Hanover were on business, after all it was his former home. However, he adapted himself to the life of a king of England by developing a taste for English beer and by stocking the Royal Park at Windsor with game—which meant that he no longer had to return to Germany for a good day's hunting.

It was on a journey to Hanover in 1727 that the monarch died. Like most of his excursions, this one seems to have been a somewhat loosely organised affair. He crossed to Holland from Greenwich in the royal yacht; the courtiers travelling in their own craft. On the far side of the North Sea, many of them had to hire carriages.

The small procession was accompanied to the German frontier by a squadron of Dutch cavalry. As was the custom, the King's bed was sent on ahead along with the rest of the baggage. On the first evening, George dined lightly off a dish of reputedly fresh carp and not much else. When he awoke on the following morning, he complained of stomach pains; there was nothing to suggest that the fish was at fault. Indeed, the surgeon diagnosed a stroke, and recommended bleeding as treatment.

The King's condition deteriorated through the day, with periods of consciousness fading away into what seemed to be unnaturally heavy sleep. Forty-eight hours later, at Osnabrück, he died.

<hr>

At Dettingen, George II achieved the distinction of being the last British monarch to accompany his troops into battle. James Wolfe, a subaltern at the time, noticed that the King 'was in the midst of the fight', though this was probably an overstatement. In any case, the King's journey to the War of Austrian Succession was only one ingredient in a military operation attended by little ceremony and no pomp. At home, the days of the ambulant courts, those seemingly endless tours of the realm, were over. The new sovereigns were content to remain in their palaces and to allow their subjects to visit them.

Throughout the reign of George II's grandson, George III, the King never ventured north of Worcester nor west of Plymouth. He journeyed neither into Wales nor Ireland nor into Scotland; he was the first British sovereign for 240 years never to visit the Continent; and his American colonies were denied so much as a glimpse of him.

Which was a pity. As one American merchant put it, 'They say King George is a very honest fellow; I should like to smoke a pipe with him.' In his foreword to *King George III* by John Brooke, Prince Charles wrote, 'The tragedy is that the American colonies never received a visit from him—if a royal tour had been a conceivable undertaking in the 18th century the leaders of the colonies might have understood him better.'

Whoever did have occasion to entertain the King found that his taste in food was modest—even humdrum. On a visit to Whitbread's brewery in London in 1787, he stood all the time and ate only bread and butter. The Queen enjoyed herself with a plate of strawberries and a cup of tea. At home, he lived on what nowadays might pass for a healthy diet, confining himself for the most part to fruit and salads, eggs, and the inevitable bread and butter. Nor was he a heavy drinker; he never took more than four glasses of wine and usually he mixed some water with it.

Nevertheless, George had all the makings of a traveller. He was a superb horseman, enjoyed riding and resorted to his carriage only when the weather was particularly bad. In 1804, at the age of sixty-six, he rode ten miles through the New Forest in the midst of a downpour. It was, he remarked afterwards, more than the Prince of Wales could have done. His greatest accomplishment, at any rate in the world of travel, was the flair with which he handled a phaeton. He drove at such speed with his daughters on board that the young princesses were frightened.

◆

In an article that appeared in the 1943 edition of *The Saturday Book*, the late James Agate remarked that, 'I cannot remember whether, when the Editor invited me to contribute . . . I was undergoing a financial crisis or not. After all, to a man who is a chronic sufferer from sick headaches, one date is very like another.'

Edward Augustus, Duke of Kent, the third son of George III, might have uttered something very similar, for he was never out of debt. As a soldier, his shortcomings were sufficient to cause the Duke of Wellington to dismiss him contemptuously as 'the corporal', a prejudice not lessened by his seemingly insatiable appetite for reviewing troops.

Possibly not the least important event in his military career was a posting to Gibraltar. The rock, goodness knows, had little enough to offer in the way of entertainment fit for a prince, but, even in these austere circumstances, Edward Augustus managed to increase his overdraft. To relieve the boredom of his situation, he paid a visit to a fortune teller. Having gone through all her conventional patter, the fortune teller suddenly and unexpectedly announced to her surprised client that he would one day become the father of a great queen.

Since he had two elder brothers, the proposition seemed unlikely. Nevertheless, the seer's words became lodged in the Duke's mind. Nearly thirty years later, he married the widow of a German princeling who already had a daughter by her previous marriage. Hard up as always, Edward Augustus and his new wife settled in the German town of Amorsbach.

By the time the Duchess became pregnant in November, 1818, the ability of the Duke's elder brothers to produce heirs to the throne had been tested and, on the whole, found wanting. Indeed, the field seemed to be sufficiently clear of rivals to suggest that there really might be some substance to the speculation of the Gibraltar clairvoyant. To make the prophecy at all possible, however, it was necessary for the child to be born in Britain.

Four hundred miles lay between Amorsbach and London. Since the Duke had no money to pay for such a journey, he sent an urgent message to the Prince Regent. He needed, he informed his brother, a substantial sum of cash, the use of the royal yacht (spelt yatcht) for crossing the Channel, the loan of an apartment in Kensington Palace, and adequate provisions for his domestic arrangements.

Sir Benjamin Bloomfield, the Prince Regent's private secretary and privy seal, replied that this was a matter for Parliament and not for the royal household, and that the Prime Minister, Lord Liverpool, had made it plain that no money was available. It was tactfully pointed out that the Duke's sister-in-law, the Duchess of Cambridge, was also pregnant and that she was prepared to give birth in Hanover—where the arrangements seemed to be perfectly adequate. Why need the Kents come all the way to London?

The young Queen Victoria leaving Buckingham Palace on a visit to the City of London. As one contemporary writer put it, the merit of her coronation in 1838 was that 'so much has been done for the people', and the public's taste for colour and pageantry was amply satisfied.

He may not have been very gifted financially, but the Duke of Kent did not give up easily once he had been aroused. If the Prince Regent and Parliament would not help, there must be others who would. He estimated that it would cost about £1,200 to make the journey in reasonable comfort, with comparatively short stages and regular rest days to ensure that the Duchess did not become overtired.

In Lytton Strachey's entertaining biography of Queen Victoria, one is left with the impression that when, at last, the Kents made their journey to London, they accomplished it in one hired carriage with a good deal of

discomfort. In fact, the Duke was not without admirers in Britain, not
least because, in an otherwise not particularly glorious military career, he
had been the first commanding officer to abolish flogging and the first to
establish a regimental school. When it came to the crunch his supporters,
encouraged by Lord Dundas and Earl Fitzwilliam, raised considerably
more than the sum required.

What was more, in the spring of 1819, the attitude of the Prince

*When a large balloon was unleashed
in Hyde Park as part of the
celebrations to mark Queen Victoria's
Golden Jubilee, a child was heard to
exclaim, 'Look! There's Queen
Victoria going up to heaven!' Adults
who thronged the route when she
drove in an open carriage to a service
of thanksgiving at Westminster Abbey,
were able to satisfy themselves that
Her Majesty was still earthbound.*

Regent became more amenable. A letter from Bloomfield promised that *Royal George*, the royal yacht, would be moored off Calais on 18 April, and that accommodation at Kensington Palace would be put at the Duke and Duchess's disposal as 'an act of kindness'.

The procession that set off from Amorsbach in late March was by no means the austere affair that Lytton Strachey suggests. The Duke, admittedly, took the reins of the specially built phaeton in which the Duchess travelled, but this was because he liked to drive and not because he could not afford a coachman. Nor was this the only vehicle. There was a landau with the maids on board, a barouche containing a lady in waiting and an eminent German female obstetrician, a large post chaise belonging to the Duchess to provide cover in case it rained, another post chaise to carry the Duchess's daughter from her previous marriage and the girl's governess, a caravan to convey the plate, two gigs transporting a clerk, a footman and the Duke's valet, a back-up phaeton, and, finally, a curricle carrying the Duke's personal physician, a retired naval surgeon.

Stopping at inns overnight, and allowing one day's rest in every four, the cavalcade covered 25 miles a day. The royal yacht was moored off Calais as promised and, although the sea was rough and the Duchess was sick, the crossing took less than three hours.

The only snag was that, as late as 10 April, the Lord Chamberlain's office had still not received the Treasury's permission to spend the £674.20 deemed necessary for redecorating the Kensington Palace apartment. Since it had been unoccupied for a considerable time it was in a sorry state of disrepair.

At 4.15 on the morning of 24 May, after $6\frac{1}{4}$ hours in labour, the Duchess gave birth to a daughter. Queen Victoria, as the child was to become, had made her first royal progress, Amorsbach to London, albeit inside her mother's womb. Before Victoria's reign was very old, steam power would transform the nature of travel; and before it drew towards its close, other advances would have improved still more the technology of communication. On 22 June, 1897, minutes before she left Buckingham Palace in the Diamond Jubilee procession, Queen Victoria walked into the telegraph room. By pressing a button, she caused an impulse to be transmitted to the central telegraph office in St Martin's le Grand. Seconds later a message from the Queen was transmitted to every part of her Empire.

It was, perhaps, the first instant royal tour.

2
REJOICING AND MOURNING

Unlike most communications in an age that seldom used a few words when several would do, Queen Victoria's message to her Empire on that Diamond Jubilee morning in 1897 was a masterpiece of brevity. 'From my heart I thank my people', she said. 'May God bless them.' The procession to Saint Paul's Cathedral that followed the message's transmission was more elaborate, though the distance was not nearly as far.

It is, indeed, a simple truth that the most important journey any British monarch makes in a lifetime is also one of the shorter. The route

On her way to the steps of St Paul's Cathedral to give thanks on the occasion of her Diamond Jubilee, Queen Victoria passed London Bridge station. The service itself was filmed by a cinematograph camera, but the Queen considered the results 'a little hazy & too rapid'.

may vary, but, in essentials it is always the same, from the Palace to Westminster Abbey and back again—the occasion is a coronation.

A coronation is one of four ceremonies organised by the Earl Marshal, an hereditary appointment that has belonged to the dukes of Norfolk since 1672. The other three are the Investiture of the Prince of Wales, state funerals (which should not be confused with royal funerals) and the state opening of parliament. The Earl Marshal's salary for all this is £20 a year; the last time that one of them received an increase was in 1483, from Richard III! The duties are, admittedly, infrequent: the only annual event being the opening of parliament. For example, the investiture of a prince of Wales has taken place only twice during the present century, whilst there have been four state funerals of sovereigns and, for one must follow the other, four coronations.

Nevertheless, when such ceremonies do take place, each one is tremendous in its size and complexity.

For a great many years, the sovereign was placed upon his throne in the great hall at the Palace of Westminster. A prodigious feast celebrated the occasion, in the course of which there were two interruptions. One occurred when the King's Champion entered on horseback. He threw down his gauntlet and thrice challenged anyone who might care to dispute the new monarch's claim to the throne. There were never any takers! In more recent times, this ritual has been regarded as unnecessary. Since the coronation of George IV in 1821, the Champion has had the less spectacular task of bearing the standard of England at the religious ceremony.

The other interruption occurred when a procession of clergy from the nearby Abbey arrived and invited the newly crowned King to return to that holy place for a service of consecration. The distance was no more than a few hundred yards, and was accomplished as quickly as possible.

As time went by, the emphasis changed. The enthronement as well as the consecration took place in the Abbey, and the feast was put in a different perspective. It ceased to be the main event and became simply a banquet to celebrate the ceremony that had just taken place. The last occasion on which it was held was at the coronation of William IV in 1831. It was so rowdy that local residents complained. Sensibly, for the day was long enough and this reproduction of a feudal monarch feasting with his barons did not seem appropriate to the enthronement of a 18-year-old girl, it was abolished for Victoria's coronation in 1838.

————————————————◆————————————————

If the royal journey to the Abbey was brief and, perhaps, lacking in popular appeal, the progress of a new sovereign through the streets of

When Henry VIII walked from Westminster Palace to the service of consecration at the Abbey, his route was covered by a red carpet. During the service, 'rude and common people' cut off pieces to keep. 'Unpardonable' behaviour that may have been explained by over indulgence at fountains flowing with wine. (From the Islip Roll c 1532.)

London on the eve of the event more than made up for it. Henry VIII's crowning took place in 1509, less than three weeks after his marriage to his former sister-in-law, Catherine of Aragon. The coincidence doubtless made the Earl Marshal profoundly grateful that royal weddings were not among his responsibilities (they are the concern of the Lord Chamberlain).

Eighteen days before this coronation, the King and Queen travelled by river from the Palace at Greenwich to the Tower of London. The ceremony was due to take place on Sunday, 24 June. On the Saturday, the royal couple showed themselves to their subjects by travelling in procession from the Tower to Westminster. As the contemporary chronicler, Edward Hall—who had a nice eye for sumptuous attire—noted, 'For a surety, more rich, nor more strange, nor more curious works hath not been seen than were prepared against this coronation.'

The cavalcade was so long that any rehearsal was impossible. The streets were decked out with tapestries and cloth of gold; the King himself, glittering with diamonds, rubies and other precious stones, looked no less magnificent. But this splendour was expected of him; the obese and decaying monarch of his later years was a very different being from this golden prince upon whom so many hopes were pinned.

Not surprisingly the public loved it, especially as, for several days, continuous streams of wine poured from three gargoyles set on a mock castle, capped with a crown, that had been erected at Westminster.

On the day of the ceremony itself, the behaviour of the King's subjects was not beyond reproach. A red carpet had been laid down along the route from Westminster Palace to the Abbey. While the service of consecration was taking place, according to Edward Hall, 'the rude and common people cut and spoiled it'—and, presumably, took the pieces home as souvenirs.

Mary I, who had yet to light her first bonfire in the cause of her Catholic faith and to the terror of the country's heretics, was invested with the glamour that became a princess. She was, admittedly, thirty-seven at the time of her coronation, but free wine flowing from fountains in Cheapside and on Cornhill probably caused her subjects to overlook her lack of youth. Her half-sister, Elizabeth, did rather better, but then, as her subsequent progresses were to show, she inspired that kind of thing.

Elizabeth was crowned in Westminster Abbey by the Bishop of Carlisle on Sunday, 15 January, 1559. Sir Edward Dynmocke (the role of Champion is hereditary) dutifully issued his challenge at the banquet in Westminster Hall, and the new queen drank his health from a golden goblet. But the real splendour of what was obviously going to be a very splendid reign had taken place on the previous day. Despite the January

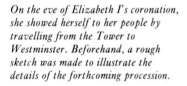

On the eve of Elizabeth I's coronation, she showed herself to her people by travelling from the Tower to Westminster. Beforehand, a rough sketch was made to illustrate the details of the forthcoming procession.

chill, the Queen set off from the Tower at two in the afternoon on a journey to Westminster. Her subjects had made certain that the progress would not be lacking in spectacle, and that it would project suitable sentiments of loyalty and morality. As for the Queen, she was determined that, so far as progress in an open carriage made possible, she should be accessible. It was as near as any pre-twentieth-century sovereign ever got, or was likely to get, to a present day 'walk-about'.

Sometimes she ordered the carriage to stop so that she might receive an armful of flowers, at other times she listened attentively to pleas. Occasionally, or so it seemed, she just paused to chat, or to thank an official for all the trouble he had taken. Her people were impressed— especially by her voice. As one spectator observed, 'She showed the wonderful spectacle of a noble hearted princess towards her most loving people, and the people [took] exceeding comfort in beholding so worthy a sovereign and hearing so prince-like a voice, which could not but have set the enemy on fire.'

At various points on the route, small stages had been erected. On some of them there were tableaux of sumptuously dressed performers, who tried hard not to wobble; on others, small playlets were mimed. In either case, a small boy usually provided a poetic commentary, the text of which was nailed to the scaffolding for the benefit of anyone sufficiently literate to read it. In some cases, a Latin version was also available. The youngster's ability to shout was severely tested, for he had to make himself heard against an orchestra playing incidental music *fortissimo*.

One of the tableaux traced the new queen's descent from Henry VII in a complex three-tier structure. On the second level stood a representation of Henry VIII happily conjoined with Elizabeth's mother, Anne Boleyn (not, perhaps, the most tactful of ideas in view of what later happened to the poor queen). Elizabeth herself, or her likeness, stood in triumph at the top.

The whole display was decked out with red and white roses to celebrate the coming together of the houses of York and Lancaster under one undisputed monarch. No doubt the moral was not lost when Sir Edward issued his traditional challenge the following evening.

Another set piece featured a pageant of virtues, Religion, Wisdom and Justice, trampling the vices, Rebellion and Insolence, Folly and Vain Glory, under their feet. Lest there was any doubt about the identity of the characters, each had a name painted on his or her breast.

Further down the road, a cast of children performed a mime in which each played one of the eight blessings, as enumerated in Saint Matthew, Chapter V. Less easy to grasp was the symbolism of an exhibit that sounds, from its description by one onlooker, to have been rickety to the

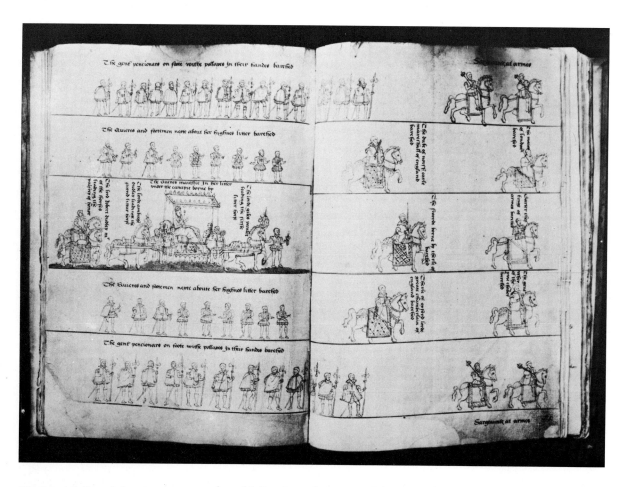

The Royal College of Arms is, next to the Earl Marshal, the authority on royal ceremonial. This volume, produced by the college, can be described as a rehearsal on paper. It shows the arrangement of the procession for the coronation of Elizabeth I.

point of folly. At each corner of the stage there was a tower; in the centre, a chair (representing the throne) was mounted on a large box. On the chair there was a palm tree rich with dates, on top of this, a table bore a notice reading 'A Palme Tree', presumably for the benefit of those who had never seen one. On the table was another chair and, seated upon it, an effigy of the Queen.

Readers who may be wondering what this strange mixture of furniture and arboreal splendour had to do with the monarchy are advised to consult Judges, Chapter IV, which reveals all (at least that was the idea; it has to do with 'Debora the judge and restorer of the house of Israel').

◆

If Queen Elizabeth I, on her progress through London on the eve of her

One of the main intentions behind the impressive coronation procession of Charles II in 1660 was to convince the public of the colourful nature of the monarchy compared with the drab years of the Commonwealth. This contemporary drawing makes all clear, including who was who.

enthronement, had watched and, by all appearances, enjoyed the various tableaux and mimes put on for her pleasure, the coronation of Charles II was a show produced by the sovereign for the benefit of his subjects. The point he was determined to make, no matter what the cost, was how fortunate they were to experience the restoration of the monarchy.

As in the case of Elizabeth, there was the eve of coronation progress from the Tower to Whitehall. Escorted by the King's footguards with their red and white plumes and the Duke of York's (later James II) men decked out in black and white, it made a fine spectacle. As did the route it followed; wine flowed from the fountains; the population—doubtless slightly drunk—was enthusiastic in its applause; and the arches through which the cavalcade passed at various points, were elegant and eloquent at the same time.

One of them featured a woman attired as 'Rebellion' in a crimson robe decorated with snakes, and holding a blood be-spattered sword in her hand. She was attended by 'Confusion', a deformed character wearing the model of a ruined castle as a crown and holding a broken sceptre in either hand.

In a brief playlet, Rebellion cried, 'I am hell's daughter, Satan's eldest child.' Immediately, a stalwart representing 'Monarchy' replied,

'To hell, foul fiend—shrink from this glorious light.' The dialogue might not have been up to the standard of the Restoration comedies to come, but Charles probably applauded its sincerity, and the public loved it and no doubt took its not very subtle moral to heart.

Among those travelling in the procession along the freshly gravelled streets were those redoubtable diarists John Evelyn and Samuel Pepys. Evelyn noted the elegance of the horses; Pepys, as was his wont, observed the many attractive women who leaned out of windows to watch the passing show.

This, in fact, was Charles's second coronation. At the earlier event in Scone Cathedral on new year's day, 1651, the ceremony of anointment had been omitted—to satisfy some of the clerics who regarded it as mere superstition. Now, in London, Charles was determined to put on the show of shows to illustrate the age of plenty about to be ushered in by the monarchy after the Commonwealth austerity. As he was well aware, a new Parliament was about to be elected and he had no intention of allowing history to repeat its mistakes.

During the weeks leading up to the coronation itself, a great many craftsmen and artists were kept busy. After the roundhead depredations, pretty well everything had to be made from scratch. A committee was appointed to examine the problem. Two crowns were required; one of them, for tradition must be preserved, should be called Saint Edward's. Charles himself is credited with the design. When it was completed, it weighed more than 5 lb; which is on the heavy side for even the most elaborate headwear. All the other ornaments of monarchy had to be provided and last, but by no means least, there was the question of the sovereign's attire. Much of it was manufactured from cloth of gold, the rest from scarcely less expensive material. The royal legs were encased in stockings of crimson satin, the royal feet in golden sandals with high heels. As Charles stood six foot two inches tall without assistance from the shoemaker's art, they made him a giant among men—which was no doubt the intention.

Nor was his horse overlooked. The saddle was embellished with pearls and gold, while a large ruby, supplied by a jeweller named William Gomeldon, glinted in rich splendour from a carefully contrived point. The cost of all this added up to £30,000.

The month leading up to the coronation had been wet and dismal. But on the day itself, the sun came out. The monarch travelled to the ceremony (and away from it afterwards) on the royal barge, bringing a bright splash of colour to the normally unglamorous waters of the River Thames.

The people's enthusiasm, the ceremony in the Abbey, the banquet in the Hall of Westminster afterwards; they were all as lavish as any king could have wished. Nevertheless, disgruntled parliamentarians found comfort in an episode that occurred just as the well-fed and contented King was leaving Westminster on his return journey down river. The hitherto beautiful coronation weather suddenly broke—in the fury of a thunderstorm. It was, the parliamentarians told themselves, an omen. Whatever fates had supported the roundhead cause had not entirely abandoned their task.

When Queen Elizabeth II was crowned on a June day in 1953, there was considerable speculation about the origin of one of the coaches. There was no doubt about the state coach in which Her Majesty drove to the Abbey. That had been built on the instructions of George III. The matter that engaged the historians concerned the carriage of the Speaker of the House of Commons. His elaborate vehicle was obviously older than the Queen's and it seemed probable that it had been built for William III. The confusion was occasioned by this scion of the House of Orange's passion for ordering stately conveyances.

Towards the end of the seventeenth century, William seems to have ordered four carriages—three of them to be built in Holland and one in France. Conceivably, one of these is now the Speaker's coach and has been for some considerable time. In 1802, for instance, we find the then current incumbent, Charles Abbott (later Lord Colchester), noting in his diary that he had paid his predecessor, Sir John Mitford (later the first Lord Redesdale), 'about £1,060 for the State Coach built in 1701 and repaired in 1801'.

Since an expert can tell that the vehicle does not reflect French workmanship, it seems probable that the coach in question was one of the batch from Holland. It may very well have been used at Queen Anne's coronation—an event that required more than the usual attention to transportation. The Queen was so overweight and so tormented by gout that she was unable to walk. Consequently she had to be carried in a sedan chair through those parts of the ceremony that were more commonly executed on foot.

Whichever vehicle became the Speaker's, it was removed from the Royal Mews in 1764 and stored away in a stable at Kensington. By the nineteenth century, it had become known as 'the old coach'. After thirty-seven years of neglect, it clearly required the repairs and refurbishing done in 1801, when Speaker Mitford acquired it.

Without doubt, one of the reasons why this particular vehicle was withdrawn from royal service was that, on 25 October, 1760 George III

The State coach, commissioned by George III and used for every coronation since George IV's. Although ornamented and modified over the years (the illustrations show 1762, 1805 and very early 20th century), it was a long time before its suspension was made tolerable. King George VI described his coronation journey in it as 'one of the most uncomfortable rides I have ever had in my life'. The box seat at the front, seen in all three illustrations was removed on the orders of Edward VII. (Below and opposite.)

ordered the construction of 'a very superb state coach'. Its cost of £7,587 19s 9½d included £314 worth of panels painted by the Italian artist Giovanni Battista Cipriani, who may well have concerned himself with other aspects of its embellishment. The new coach took two years to build, at the works of James Butler in Great Queen Street, Lincoln's Inn Fields, and it eventually arrived at the Royal Mews on 24 November, 1792. Eight cream ponies from Hanover were harnessed to it, and this most elegant of conveyances made a brief journey to convince the authorities that it was in satisfactory running order. On the following day, the King travelled in it to the state opening of parliament.

On this occasion, the crowd was in one of its less friendly moods. The window on one of the doors was smashed and the handle was broken. Three years later, when the King was returning along Pall Mall from Westminster, all of the windows were shattered by the mob. The coach was modified to reduce the area of glass.

For his coronation on 22 September, 1761, George III did not avail himself of 'the old coach', and his future 'very superb' vehicle was still

His Majesty King George the Thirds New State Coach.
Eng. for the LONDON Magazine

under construction. On their journey from Saint James's Palace to Westminster, he and his wife, Queen Charlotte, were carried in sedan chairs. As one onlooker observed, 'they were just like ordinary citizens going to the theatre.' The procession set off at eleven o'clock in the morning; at 3.30 in the afternoon, George was crowned, and the royal couple eventually returned to the Palace at 10.00 in the evening after the inevitable banquet in Westminster Hall. They were, we are told, 'rather tired' which is not surprising; it had been a long day.

For many of those who had watched the ceremony, the day had been even longer. William Hickey, the future diarist, was a boy at the time and he was taken by his father to see the proceedings in the Abbey and, later, in Westminster Hall. For £50, the elder Hickey had secured a box in a nunnery at the head of the giant columns that support the Abbey roof. The box was able to accommodate twelve family and friends and two servants.

Mr Hickey had planned the excursion carefully. Whatever else might happen, he was determined that nobody should go short of food. His servants moved into the nunnery in good time, taking with them an assortment of 'cold fowls, ham, tongues, different meat pies, wines and liquors of various sorts'. He and his guests ate supper on the evening before in a house near Piccadilly Circus. At midnight, they set off for the Abbey in three carriages. The going was uncommonly slow. 'At the end of Pall Mall,' William noted, 'the different lines of carriages, nearly filling the street, our progress was consequently tedious; yet the time was beguiled by the grandeur of the scene; such a multitude of carriages, with servants behind carrying flambeauxs, made a blaze of light equal to day, and had a fine effect.'

Opposite the Horse Guards, the traffic came to a standstill for an hour. There was another hold-up later, caused by coachmen who should have been in the lane reserved for Westminster Hall, making a mistake and finding themselves trapped in the Abbey-bound throng. 'This,' wrote William, 'created much confusion and running against each other, whereby glasses and panels were demolished without number, the noise of which, accompanied by the screeches of terrified ladies, was at times truly terrific.'

It was past seven when the Hickeys arrived at the Abbey and made their way by a private staircase to their rooftop perch. The servants had been busy preparing breakfast 'which I enjoyed, and proved highly refreshing to us all'.

———————————————◆———————————————

Before George IV made the journey to the Abbey in 1821, he ordered the state coach, which had been completed too late for his father's coronation, to be restored to its original design by the replacement of the missing windows. The public was consequently to be afforded a better view of His 51-year-old Majesty. Anyone who hoped to catch a glimpse of the Queen was disappointed. Having recently disgraced herself at a ball in Geneva, the King was afraid that she might cause him further embarrassment, and took great pains to ensure that she was unable to attend.

Doubtless he had his subjects' interests at heart when he expanded the state coach's area of glass: he might have served himself and his descendants better if he had concerned himself with the suspension as well. The vehicle, whilst beautiful to look at, was damnably uncomfortable inside. After suffering its unpleasant motion, William IV, appropriately for the 'Sailor King', compared it to a ship in a rough sea. Queen Victoria disliked it intensely and after 1861 refused to use it, no matter how appropriate the occasion might be.

Edward VII decided to amend its appearance by removing the box-seat and its elaborate scallop-shell footboard, thus providing an even better view of its illustrious passenger. This did away with the coachman, who used to drive a team of horses 'six-in-hand'. He was replaced by two postillions riding the leading animals. This, again, was to the public's advantage, but not to that of its occupants, who remained as uncomfortable as ever.

King George V had a shot at improving matters by replacing the springs and fitting rubber tyres. Probably he realised that the problem had not been completely solved, for in 1911 he bought the so-called 'Glass Coach' for use at his coronation. Completed a year earlier, it had been designed as a sheriff's town coach. His son, George VI, suffered the rigours of the state coach on his journey to the Abbey in 1937. He described this as 'one of the most uncomfortable rides I have ever had in my life.'

However, if you work on something that is solvable for long enough, you will eventually discover the solution. By the time the present Queen set off in procession to Westminster Abbey, the ill-suspended coach had been rendered tolerable. Even antiques, it seems, are susceptible to modern technology.

◆

When Victoria travelled to her coronation on a summer day in 1838, she had to endure the worst excesses of her grandfather's unfortunate dream coach. Nevertheless, she must have found comfort during the journey in the nation's enthusiasm for the prospect of a girl queen. The extent of enthusiasm was reflected by Parliament's contribution to the proceedings. Whilst the MPs had voted only £50,000 to be spent on William IV's coronation, seventeen years later they approved £200,000 for hers.

Inside the Abbey the decorations were a dazzling arrangement of scarlet and gold. Outside, Londoners applied themselves to making plans for a tremendous two-day celebration. Bands would be playing in the parks; there would be a fair; ascents by balloons; illuminations and a breath-taking firework display. After the enthronement of George III, the formal state procession of the new monarch through the capital had been discontinued. Now there were ideas of reviving it, at a cost of £26,000. The young queen would be seen in her coronation robes, carrying the orb and the sceptre.

As the chronicler Charles Greville put it, 'The great merit of this coronation is that so much has been done for the people.' Nobody could dispute this, the pity was that during the ceremony itself, so little was done for the star player.

The Prime Minister, Lord Melbourne, was much more than his official title suggested. To the 19-year-old queen, he was a friend and confidant—an adult figure upon whom she leaned for support and advice. The monarch and the politician rode together each morning. On these outings, the talk ranged far beyond matters of state. Nevertheless, Melbourne had little to offer in the way of advice for the ceremony that was now arranged for the 28th June.

He remarked that it was imperative that cream-coloured ponies be brought from Hanover to haul the state coach. Any other horses, he said, would look more like 'rats and mice'. He also suggested that she might visit the Abbey to try out the thrones. It was just as well. Both of them were too low, and last-minute modifications had to be made.

On the day before the coronation, Victoria drove round her capital in an open carriage. Greville noted that, 'It is as if the population had been all of a sudden quintupled; the uproar, the confusion, the noises are indescribable.' Victoria herself was delighted by the 'crowds in the street and all *so* friendly'.

That night, she slept badly, haunted by 'a feeling that something awful was going to happen tomorrow'. She rose at seven o'clock; failed on her first attempt to eat breakfast, but was rather more successful on the second (Melbourne had told her: 'Oh, you'll like it when you are there'). She dressed at 9.30 and an hour later climbed into the state coach. The route to the Abbey lay via Constitution Hill, Piccadilly, Saint James's Street and Trafalgar Square, and thence to Westminster. Wherever she looked, there were masses of people, with soldiers guarding and bandsmen thumping out suitably loyal and rumbustious tunes.

As she entered the Abbey with her eight train-bearers, she seemed to one observer, 'gay as a lark—like a girl on her birthday'. Nor had it escaped people's notice that a day which had begun wet and cloudy had now improved, and the sun was shining. It was, they suggested, a favourable portent.

For want of any rehearsal, the Abbey ceremony was unable to reflect this timely improvement in the weather. The Bishop of York missed his cue to hand the Queen the orb, which, in any case, was almost too heavy for her to hold. The Archbishop of Canterbury forced the ring on to the wrong finger, which caused Victoria considerable pain. The Bishop of Bath and Wells accidentally turned over two pages in the prayer book and lost his place. In Saint Edward's chapel, the altar was littered with the remains of sandwiches and half-finished bottles of wine, and when the peers paraded to pay their homage, the 82-year-old Lord Rolly tripped over his gown on the steps leading to the throne. Even the distribution of medals to commemorate the occasion went wrong. Instead of receiving them in an orderly manner, the Abbey guests had to scramble for them in an unseemly free-for-all.

Throughout all this fumbling the young Queen ad libbed splendidly. Afterwards she was driven back to the Palace by the same route she had followed earlier in the day. By all accounts, she immediately ran upstairs to carry out the rather more domestic, and certainly much less earnest, task of giving her favourite dog, Dash, his bath.

Edward VII's coronation had been planned for 26 June, 1902. On the 14th of the month, he fell ill while on a visit to Aldershot. It appeared to be a chill, although, next day, the press was told that he had suffered a 'severe attack of lumbago'.

During the following days, his condition deteriorated. He was irritable and depressed, and unable to enjoy his food. He observed, in one of his darker moments, 'If this goes on, I shall give it up. I shall abdicate.'

Nevertheless, and despite his talk of abdication, he was determined that the coronation should take place as arranged. The people were looking forward to it, and he had no intention of disappointing them. Even when his doctor, Sir Francis Laking, informed him that he was suffering from a severe appendicitis accompanied by peritonitis, the King refused to change his plans.

However, matters reached a point when it seemed that, unless an operation was carried out, the King would surely die. The proposed dress rehearsal in the Abbey, to be conducted by the Bishop of London, was replaced by a service of intercession for the sovereign's health. Next day, 24 June, Sir Frederick Treves removed the King's appendix, in a room at the Palace that had been converted into an extempore operating theatre. It

In January, 1903, a great durbar took place at Delhi to celebrate the coronation of Edward VII, King of Great Britain and Emperor of India. As his Majesty was unable to be present, he was represented by the viceroy, Lord Curzon, who had a liking for pomp and ceremony.

was reported that, on coming round from the anaesthetic, the King's first words were, 'Will my people ever forgive me?' This was a pleasant fiction. What he said was, 'Where's George?'—referring to the Prince of Wales.

The ceremony eventually took place on 9 August. In view of what had happened, it was considerably simplified. Before setting off from the Palace, the King paraded before his grandchildren in his coronation dress. 'Good morning, children', he said. 'Am I not a funny-looking old man?'

Within the Abbey, there was a special compartment for the King's 'lady friends'—irreverently referred to as 'the King's loose box'. When asked afterwards what had impressed him the most, the sovereign replied, 'The white arms [of the peeresses putting on their coronets] arching over their heads,' reminded him, he said, of 'a scene from a beautiful ballet.' (Peeresses' arms seem to have remained one of the more attractive features of coronations. At the crowning of Queen Elizabeth II, that amiable politician and socialite, Chips Channon, likened them to the necks of swans.)

THE CROWNING OF THE KING BY THE ARCHBISHOP OF CANTERBURY
The Dean of Westminster and the Bishop of Bath and Wells standing beside the Throne

Whatever else it may have signified, Queen Victoria's coronation was notable for two things. One was that it made clear the need for proper rehearsals; when all is said and done, and quite apart from its temporal and spiritual importance, a coronation is (or should be) a superb piece of theatre. The other notable thing was Victoria's first action once the pomp and ceremony had ended. There was no rowdy banquet in Westminster Hall; instead she bathed her dog.

Similarly, after George V's coronation in 1911, the monarch (his words), 'Worked all afternoon . . . answering telegrams and letters of which I have had hundreds.' For this coronation fifty thousand troops under the command of Lord Kitchener lined the streets. Whilst the

Fifty thousand troops under the command of Lord Kitchener lined the streets of London for the coronation of George V in 1911; the last great gathering of European royalty. In the half year that followed his coronation George V invested his son as Prince of Wales at Caernarvon castle and then set sail for India, where he held a durbar at Delhi which he insisted upon attending in person.

ceremony itself followed a now well-tried formula (the drive to the
Abbey, the service, and the return journey to Buckingham Palace), there
was an interesting contrast between the old and the new in the streets of
London beforehand.

The motor car was now an established member of London's traffic
population. Nevertheless, those peers who still owned state coaches were
asked to use them for their journeys to and from the Abbey. These ancient
vehicles were taken out of store, greased and refurbished, and brought up
to the capital by train.

This much was simple enough; the trouble was that they required
horses to haul them. The beasts, which had been enjoying quiet lives in
the country, were unaccustomed to streets dominated by the internal
combustion engine; nor were they used to pulling state coaches. Consequently they, too, needed a period of rehearsal. The result was that the
traffic jams, already rather less than tolerable, were made worse by unhappy and recalcitrant animals wondering what strange hell was trying to
absorb them.

During the days before and after the coronation, anyone in a hurry
in London very prudently travelled by the underground. For the crowning of King George VI and later Elizabeth II, this provided the solution
for a number of the guests at the Abbey. On each occasion, a special tube
train was dispatched from Kensington High Street station to Westminster
carrying 800 peers and MPs. According to a present-day spokesman for
London Transport, 'I'm sticking my neck out, but you could say that this
was unique. We might run a *special* when a new line is opened; but,
otherwise, we don't go in for this sort of thing. For example, *you* couldn't
charter a special train.'

◆

Queen Elizabeth II was crowned on 2 June, 1953. More than a year
earlier, in April 1952, a coronation commission had been set up under the
chairmanship of Prince Philip. Not the least of the matters it had to
decide was what should be his own means of proceeding to the Abbey.
There had been no coronation of a queen with a male consort since
Queen Anne's coronation in 1702. But the details of that ceremony had
been lost, nor, in any case, would they have helped much. Queen Anne
dodged the issue by leaving her husband, Prince George of Denmark,
at home.

There were several alternatives; Prince Philip might go in a coach
of his own; he might ride to the Abbey on horseback; he might (as he did)
accompany the Queen in the state coach.

As mentioned, the state coach was originally drawn by cream ponies, imported from Hanover; however, the last members of this line had been sold during World War I. For the state opening of Parliament in 1921, blacks had hauled the Irish state coach; which, by tradition, is used for these journeys. Bays had been harnessed to the George VI coronation coach in 1937 and Elizabeth II was taken to the Abbey by eight of the famous Windsor Greys, each with a postillion on its back. Five of the greys had been presented to her father by the Queen of the Netherlands in 1946. The postillions, like the coachmen who drove the other vehicles, were recruited from the grooms employed in the Royal Mews at Buckingham Palace—a small world of horses and cars, coaches and carriages, managed by the Crown Equerry.

Since 1839, the Speaker's coach has been hauled by a team of shire horses provided by Whitbread, the brewers. On his journey from the City, the Lord Mayor of London is traditionally escorted by pikemen and the musketeers from the Honourable Artillery Company. This territorial army regiment, every member of which, no matter what his rank, is regarded as officer material (hence the preface of each word of command by 'Gentlemen . . .') still uses a manual of pike drill that was originally published in the sixteenth century. It is also responsible for firing salutes from the Tower of London on appropriate occasions. In Hyde Park, this duty is performed by members of the King's Troop of the Royal Horse Artillery. Since these men are full time soldiers, they are able to parade earlier than the HAC's representatives—with the result that the two salutes seldom coincide. As a member of the HAC told the present author, 'Most of our chaps are working in the City, and they have to carry out this job in their lunch hours. They change into uniform, fire the guns, have a quick beer and then go back to work again.'

When Queen Victoria sent her telegraph message just before departing on her Diamond Jubilee procession, she used a new technology to communicate with her people. The coronation of Queen Elizabeth II, carried the art of communication a great deal further. Radio had enabled families throughout the world to *listen* to the coronation of her father. Admittedly, the occasion had also been televised, but the quality of the picture was poor, and, in any case, most people had no access to a television set. Now the state of the art had taken a massive leap forward, and millions of viewers could see the events as they happened, if not yet in colour, then at least in crisp black and white. This did not, however, prevent an estimated 30,000 people from staying up throughout a wet night in the Mall, to obtain the best view of the procession. Nor did it diminish the demand for windows overlooking the route, nor reduce the ocean of people that lined the royal route via the West End to Hyde Park Corner, to Marble Arch and to Oxford Circus, down Regent Street to

Londoners spent £¼ million on street decorations for Queen Victoria's Diamond Jubilee. The sun shone and the Queen reflected to herself that she had now occupied the throne of Britain for one day longer than her grandfather, George III, who had, until then, held the record for the longest-reigning monarch.

Piccadilly Circus, and thence by way of Haymarket and the Mall back to Buckingham Palace. Despite the fact it poured with rain for most of the time, the spectators were undaunted.

◆

There has always been an interval between the accession of a new sovereign and his or her coronation. In the case of Queen Elizabeth II, it amounted to sixteen months, which some people said (wrongly) was unusually long. The length of the period depends upon such factors as the duration of official mourning for the deceased monarch; a very reasonable preference for coronations to take place in the summer; the time required to arrange the finance and to recruit the necessary staff; and the time needed to enable foreign guests to fit the occasion into their busy schedules. To which might be added; the need to give the Earl Marshal a respite, as he winds up the organisation of a state funeral and prepares for a very much happier ceremony.

State funerals should not be confused with royal funerals, which are organised by the Lord Chamberlain. Only the sovereign is automatically entitled to the former. Very occasionally, at a monarch's discretion, an outstanding national figure is accorded the honour—though this is very rare indeed. During the past two centuries, only three people have received it.

The Duke of Wellington, like Nelson, was one of the very few people other than a reigning sovereign to be accorded a state funeral. Prince Albert supervised the design of the Duke's highly ornate funeral car, which was 21ft (6.4m) long and weighed eighteen tons.

Nelson was given a state funeral in 1806, when he was entombed in Saint Paul's Cathedral in a coffin fashioned from the mainmast of *L'Orient*, the French flagship at the Battle of the Nile. When the Duke of Wellington died in 1852, Queen Victoria insisted that his body should 'rest by the side of Nelson'. A special funeral car, manufactured from the metal of captured guns, was built in eighteen days by a work force of a hundred men. The coffin was designed by Prince Albert, who seems to have been inspired by the reputation of the Duke rather than by his dimensions. In any event, it was an uncommonly large container for a normally-sized corpse.

The tomb in which it was enshrined took a good deal longer to complete; twenty years, which is a long time, even by the slowest standards of elaborate monumental masonry.

Winston Churchill was the third member of this illustrious trio. His death in 1965 was the occasion for a parade through London from Westminster Hall (where he had lain in state) to Saint Paul's Cathedral. However, unlike Nelson and Wellington, he did not remain there. His body was taken by train to the little churchyard at Bladen near his birthplace at Blenheim, where it was interred. Unlike the extravagance of Wellington's final resting place, Churchill's is marked by a modest and conventional gravestone.

Since a sovereign's consort is not eligible for a state funeral, Prince Albert had to be content with the royal version. Queen Victoria enjoyed arranging these sorry occasions, and she had left very clear instructions for her own funeral. After lying in state for ten days at Osborne (where she died), her body was brought to Gosport in *Alberta*, one of the smaller royal yachts. A special train took it to London. As it hurried by, people working in the fields fell on their knees. In the capital, the coffin was borne on a gun-carriage to Paddington station, *en route* for Windsor. The royal standard, true to the Queen's wishes, was 'thrown partially over the Pall'.

Queen Victoria had studied various accounts of the funeral rites carried out at Saint Peter's in Rome. What impressed her was the brilliance of these occasions, the gold used in the decorations and the colourful uniforms. Even the music seemed more suited to a thanksgiving.

This, the Queen felt, was how things should be. Instead of Handel's funeral march, she chose works by Chopin and Beethoven, with, now and then, a Highland lament. Above all, there was to be no use of black. Instead, the London streets were to be adorned with purple cashmere decorated by white satin bows.

At Windsor station, another gun-carriage, with a team of horses harnessed to it, was to wait to take the coffin up the hill to Saint George's Chapel. In her will, the Queen had expressed her dislike of this manner of conveyance: it was, she wrote, 'very rough jolting and noisy'.

The fact that she would not be aware of the discomfort did not seem to be relevant. A queen, presumably, must always travel in comfort; even a dead queen. But the gun-carriage was a tradition that even Queen Victoria could not overrule. A monarch must make the final journey by this method and that was that.

In the event a potential disaster led to a now hallowed tradition. It was a cold February day, and the horses at Windsor became restless. One, more impatient than the rest, suddenly reared up and snapped its traces. The train from Paddington was due to arrive at any minute, and this one beast had thrown all of the carefully worked-out preparations into disarray. Happily, one of the ADCs, Captain the Hon. Hedworth Lambton, was quick to see a solution. Pointing to the Naval guard of honour, he suggested that the remaining horses be removed, and the sailors take their places. And so, on her last journey, Queen Victoria was taken to the chapel by a team of bluejackets.

Thus an emergency measure became a tradition. Thereafter, the horses of the Royal Horse Artillery (which still provides the gun-carriage)

Shortly before the train carrying the mortal remains of Queen Victoria arrived at Windsor, one of the horses that should have hauled the gun-carriage shied and snapped its traces. The Royal Navy came to the rescue by providing a team of bluejackets to drag the vehicle from the station to St George's Chapel. From this act of improvisation came a tradition.

were relieved of their duties at state funerals, and naval ratings were used instead. At King George VI's funeral in 1952, a hundred and thirty-eight ratings drew the gun-carriage through the streets of London, no doubt making the journey less 'jolting and noisy'.

Victoria's abhorrence of black for her own funeral was in marked contrast to her attitude after the death of Prince Albert nearly forty years earlier. On that occasion, virtually anything that could be draped in this most sombre of colours was so covered. When, more than a year after-wards, the Prince of Wales (later Edward VII) was married to Princess Alexandra at Saint George's Chapel, Windsor, the Queen made it clear that she wished the church to be decorated in black. She was dissuaded only when the Prince told her that, if such were the case, he would bring his bride to the ceremony in a hearse. Nevertheless, Victoria won a small victory. Her dress for the occasion was black—relieved only by the Order of the Garter. (Students of rail travel may care to note that leading politicians were conveyed from Paddington to Windsor in a special train. On the return journey, they were crammed into a third class carriage.

The over-crowding was such that Disraeli was compelled to travel on his wife's lap.)

Queen Victoria's last rites marked a turning point, as far as state funerals were concerned. Since her successors did not share her almost obsessive attachment to Osborne, they lay in state in Westminster Hall before travelling to Paddington and thence to Windsor. When Edward VII died in 1910, it was estimated that about two hundred and fifty thousand people filed past the *catafalque* at Westminster. Among those who rode in the procession on 20 May were nine kings. The German Kaiser, Wilhelm II, who had never enjoyed an easy relationship with his uncle, was nevertheless conspicuous in his devotion to the dead king. Visitors to Westminster Hall had seen him kneeling in prayer by the coffin. Now, he was suitably attired in the uniform of a (honorary) field marshal in the British Army.

Possibly less impressive, though more moving for all that, was an unhappy four-footed figure that followed immediately behind the visiting sovereigns. It was the late King's fox-terrier, Caesar, attended by one of the servants from Balmoral.

———————————————◆———————————————

The route taken from Westminster to Paddington is 3½ miles long. When King George VI died in 1952, it was lined by ten thousand troops. The cortège, marching at the obligatory 65 paces to the minute, was one mile long.

One difference between a state funeral and a royal funeral is that the state pays for the former. The preliminary work is carried out by the Earl Marshal at the Royal College of Arms in London (President, the Duke of Norfolk; members, the thirteen officers of the college—three kings of arms, six heralds and six pursuivants). Just as the obituary of a distinguished person is written during his or her lifetime, and updated when appropriate, so the preparations are begun some while before a sovereign's death. It is, after all, far too complex a matter to be arranged in a matter of days. By the time the monarch has died, a great many people, including the heralds, officials at the Lord Chamberlain's office, the police, senior officers in the services, and many other people who will be involved, know about the plans. But discretion is everything.

In *The British Monarchy*, John Brooke-Little, Richmond Herald of Arms, recalls that in the case of Winston Churchill's state funeral, 'In these circumstances it is hardly surprising that the secret leaked out to the Press but, to its everlasting credit, it held its peace. Not a single newspaper made cheap capital out of the Hope Not story . . .' (Operation Hope Not was its code name.)

But these events are very rare indeed. The Duke of Windsor, though once—if briefly—a sovereign, was not entitled to a state funeral when he died in 1972. Nor did he want one. Having lived in what amounted to exile for a great many years, he wished the homecoming that death would make possible to be a quiet occasion.

His body was flown in a VC10 from Le Bourget airport on the edge of Paris to the headquarters of the Queen's Flight at RAF Benson in Oxfordshire. That night, the coffin rested in the station's small church. Next day, it was taken by hearse to the Prince Albert Memorial Chapel (part of Saint George's Chapel) at Windsor. The Duchess should have accompanied the coffin, but she felt too ill and too tired to travel. Instead, she followed two days later, when an Andover of the Queen's Flight brought her to Heathrow.

The only evidence of the occasion seen by Londoners occurred at the Trooping the Colour, which took place on the day before the funeral. On the Queen's insistence, it was preceded by an Act of Remembrance in which pipers of the Scots Guards played *The Flowers of the Forest*. The

During their visit to Canada in 1951, Princess Elizabeth and the Duke of Edinburgh made a brief journey in a mail coach, escorted by Mounties, cowboys and Indians! The use of the Prince of Wales emblem on the door poses an interesting question. Had the coach previously been used by the Princess's uncle (Edward VIII) on one of his trips to Calgary? Although heir to the throne, Princess Elizabeth was not Princess of Wales, and so its use for her or for Prince Philip would have been inappropriate.

When Queen Elizabeth II went to Ethiopia, she drove through the streets of Addis Ababa with Emperor Haile Selassie. The latter's state coach seems to have been strongly influenced by the European concept of these vehicles.

Highland lament that had been rendered more than thirty years earlier when, as Governor General of the Bahamas, the Duke had arranged a memorial service to his brother, the Duke of Kent.

The man who had been Edward VIII was not without honour. As his body lay in state in the Albert Memorial Chapel, no fewer than sixty thousand people filed past it to pay their respects.

It was, perhaps, particularly appropriate that his coffin's arrival in England should have been undertaken by the Queen's Flight, and that its first night in the country should have been at Benson. For it was Edward VIII who, in 1936, had formed the King's Flight to bring royal travel up-to-date.

3
ROYALTY AFLOAT

One morning in the summer of 1660, Charles II glanced out of a window in the Palace at Whitehall, and noticed a familiar vessel moored a few yards away in the Thames. She was the brig *Surprise*, now scrubbed clean of her coal-carrying drabness. The astute Captain Tettersell had decided that a visit to London could do him no harm. At the very least, the ship in which the recently restored monarch had fled to France would attract sightseers. The sight of her might even stir a grateful chord in the royal memory—possibly producing the rewards that Tettersell felt were his due.

The Captain was not disappointed. Charles ordered *Surprise*'s name to be changed to *Royal Escape*. This drudge of the coastal trade was converted into a fifth rate warship and, with a master and two seamen aboard as caretakers, she was permanently moored within sight of the Palace. Tettersell was given a pension, a commission in the Royal Navy, and command of another fifth-rater.

Royal Escape (as we shall now call her) has often been described as the first royal yacht. In fact, this distinction more properly belongs to a Dutch-built vessel named *Mary*. During his exile, Charles had made a trip from Breda to Delft in a similar ship. He had liked her so much that, on his return to England, he was presented with a replica. The bill, for £1,335, was paid by the Dutch East India Company. Pepys described her as 'one of the finest things I ever saw for neatness and room in so small a vessel.'

Hitherto there had been no precise word for small ships that were dedicated neither to commerce nor to war, but existed simply for pleasure. Now, from Holland, came the word *jaght*, which was quickly absorbed into the English dictionary as 'yacht' (though for many years spelt as 'yatcht').

Charles II, an able navigator and a man who was prepared to take the helm or haul on a sheet, conceived a passion for such craft. At one time, he owned no fewer than twenty, most of them built by a Thameside family named Pett. In *Mary*, he raced his brother James's *Anne* from Greenwich to Gravesend and back for a wager of £100. *Anne* led on the way downstream, but *Mary* overhauled her on the final stretch. Among his other boats, *Bezan* (also a present from Holland) and *Jamie* were built for speed, while *Fubbs* was built for comfort. She was named after one of his mistresses, Louise Duchess of Portsmouth, whom he had nicknamed 'Fubbs' on account of her figure (the word was used with affection to denote a small but plump woman). Among the furniture in the sovereign's accommodation at the after end was an ornate four-poster bed, where, we must assume, he was wont to entertain the buxom Louise.

The ship outlived her monarch and his mistress. *Fubbs* was scrapped towards the end of the eighteenth century after 99 years in service.

Although built for pleasure, in times of war the yachts were required to do their bit. Prince Rupert's *Fanfare* actually took part in an engagement against the Dutch fleet. Mostly, however, the yachts were used as 'advice boats' to carry orders and dispatches to and from their fighting sisters. It was a task that required speed rather than pugnacity, and *Jamie* and *Bezan* (the faster of the two) were ideal for such purposes.

During the next 150 years, royal yachts grew in size until there was little to distinguish them from men-of-war. They reached a pinnacle of perfection in 1817, when the 330 ton *Royal George* was built to the order of the Prince Regent. When she was laid up, her crew was transferred to the 10-gun brig, HMS *Pantaloon*, in which the men were employed carrying mail and on fishery protection duties. William IV had other ideas, and insisted that, when the royal yacht was out of commission, her sailors should work at Portsmouth dockyard as riggers.

Royal George had been the vessel that carried the Duke of Kent and his pregnant duchess across the Dover Strait to ensure that their child should be born in London and appropriately enough it was in the *Royal George* that Queen Victoria (as the unborn baby had now become) made her first sea voyage.

The year was 1842; the destination, Leith. Victoria and Prince Albert embarked at Woolwich, and *Royal George* was towed down river by the steam tug *Monkey*. Pleasure boats crammed with spectators watched the departure. Seven warships were in attendance as was the Trinity House yacht *Vestal*.

The voyage was not a success. It took 66 hours to cover the 404 miles up the east coast, averaging six knots. Victoria noticed with impatience, the steamers that overtook them making, it seemed to her, easy work of the passage, while *Royal George* struggled against adverse winds and sometimes had to be taken in tow. When the time came to make the return trip, she insisted that a 1,000-ton paddle steamer should be

·VICTORIA & ALBERT 1843-1855·

·VICTORIA & ALBERT 1855-1904·

·VICTORIA & ALBERT 1899-1955·

·BRITANNIA 1953·

·BRITANNIA·
RACING CUTTER
1893-1936

chartered. Back in London, she sent a note to her Prime Minister, Sir Robert Peel. The gist of it was that *Royal George* was hopelessly out-of-date; a new royal yacht should be built and it should no longer depend upon the caprice of the wind for its propulsion.

Peel was quick to reassure her. 'The Admiralty', he replied, 'is now building a large vessel to be worked by steam power . . . Sir Robert Peel will leave nothing undone to ensure Your Majesty's comfort and safety in any future naval excursion that Your Majesty may be pleased to make.'

The days of the *Royal George* as the transporter of sovereigns were over. Nevertheless, the old ship was far from dead. She was laid up at Portsmouth, where she served as a hulk in which the crews of her

The main royal steam-yachts, from the original Victoria and Albert *to the present day* Britannia. *The racing yacht's hull at the foot of the picture is that of George V's beloved* Britannia—*a J-Class cutter after which the present royal yacht is named.*

successors lodged when not at sea. Eventually, she was scrapped in
1905, on the orders of Edward VII. In fact, she had been idle since 1902,
when a reporter on the *Daily Graphic* anticipated her demise by writing
that the 'royal yacht *Royal George* to be moved from her moorings in
Portsmouth Harbour that she has so long occupied, and towed off to
"Rotten Row" to lie there awaiting the signing of a formal order that will
hand her over to the ship-breakers. So passes a relic of England in the
far-off days of the Regency, the oldest royal yacht in the world, the third
oldest ship in the Royal Navy.' *Victory* was the oldest.

Royal George's successor was laid down on 9 September, 1842, and
launched at the Royal Dockyard, Pembroke, by the Duchess of Cawdor
on 26 April in the following year. She was built mostly from Danzig oak;
a groove was cut into the forepart of her sternpost and a small copper box
containing coins of the realm lodged inside. *Victoria and Albert*, for such
was her name, was a steamer with one funnel and a pair of hefty paddle
wheels that propelled her through the water regardless of what the wind
might be doing. In June, 1843, she was brought round to the Thames,
where Prince Albert inspected her and pronounced himself satisfied. On
1 July, commanded by Captain the Rt. Hon. Lord Adolphus Fitz-
Clarence, and with the Queen, Prince Albert and the Duke of Wellington
aboard, she set off on a cruise to ports along the south coast.

Victoria and Albert behaved faultlessly, though the weather was bad
and the trip was not without its misadventures. At Ryde, on the Isle of
Wight, the weather was so bad the mayor offered Victoria his robes of
office to protect her against the rain on her way ashore. As she walked
down the accommodation ladder, the mate—a Mr Warren—edged
backwards to give her more room and fell overboard. He was fished out
of the water unhurt.

Later, the heavily escorted royal yacht called at Weymouth, Dartmouth and Plymouth. At each town the local worthies came on board to
be presented to the Queen. At Weymouth, the mayor misjudged his
footing and shared the fate of the luckless Mr Warren. He tumbled into
the bay clutching his mace, with his robes billowing around him. The
mayor was recovered; the mace, which he had to abandon in his efforts to
swim, was not.

One of Queen Victoria's early voyages in *Victoria and Albert* took her
to France, where she and the Prince Consort were to spend four days
with Louis Philippe at his country house, the Château d'Eu. If the
weather was fine, Victoria was in the habit of sitting on deck and passing
the time by plaiting lengths of paper into tiny bonnets. On this occasion,
she and two companions, Lady Bloomfield and Lady Channing, were
seated in the lee of one of the paddle-boxes. The Queen was perched on a

camp stool and they were all busily plaiting paper. 'Suddenly', wrote Lady Bloomfield, 'we observed a commotion among the sailors, little knots of them talking together in a mysterious manner. First one officer came up to them, then another, looking puzzled, and at last Lord Adolphus Fitz-Clarence was called. The Queen, much puzzled, wondered whether a mutiny was brewing. Lord Adolphus laughed and asked her whether she would move her seat.'

' "Move my seat?" said the Queen. "Why should I? What possible harm am I doing here?"

'Lord Adolphus explained: "Well, ma'am, the fact is Your Majesty is unwittingly closing up the door of the place where the grog tubs are kept, so the men cannot have their grog."

'Victoria: "Oh very well, I will move on one condition, namely that you bring me a glass of grog."

'Having sampled it, the Queen observed, "I am afraid I can only make the same remark as I did once before, that I think it would be very good if it were stronger." '

The royal party was disembarked at Le Tréport. *Victoria and Albert* had to lie offshore and a barge used to ferry the Queen and her attendants to the beach. This posed a problem. Her Majesty could not be expected to wade ashore and any thought of carrying her was out of the question. The problem was solved by bringing a bathing machine into the water. Victoria stepped out of the boat and into its discreet interior. A horse then hauled it up the shore, to a place on dry land where Louis Philippe was waiting to greet her.

In 1842, Victoria and her husband had stayed with Lady Blatchford at Osborne House on the Isle of Wight. The Queen was greatly taken with the place and three years later she bought it for £26,000. Prince Albert insisted that it would not do in its present form. It should be pulled down, and he would design something better. Taking his inspiration from a modern Italian villa overlooking the Bay of Naples, Albert sketched out something that has been variously likened to a large crematorium and a prison. Work on the new building began in 1845 and was completed in 1848. Whatever its aesthetic shortcomings, Queen Victoria loved it, and resolved to spend as much time as possible in her island home.

Victoria and Albert was a very splendid ship, but she drew rather a lot of water, meaning that she was unable to proceed up rivers such as the Tamar in Devon. To assist the royal progress in more shallow surroundings, Victoria ordered two smaller steamers to be built. *Fairy* was launched in 1844 and *Elfin* in 1848. One or the other nearly always accompanied the royal yacht on her journeys; to act as a tender in much the same manner as lesser pleasure boats now employ dinghies.

When the Prince of Wales and his wife, Princess Alexandra, paid a visit to Sweden in 1864, they travelled in what had formerly been the royal yacht Victoria and Albert *(I), and was now—with the coming of* Victoria and Albert *(II)—renamed* Osborne. *The port of disembarkation was Gottenborg.*

But as the royal family spent more and more time at Osborne, *Elfin* seldom strayed far from Spithead and the Solent. Under the command of Staff Captain Watts, she became to all intents and purposes a ferry boat between the mainland and the island.

Each day, she would depart from Portsmouth at 10 am, carrying the morning newspapers and official letters. Having landed them on the shore of Osborne Bay, she would proceed to Cowes, where the Queen's messenger boarded her. He and his dispatches were then taken to Southampton, where he caught the train for London.

Another Queen's messenger was waiting to embark in *Elfin* for Cowes. Having dropped him, the small steamship dropped anchor in the roads and, unless there were any other demands for her services, there she would remain until seven o'clock the next morning, when she would depart for Portsmouth. By ten, she was ready to resume her daily round; a procedure that was carried out with such regularity that *Elfin* soon became known as 'the milk boat'.

She served in this capacity for more than fifty years, until, in 1901, her crew was disbanded and she was dismantled. Her masts and some of the scroll work that adorned her hull were preserved in Portsmouth dockyard. In February, 1929, when George V repaired to Craigwell House, Bognor, to recuperate from his first serious illness, somebody remembered that *Elfin*'s mainmast was still there. It was hastily taken out of store, and erected in the grounds as a flagstaff from which the royal standard was flown.

Victoria never reached Charles II's considerable total of yachts, though, at one time or another, she was the proud possessor of seven steamers, which, even by the standards of monarchy, was not unimpressive.

Although the Queen was certainly very attached to her ships and, by all accounts, enjoyed a sea voyage (though ill on at least one Channel crossing), there was an undoubted sincerity in the message she conveyed to a French engineer who was busy designing a Channel tunnel. 'You may tell [him],' she wrote, 'that if he can accomplish it I will give him my blessing in my own name, and in the name of all the ladies of England.'

During the latter part of her reign, on one rough winter's crossing in the royal yacht to Cherbourg, her servant John Brown made frequent trips to the bridge. On each occasion, he asked the navigator whether the gale and its attendant snowflakes were likely to abate. According to one observer, he explained that, 'The puir boddie downstairs does not feel at all well.' When, at last, the navigating officer was able to report that the French coast was in sight, Brown was relieved. 'That', he said, 'will cheer her up. I will tell her.'

In matters relating to her fleet of royal yachts, Victoria was, as in so many other matters, a collection of contradictions.

She was eager for change, to keep, so to speak, up-to-date. And yet, when changes were made, she was anxious to retain much that they replaced. Although fond of her sailors and their officers, her manner was often imperious. For example, on one occasion when the royal yacht docked at Dover, a guard of honour commanded by a major general came on board to receive her. When she was told of their arrival, she snapped that she was not yet ready for them—and that they should wait on the quayside until she called for them.

Nevertheless, as many historians have noted, there was something reassuringly middle class about Victoria and Albert. If there were any way of measuring the supposedly aristocratic qualities, many of their courtiers would have received a far higher rating than would the royal couple. The interiors of all the royal yachts were nothing if not homely. When, in 1854, it was decided to replace the first *Victoria and Albert* with a larger vessel, of 2,470 tons compared with 1,034 tons, the decoration could hardly have been considered elegant. The furnishings were mostly heavy pieces made from mahogany, while the fabrics were of chintz, designed by Prince Albert.

Having persuaded parliament that a new royal yacht would be in order, the question arose as to what to do with the old one. To scrap a vessel that still had life in her would be a foolish extravagance. As for selling her, that, in Victoria's mind, was quite out of the question. She should be retained for more general duties; as a back-up ship. She might also come in useful for the Prince of Wales, who would soon be growing out of the white sailor suit in which he had first been glimpsed on the deck of *Fairy* during a tour of England's West Country.

There was also the problem of names. *Victoria and Albert* was a celebration of the union of Victoria and Albert. In future, or so it seemed to the Queen, royal yachts should be named after royal residences. They were, after all, floating palaces. Initially, she decided that the newcomer, which was laid down at Pembroke dock, should be called *Windsor Castle*. But then she had second thoughts. In a perfect world there would always be Albert, so there was no reason why their two names should not be perpetuated in their ship of state. *Victoria and Albert* (Mk I) should be renamed *Osborne;* the new ship should inherit her name and become *Victoria and Albert* (Mk II).

The original intention had been that the new royal yacht should be ready for launching in the summer of 1855 and that the Queen herself would perform the ceremony. But the outbreak of the Crimean War put a strain on the dockyard's resources. The slipway on which the new royal yacht was under construction was urgently needed for the building of a line-of-battle ship to be named HMS *Alma*. Consequently, matters were hurried up and, on 16 January, 1855, the vessel was christened by Lady Milford, who smashed the obligatory bottle across her bows and sent her gracefully down to the water. The weather had been bad, but, towards evening, the sun came out and (in the words of an *Illustrated London News* reporter) 'illuminated the interior of the ship in a most beautiful manner'.

Owing to the rush, she was, it appeared, 'in a rather unfinished state'. Nevertheless, her shape commanded respect. Once again quoting the reporter on the ILN, 'her lines would warrant the impression that she will be the fastest vessel in the world.' This was an overstatement, as was his assertion that she was nearly as large as the P & O troopship *Himalaya* (3,438 tons), which, at that time, was the biggest steamer in the world. In fact the new *Victoria and Albert* was nearly 1,000 tons smaller than

Brunel's *Great Britain* built twelve years earlier.

The royal family's accommodation was situated in the after part; that of the officers and ratings in the forward part. There were two tea-houses, a chapel, a nursery for the royal children, sumptuous apartments for the Queen and Prince Albert, and a large dining room on the upper deck, glazed all round, providing an excellent and completely unobstructed view of the surrounding ocean.

As always with Victoria, there were plenty of homely touches, such as a collection of watercolours depicting Her Majesty's ships executed by the 'mathematical' boys of Christ's Hospital. Two tiny brass bedsteads were installed in the cabin that the Prince of Wales would have to share (until he grew older, at any rate) with his brother, the Duke of Edinburgh. There were family portraits in oval frames, and Albert's chintz.

Illumination was provided by candles until 1888, when electric light was installed. Victoria, for some reason, was against it (Albert would have loved the idea, but, by this time, Albert was dead). It required the persuasion of her occulist to convince her that it might be an improvement and that the dim light was harmful to her eyesight. All the same, she insisted that the silver candlesticks should remain in position.

From her berth in Pembroke dock, *Victoria and Albert*, was towed to Portsmouth by the tug *Dragon* and it was here, in the early spring, that her machinery was installed and the fitting-out completed. On 5 July, she carried out her trials, on which, to everyone's satisfaction, she produced a maximum speed of 15 knots.

Unlike her predecessor, she had two funnels. Although the *Great Britain* had already removed the last remaining prejudices against the screw as a means of propulsion; and although nearly all warships were now so designed, for the very good reason that they were less likely to be put out of action by gun fire; *Victoria and Albert* was another paddle steamer. She was manned by a crew of 240 officers and men, most of whom were old hands in the business of navigating royal yachts.

Some years later, *Osborne's* captain, Commander Charles Beresford, RN (later Admiral Lord Beresford), suggested to the Prince of Wales that it might be a good idea if the officers in the royal yacht were changed from time to time. If this were done, his argument ran, Her Majesty would be able to meet more members of her fleet. When Beresford put the proposition to her, she seemed to be worried. Why should he wish to change her officers? Did he insist on doing so?

Beresford smiled respectfully. 'No, ma'am,' he said. 'I have no such power. I only made a suggestion to the Prince.'

Victoria thought for a moment or two. 'You may be right,' she said, 'but I am an old woman now, and I like to see faces I know about me, and not have to begin again with new faces.'

The idea was abandoned.

Fairy and *Elfin* had gone about their duties faultlessly and had given nobody cause for complaint. But with a bigger, and perhaps better, royal yacht, it now seemed appropriate that the Queen should have something more impressive than these diminutive (though, none the less, elegant) little ships as her tender. For this reason the 370 ton *Alberta* was built in 1863. Five years later, the original *Victoria and Albert* (now *Osborne*) was

In 1868, the early Osborne *(formerly* Victoria and Albert*) was scrapped, and replaced by another steam yacht also named* Osborne. *These pictures of the new yacht show the royal apartments:* (top) *the sleeping saloon, and* (bottom) *the pavilion and dining room. They were drawn when the Duke and Duchess of Connaught used the yacht for their honeymoon in 1879.*

scrapped and replaced by a new *Osborne*, 816 tons larger and primarily intended to take the Prince of Wales about his duties and pleasures. The royal steam ship fleet was at its zenith.

The *Victoria and Albert* was kept busy. At the end of the Crimean War, the Queen used her to review the fleet. Then there were the summer cruises along the south coast, which had now become annual events. When the weather was fine there was the yearly trip to Aberdeen *en route* to Balmoral (when the forecast boded ill, Her Majesty very sensibly preferred to travel by train). In 1858, the *Victoria and Albert* took the newly married Princess Royal and her husband, Frederick of Prussia ('Fritz'), from Gravesend to Antwerp on the first stage of their journey to Potsdam. To mark the occasion, all the gaff ends were garlanded with flowers.

On his journey to India in 1875, the Prince of Wales travelled in the troopship Serapis, *which was specially fitted-out for the voyage. Seen here entering the Suez Canal at Port Said,* Serapis *is the centre ship: one of the escorting frigates (either* Pallas *or* Hercules*) is leading, and* Victoria and Albert *(II) is in attendance astern of the large trooper.*

Five years later, she brought Princess Alexandra of Denmark from Flushing to Gravesend for her marriage to Edward Prince of Wales. Edward, always the romantic, had filled his bride-to-be's cabin with roses. When the royal yacht came alongside the landing stage, he ran up the gangway and, to the great delight of the crowd, kissed his 18-year-old fiancée in public.

A rather less happy voyage took place in 1860, when Victoria loaned

Victoria and Albert to the Empress of Austria for her annual migration to Madeira. *Osborne* kept her company in case anything should go wrong, which, in view of the weather, was a very prudent precaution.

The royal yacht had sailed from London on 24 November at three in the afternoon. According to one of the Empress's attendants, 'There arose a strong wind which made the ship rock and we dared not descend into our cabins for fear of making our situation worse.' Somehow, this perilous journey was accomplished. 'As darkness drew on,' she continued, 'we were scarcely settled in our cabins, when we all became so ill and prostrate, that the good people on the ship knew not to whom first to give aid.'

Dr Minter, the royal yacht's physician, was kept continually busy. The commanding officer, Captain Deman, made trips below to 'console and comfort' his unhappy passengers. But he, too, had his troubles. At least one sailor fell from the mast, several suffered broken legs and sprains, and many of them were ill. But even worse was to come.

As *Victoria and Albert* wallowed through the Bay of Biscay, 'no imagination can picture how terrible it was; the ship groaned and cracked in her innermost parts, she rose and tossed about and struggled with the foaming and furious waves . . . it seemed as if all the evil water sprites had combined with the elements to destroy us.'

The Empress and the Princess Windischgratz suffered less than the others if this account is to be believed. But was the writer being tactful? She admits that the former 'had to lie down as it was impossible to walk and from Saturday she didn't eat a morsel, although we were always being persuaded to try to eat, for we were told that our sufferings would be greater on a fasting stomach.'

Eventually, the sun came out and Madeira appeared on the skyline. The lady in waiting wrote, 'We must indeed thank and praise God that our dreadful ordeal has come to a happy termination; what we all suffered on the ship it is not in my power to describe.'

Significantly when, six months later, the Empress returned to Austria and *Victoria and Albert* was again put at her disposal, she directed the captain to Trieste. It was the only occasion on which this particular royal yacht ever ventured into the Mediterranean.

Considering the number of disasters at sea in the nineteenth century, the vessels in Queen Victoria's fleet did well. When the Princess Royal and her husband travelled to Antwerp on their way to Germany, *Victoria and Albert* collided with a brig and damaged one of her paddle boxes. But this did not impede her progress. On a return journey from Denmark, the Prince and Princess of Wales were in jeopardy when *Osborne* steamed into a gale. Her starboard paddle-wheel was damaged on a piece of wreckage,

Officers and ratings of Osborne *pose for a picture with members of the royal family. They include Princess Victoria, Princess Alexandra (later Queen Alexandra), Princess Maud (later Queen of Norway), Lord Charles Beresford (Osborne's captain and later Admiral Lord Beresford) and Prince Louis of Battenberg (father of Lord Mountbatten).*

and the anchor had to be dropped while repairs were carried out. Not far away, it was possible to discern another ship being driven aground on the Danish coast. Her engine had broken down and she had been caught on a lee shore.

Alberta was in trouble in 1875, when she ran into the schooner *Mistletoe*. The Queen, Prince Leopold and Princess Beatrice were on board at the time. Apparently, Staff Captain Welch, who was in command, was shaping a course that should have taken him past the sailing ship's stern. Suddenly, when *Alberta* was too close to do anything about it, *Mistletoe*'s skipper put about and a collision became inevitable. The master of the sailing vessel and two of her passengers were killed. At the subsequent inquest, the coroner's jury was unable to reach a decision. There was a difference of opinion about *Alberta*'s speed.

But these misfortunes pale into insignificance beside the fate of the Russian royal yacht *Standart* in 1907. It was teatime on a brilliant summer afternoon. The ship was steaming along a narrow channel towards the sea, when she struck a rock. Soon afterwards, water began to pour into the hull and she developed a heavy list. The Tsarina and her children were quickly taken off in the boats, carrying with them as many jewels, icons and other precious possessions as they could. The Tsar remained on the bridge, giving the impression that he was about to go down with his ship. Indeed, at one point, he remarked to the commanding officer that he estimated the *Standart* to have twenty minutes more to live.

The Tsar of Russia and his family on board his yacht Standart. *Left to right: the Grand Duchess Olga, the Tsar, the Grand Duchess Anastasia, the Tsaritsa, the Grand Duchess Tatiana, and in the foreground the Tsarevitch Alexis and the Grand Duchess Marie. The design of the* Standard *strongly influenced the shape of the third British royal yacht to be named* Victoria and Albert.

In fact, she survived. Everybody was rescued by the cruiser *Asia* and presently transferred to the other imperial yacht, the *Poliarnaia Zvesday* (Pole Star).

◆

After the death of Prince Albert in 1861, Victoria withdrew into herself. She had seldom travelled far from the coast of Britain, although, even now, she made a good many Channel crossings on private journeys to her villa at Cimiez in the South of France.

The theme of the 1889 international exhibition held in Paris (which coincided with the opening of the Eiffel Tower) was 'Means of Transport'. It seemed appropriate that a *de luxe* cross-channel service should be introduced to mark the occasion. Among the units was a new steamer named *Calais-Douvres*. This ship was far more elegantly appointed than the other packet boats and somewhat quicker. Consequently, it seemed possible that she might serve to convey Victoria to France. A special cabin was built for her on the boat deck and it was, on her insistence, crammed with furniture from *Victoria and Albert*. The journey does not seem to have been a complete success, for she never repeated it. But this may have been due to the fact that *Calais-Douvres* was, herself, unsuccessful. Her appetite for coal was disproportionate to the number of customers prepared to pay extra for her comfortable accommodation.

After a short life, she was withdrawn from service.

———————————◆———————————

By the turn of the century, *Victoria and Albert* was an old ship and the Queen that accounted for half her name was an old woman. The Queen and the yacht were so entwined that, in a manner of speaking, they both died at the same time.

On 22 January, 1901, Victoria passed away peacefully at Osborne. Ten days later, *Alberta* carried her body to Gosport, preceded by eight destroyers and followed in line ahead by *Victoria and Albert, Osborne*, the Kaiser's mighty steam yacht *Hohenzollern,* and the Trinity House yacht *Enchantress.*

The coffin remained on board *Alberta* that night. On the following morning, twelve bluejackets from the fleet bore it to the train for London. On *Victoria and Albert,* the former Prince of Wales, now Edward VII, lowered the royal standard for the last time. He had hoped to use the yacht the next year for a coronation review of the fleet, but the authorities at Portsmouth dockyard reported that the cost of a refit would be exorbitant. In any case, it would take too long. Not that it mattered very much, for a new royal yacht, the third *Victoria and Albert*, was already nearing completion.

However, having retired *Victoria and Albert*, nobody, Edward VII least of all, was prepared to consign her to the scrap yard. She lingered on

Victoria and Albert *(III) at Spithead for the coronation review of the fleet in 1911. As originally designed, she turned out to be top heavy: the height of her funnels had to be reduced and her forecastle removed.*

until 1904 when, at last, she was towed away to the breakers. The *Royal George* which, admittedly, was a lot older, was dealt with rather more quickly. Edward decided that there was no need for a hulk to house the crews of royal yachts when the ships were out of service. Nor, one must assume, did the emerging shape of warships provide much scope for riggers.

In this instance, the duties of hands on British royal yachts differed from those who manned the Tsar's ship. Most of the latter were impressive looking individuals, six feet or so tall, who, during the winter, were often called upon to play the parts of warriors in the opera house at St Petersburg. *Aida*, especially, benefited from their services—though they are said to have looked rather self-conscious on stage.

◆

Britain may be an island; but there was scarcely a European sovereign who did not have some sort of kinship with Queen Victoria. The German Kaiser was her grandson (and Edward VII's nephew); Nicholas II of Russia was a grandson by marriage; the kings of Belgium, Denmark, Spain and Greece could all be arranged on the family tree. The royalty of Europe were inextricably linked by blood and marriage; and they had something else in common—a passion for yachts.

Victoria did not acknowledge any rivals, and she certainly did not wish for any vessel better than *Victoria and Albert* (Mk II), although her son, Edward VII, clearly believed that the art of shipbuilding had advanced since the old paddle-steamer's keel had been laid down nearly half a century before. The Kaiser *knew* that he had the finest steam yacht in the world in his incomparable *Hohenzollern* (had she not crossed the Atlantic, with his brother, Prince Henry of Prussia, on board? What other royal yacht had done *that?*). The Tsar, who looked like a rather watered-down replica of George V, was suitably proud of *Standart* and certainly felt more happy aboard her than he did anywhere else. The only snag about his ship was the ratings' accommodation. It was situated deep in the forward end, with no portholes and horribly low deckheads on which the burly crewmen were constantly bumping their heads. Furthermore, while *Hohenzollern* was ugly to a fault, *Standart* was a graceful ship, combining the elegant lines of, say, a clipper with all the advantages of steam.

Standart it was that inspired the new British royal yacht, which was launched by the Duchess of York at Pembroke dock on 6 May, 1899. Once again, there was a confusion of names. In this case, the idea had been to call the newcomer *Balmoral*, but just as the name *Victoria and Albert* had once triumphed over *Windsor Castle*, so was it again preferred.

Having come to this decision, Victoria lost interest in the project. She once glimpsed the ship coming up Spithead on passage to Portsmouth, but her curiosity was not excited and she never went on board. The past was beyond recall and was peopled by Albert and the children and holidays at Osborne and Balmoral, and the old *Victoria and Albert* of so many happy memories now, like the sovereign herself, too antique to carry on for much longer.

Perhaps we should regard the use of *Standart*'s plans for the Mk III edition of *Victoria and Albert* as an early argument for Britain adopting metrication. At all events, somebody got the sums wrong. She glided impeccably down the slipway at the Duchess's command; the first signs of trouble appeared later, when, apparently complete and ready for whatever tasks lay in waiting, she was floated out of drydock. Instead of gently coming alive as the water grasped her, she keeled over until she touched the dockside and, in the process, damaged her bottom. This, obviously, was not good enough. The authorities scratched their heads and audibly wondered whether she would ever be fit for use as a royal yacht.

Nevertheless, they adjusted her ballast in the rather forlorn hope that it might improve matters, and sent her to Portsmouth. A programme of trials and various complex calculations occupied the next few months. The outcome was that the funnels were shortened, the forecastle removed, a lot of concrete ballast added, and several particularly heavy fittings taken away.

The bill for all this came to nearly £$\frac{1}{2}$ million, which was almost as much as the ship had cost in the first place. But never mind; at least she was stable and fit for a king! Her interior suggested an opulent and rather pleasant country house; her exterior was even more pleasing than *Standart*'s graceful shape.

She was commissioned on 23 July, 1901, and manned by a crew of 367 officers and men. When the sovereign was on board, there were usually about forty servants from Buckingham Palace as well.

◆

King Edward, like his nephew the Kaiser, liked to visit the Mediterranean. He made several trips in *Osborne* (Mk II). On one of them, when he was Prince of Wales, a sea monster had been sighted. It was on 2 June, 1877, at five o'clock in the afternoon. The ship was on passage, off the north coast of Sicily, when the commanding officer (Captain Pearson) 'distinctly saw a seal-shaped head of immense size, large flappers and part of a huge body'. Lieutenant Hays, who was also on the bridge, noticed 'a head, two flappers, and about thirty feet of an animal's shoulders'. The head, he estimated, was about six feet thick; the neck narrower—perhaps four or five feet. The creature's shoulders seemed to be about fifteen feet across, and each flapper about fifteen feet long.

His colleague, Lieutenant Forsyth, thought that the head was even bigger. He put its length at fifteen or even twenty feet. Whatever its dimensions, this titanic seal (if such it was) displayed a healthy mistrust of *Osborne* and made off at speed in a south-easterly direction. By the time the Prince came on deck to view it, it had vanished.

Edward VII spent less time afloat than his German nephew who, it was calculated, lived aboard *Hohenzollern* for more than one-third of his total reign (in one year alone he spent 200 days). When Edward was cruising in the Mediterranean, he often extemporised his route, much to the consternation of the First Lord of the Admiralty in London, who would have liked notice of the sovereign's plans.

There was, for example, the unhappy occasion in 1909, when *Victoria and Albert* was steaming towards Malta. At any moment, the huge grey shapes of the fleet should have loomed up on the horizon, hastening to welcome the King. But no such shapes appeared, and when the royal yacht entered harbour, there were no warships to be seen.

Somewhat testily, Edward wanted to know where they were. He was told that there had, it seemed, been an uprising in Turkey and His Majesty's men-of-war had been dispatched on a flag-showing mission to the coast of Asia Minor.

Why, he asked, had he not been told about this? Winston Churchill, the First Lord, was quick to point out that the King would certainly have been informed—had anyone known precisely where *Victoria and Albert* was. The art of communication at sea still had its limitations.

There was also the monarch's fondness for travelling, as he believed, incognito. In 1903, to mention only one case, the royal yacht arrived at Naples escorted by eight battleships, four cruisers and eight destroyers. Such an array of naval might could scarcely be expected to escape notice. Nevertheless, he decided to go ashore in what he insisted was the guise of a tourist, accompanied by the Queen of Portugal and Mrs Gloria Vander-bilt, herself no stranger to the world of large yachts. Her husband, the self-styled 'Commodore', owned a 2,300 ton vessel that included a marble dining room and a bathroom occupying half the length of one deck. 'Disguised' as tourists, the trio set out to explore the town's slums.

Good sea boat that she was, once the matter of her stability had been corrected, *Victoria and Albert* behaved just as uncomfortably as any commoner's ship when conditions were rough. Admiral Lord Fisher, who frequently attended the King on his voyages, described a trip to Russia in June, 1908. 'We had', he wrote in a letter to his wife, 'a horrible knocking about in the North Sea. Every one ill from the King downwards. I wasn't actually sick, but a horrible sick headache, which was worse. The Queen lay on deck like a corpse! and Princess Victoria beckoned me to her (when I went on deck in a quiet interval) and said she had been continuously sick and could not keep down a biscuit. Everything in my cabin went mad. The armchair went head over heels through the door and teapot and milk jug emptied themselves on to my hairbrushes, and everything upset . . .'

Not all the storms were created by the weather. The King was not the easiest of men; when he fulminated he did so in the grand manner.

There was one particularly upsetting episode in the summer of 1902. The Shah of Persia was on a visit to England, and somebody conceived the idea that he should be invested with the Order of the Garter. Edward would have none of it. Ignoring the fact that his mother had conferred it upon the Sultan of Turkey (aboard *Victoria and Albert* [Mk II], as it happened), and had thereby created some sort of precedent, he protested that this was a Christian order of chivalry and not for infidels such as the Shah.

Knowing that the visitor was expecting something the foreign secretary, Lord Lansdowne, went to see the Court jewellers (Messrs Garrard). In the remarkably short time of three days, they produced a non-Christian version of the Garter star and badge, by cleverly omitting the cross. In triumph, Lansdowne set off to show it to the King.

Victoria and Albert with Edward aboard was at anchor off Pembroke dock. Edward was less than appreciative of his minister's ability to compromise. If he had said there should be no such award; there *would* be no such award. In a moment of fury, he flung the precious bauble through an open porthole. As it happened, a steam pinnace was a few feet away. A stoker caught it and returned it to the ship. It may have been a fortunate coincidence, but it did nothing to change the royal mind. The Shah returned to Persia undecorated.

In matters of clothing, Edward was a stickler. He changed the appearance of men's trousers when, by accident, his valet pressed a pair of trousers with the creases fore and aft, rather than, as was the custom, on either side. Edward liked it and trousers have never recovered from the error.

Nevertheless, in most matters, he insisted upon orthodoxy, even to the point of merging by degrees into what he regarded as suitable attire. For instance, on approaching Scotland by sea, he did not suddenly don the kilt; he worked towards it. One evening, as *Victoria and Albert* crept northwards up the coast, Edward instructed his man to produce, 'Un costume un peu plus écossais demain.'

He expected his companions to observe a similar awareness of what was, and what was not, suitable; which, given such subtle transitions, must have been difficult. There was, however, one rule that had to be obeyed wherever the royal yacht might be. Knee-breeches were strictly taboo. As Edward pointed out on more than one occasion, 'trousers are always worn on board ship'.

───────────────◆───────────────

Victoria and Albert was, literally, the ship of state; a floating palace where the sovereign and his peers sat down to dinner with guests ranging from, on one occasion, sixteen admirals to, on another, half-a-dozen crowned heads. For shorter journeys and less important occasions, Edward ordered a smaller steamer, the *Alexandra* (2,050 tons), which was completed in 1908. She was mostly used on trips across the Channel to France.

Charles II might reasonably have claimed to have invented yacht racing. His successors, whether Stuart or Hanoverian, encouraged the sport. George IV, having joined the Yacht Club when Prince Regent, caused it to be called the Royal Yacht Club on his accession in 1820. In 1833, William IV, who devised a system of handicapping, changed its name to Royal Yacht Squadron, the present day organisation of the few who are allowed to fly the White Ensign. These monarchs did not, however, take part in many events.

As Prince of Wales, Edward decided that his by no means meagre leisure would be the richer for a racing yacht. The Kaiser owned five large sailing boats in ten years, all of them named *Meteor*. Edward contented himself with one, which he passed on to his son George V, and which survived to the ripe old age of 42. Designed by G L Watson and built by a Glasgow firm named D & W Henderson, *Britannia* (as he called her) registered 212 tons, was one hundred feet from her graceful stem to her no less comely stern, and drew 12ft 6in. of water. There was more than sufficiently comfortable accommodation within her hull. She was manned by a professional skipper and a crew of twenty-four.

Edward used to sit in a chair at the stern, invariably wearing a panama hat and smoking a cigar. Initially, *Britannia* did very well in races at venues ranging from the Clyde to Cannes. Unfortunately, in what was an ill-advised gesture, the Kaiser had been given honorary membership of the Royal Yacht Squadron. As anyone who knew Wilhelm would have realised, he was incapable of leaving well alone. He disagreed with the squadron's system of handicapping, and he produced a plan whereby smaller vessels were able to race alongside larger ones. Edward, who always found his nephew hard to tolerate, became fed up. Speaking of

Queen Mary aboard a steam pinnace leaves one of the royal yachts in August 1911. (Top.)

George V at the wheel of his much loved racing yacht Britannia. *The original of this photograph is mounted on the wheelhouse bulkhead of the present royal yacht.* (Bottom.)

Cowes week, he said, 'The Regatta used to be a pleasant recreation for me. Since the Kaiser takes command, it is a vexation.'

One result of this vexation was that, in 1897, he sold *Britannia*. This obviously left some sort of gap in his life, because four years later he bought her back. But he was done with racing. Thereafter, he used her only for cruising. It was left to his son, George V, to restore her to the world of regattas in which, summer after summer, she and her peers, those stately J class vessels such as *Shamrock, White Heather, Velsheda* and *Endeavour,* raced against one another at Cowes and thence at events round the coast.

Britannia was the star. As Major B Heckstall-Smith wrote in *All Hands on the Main Sheet,* 'It is a fact that if *Britannia* attends regattas they are successful. I am not speaking of fashionable places like Cowes or the Solent, but the people's regattas at the outports. To the people of these places a regatta means a holiday, and to the shop-people and water-side folk a harvest. If the Royal Yacht arrives, it means a success, if she does not it very often means a failure.'

———————————————◆———————————————

At the end of World War 1, the British fleet of royal yachts was much as it had been at the beginning of the war, which was more than can be said for the European royalty and theirs. A new vessel ordered by the Kaiser in 1913 lay uncompleted on the slipway and was taken to pieces. *Hohenzollern,* her owner now exiled in Holland, was scrapped in 1923. *Standart* was taken over by the Bolsheviks, converted into a mine-layer, and renamed *Marty. Poliarnaia Zvesday* became some sort of floating prison, where the Tsarina's confidante, Anna Vyrubova, was jailed in the stokers' quarters after the execution of the Russian royal family.

In Britain, *Alexandra* was sold in 1925 to the Norwegian Shipping Company (Nordenfjeldske Dampskibsselshab) of Trondheim, which converted her into a small cruise liner and renamed her *Prins Olav. Victoria and Albert* still went about her not very exacting business, and *Britannia* continued to charm the crowds at seaside-resort regattas. Unlike Edward VII, George V liked to take the helm himself and was perfectly able to act as skipper. In his study at Buckingham Palace, he spent quite a lot of time with designer Charles Nicholson—discussing ideas to improve her performance. In 1931, he ordered her conversion to Bermuda rig, which brought her in line with the other J class competitors.

George V loved *Britannia*. When he died in 1936, she was not, on his insistence, allowed to survive him. Her 50ft boom was erected in the keep of Carisbrooke Castle on the Isle of Wight, to replace a flagstaff that

Faced with the problem of finding their 19-year-old son something worthwhile to do during the long vacation, Victoria and Albert decided to send the Prince of Wales (later Edward VII) to Canada and the United States in July, 1860, aboard the screw-driven battleship HMS Hero. The return trip in November of that year was something of a nightmare. High seas and adverse winds slowed the ship down and the passage took twenty-six days. (Left.)

The troopship Serapis *took the Prince of Wales to India in 1875. She was one of five sisters—all built in 1866. When not employed on royal duty, she could transport a battalion of infantry and the soldiers' families—all told, about 1,200 people.* (Bottom.)

had been shattered by lightning. Her fittings were sold at auction, where they raised £1,025 for George V's Fund for Sailors. Her furniture and crockery were sent to Queen Mary at Buckingham Palace.

All that remained of her now lay on a slipway at Marvin's yard, Cowes. In early July, 1936, carrying out his father's wishes, Edward VIII signed *Britannia*'s death warrant. The yard foreman placed a garland of wild flowers over her stem head, and a party of schoolboys helped to warp her down into the water. For the next two days, she lay at anchor in the roads.

Just before midnight on 9 July, two destroyers—HMS *Amazon* and HMS *Winchelsea*—took her in tow to a mark off St Catherine's point. A squad of sailors went aboard and placed charges of explosive in suitable points. Then the warships withdrew to a safe distance. Five minutes later, there was an explosion and *Britannia* vanished.

The feelings of many people were summed up in a letter to *The Times* by a Mr G H Nicolson of Winchester, who wrote,

> No yachtsman can visit Cowes this year without feeling an aching void at the absence of our dear old idol. The undisputed 'Queen of Cowes Roads', all other yachts shrank into insignificance beside her . . . We loved her because she was no gimcrack racing machine but a ship, fit for all weathers, and her place in our hearts can never be filled. It would have been indeed harrowing to see her descend like many other famous ships to an unhonoured end rotting on the mud of some remote estuary.

If Mr Nicolson is still alive, it will no doubt please him to learn that the wheel of *Britannia* continues to fulfil a useful purpose. It is used to steer her present day namesake. Nearby, on the wheelhouse bulkhead, there is a photograph of King George V at the great sailing yacht's helm. It was taken in 1926.

Nor is this the only item of history on today's royal yacht. An ornate gilded binnacle, a survivor of *Royal George*, is installed on the verandah deck immediately outside the sun lounge. It still houses a compass, though, in this respect at least it has been brought up to date. It is a repeater from the ship's main gyro compass.

◆

Although King George V sailed in *Victoria and Albert* on numerous occasions, he only once travelled to the Mediterranean in her, in 1925. Edward VIII made no use of her at all. The one voyage of his reign was in a steam yacht named *Nahlin*, which he chartered from Lady Yule. The

fact that the trip took place in the company of Mrs Simpson rather obscured the fact that it was, officially at any rate, a state visit to Turkey.

Edward decided that *Victoria and Albert* was obsolete, and that she should be scrapped. George VI had fonder memories of the admittedly ageing ship—possibly because he had been much closer to George V than Edward ever was. As a boy, he had stood by his father's side at fleet reviews. On one occasion, at Portsmouth in 1912, a submarine came alongside and father and son made a descent in this latest, though still rudimentary, weapon of war. The boat was the D4, whose commanding officer, Lieutenant Martin Dunbar-Nasmith, won the VC some years later for destroying 96 Turkish ships in the Sea of Marmora.

On this same visit, the future George VI (Prince Albert as he then was) met Winston Churchill for the first time. Albert was a cadet at Dartmouth; Churchill a thrusting young First Lord of the Admiralty.

During the brief period between his coming to the throne and the outbreak of World War 2, George VI used *Victoria and Albert* for the coronation fleet review; for a trip to Aberdeen *en route* to Balmoral in 1938; and for a cruise to the West Country in 1939. But when he and the Queen went on a state visit to France in 1938, they crossed the channel in a sloop named HMS *Enchantress*. As even the King had to admit, the royal

During his visit to Canada in 1919, the Prince of Wales, ever adventurous, used more modest water transport than was normal for an heir to the throne.

yacht was now a long way past her prime. Among the items that appeared in the 1939 navy estimates was the authorisation for a replacement.

There was, however, a happy conclusion to *Victoria and Albert*'s career as a royal yacht, though it did not seem particularly significant at the time. During the West Country cruise of 1939, the King visited the Royal Naval College at Dartmouth. This establishment was in the throes of a combined epidemic of mumps and chickenpox. One cadet who, fortunately, was not affected by it was the young Prince Philip of Greece. That night, he dined on board the yacht; and that is how he made the acquaintance of his distant cousin, the Princess Elizabeth.

------------------------◆------------------------

World War 2 put a stop to the building of a new royal yacht. Afterwards, with George VI in poor health, the plans were taken out of store and revised. More family accommodation was included, and the vessel, to be called *Britannia*, was so designed that, in the event of a future war, she could be converted into a hospital ship. There was some urgency in her construction. It was felt that, once she was completed, the monarch could cruise to warmer climates, which might improve his condition.

Meanwhile, *Victoria and Albert* remained in commission, though no longer as HM Royal Yacht. During the war she had served as an accommodation ship attached to HMS *Excellent*, the gunnery school at Whale Island, Portsmouth. She was finally broken up in 1955.

Britannia was not completed in time to take George VI to those sunny places that people felt might be good for him. He died in February, 1952, more than a year before his new yacht was ready for launching. For want of a royal yacht, Queen Elizabeth II had to rely on stop-gap measures during her coronation year of 1953. For the coronation review of the fleet in the summer of that year, the despatch vessel HMS *Surprise* (she had been built as a frigate named HMS *Gerrans Bay*) was put at the Queen's disposal and suitably modified for her needs. Later, for much of the coronation world tour of the Commonwealth in 1953–1954, a passenger liner named *Gothic* was chartered from the Shaw Saville and Albion Line.

When the Queen and the Duke of Edinburgh departed from London Airport on the first stage of the Commonwealth tour, which was to take them round the world, *Britannia* was being fitted out. On 16 April of that year, Her Majesty had been to her builder's yard, John Brown & Co of Clydebank, to carry out the launching ceremony. After she had given her ship a name, and when she had sent the yacht down the slipway and delivered *Britannia* to her natural element, the Queen said,

'I am sure that all of you who are present here realise how much the

A navy is as much a status symbol to a newly emerged nation as an airline and in 1961 Pakistan was justly proud of its collection of warships. When the Queen and the Duke of Edinburgh (in the uniform of a British admiral of the fleet) arrived on a state visit, they were invited to review the fleet from the deck of a destroyer. (Left.)

When Queen Elizabeth paid a visit to Borneo in 1972, she travelled in the royal barge of the Britannia *up the river in Kuching, where the local population turned out to greet her in less elaborate—though, more colourful—river-craft. In Brunei, on the same royal tour, the Queen drove through the capital in a chariot drawn by forty men. (Bottom.)*

building of this ship meant to the late King, my father. He felt most strongly, as I do, that a Yacht was a necessity and not a luxury for the Head of our great British Commonwealth, between whose countries the sea is no barrier but the natural and indestructible highway.'

As she also pointed out, the royal yacht was 'to be at times the home of my husband and myself and of our family'.

Since *Britannia*'s maiden voyage, the nature of long distance travel has changed considerably. Jet aircraft have replaced ocean liners, and the few that remain are, with very few exceptions, used for pleasure cruising. The Queen herself makes considerable use of aeroplanes; nevertheless, *Britannia* has covered more miles than the sum of voyages by all previous royal yachts. The three *Victoria and Albert*s seldom strayed far from the English Channel or the North Sea. A trip to the Mediterranean was a rarity. *Britannia*, on the other hand, has circumnavigated the globe; she has travelled south to the edge of Antarctica; and she has crossed all the great oceans. As the Queen remarked, she is a 'home', but she is also a ship for all seasons, and a very sturdy one too.

4
JOURNEY BY TRAIN

On 16 May, 1977, the Queen and the Duke of Edinburgh attended the Chelsea Flower Show in London. Next morning they were due to be in Glasgow Cathedral for a national service of thanksgiving, followed by a civic lunch in the City Chambers. The occasion for rejoicing was the Silver Jubilee. Her Majesty had just completed twenty-five years as sovereign of the United Kingdom and as head of the Commonwealth.

The journey to Glasgow was to be made overnight in a new royal train. On arrival at Euston, the Queen and the Duke were met by Sir Peter Parker (then Mr Parker), chairman of British Rail. During the latter years of the 1960s it had been decided that the royal saloons—which are the heart of this illustrious collection of carriages—were due for replacement. They had, after all, been in service for a long time. No less to the point was the fact that they had been built for rail travel in the days when 70mph (112km/h) was regarded as fast. Since then, the pace had quickened and speeds of 100mph (160km/h) were by no means uncommon.

But the royal coaches could not travel at more than seventy with any promise of comfort or safety. Nor were they equipped with modern air-conditioning, a refinement that travellers on ordinary Inter-City services had been enjoying for several years. It was, someone said, time that the royal train was brought up to date.

The project had begun in 1974 at that manufactory of regal rolling stock, the Wolverton Works of British Rail Engineering Ltd in Buckinghamshire. Now the task was done, and there, beside a Euston platform, stood the new saloons—one for the Queen and one for the Duke, each painted in that subtle shade of royal claret that is peculiar to royal vehicles, and which is so dark that, in bad light or at a distance, it can easily be mistaken for black.

Mr Parker hoped that Her Majesty would be pleased with the new coaches. He presented her with a key that would unlock the door of her saloon, and with an album of pictures featuring not only the new train but also prints depicting royal rail travel in the nineteenth century. Other evocations of these early royal trains hung on the walls inside. One, for example, showed Queen Victoria with Prince Albert, Prince Albert Edward (who later became Edward VII) and the Princess Royal, setting off for Scotland on the Great Northern line from a temporary station in Maiden Lane, London. This, as any railway buff could have told Her Majesty, must have been before the company's London terminus at King's Cross was opened in 1852.

The royal party climbed aboard. On a wall of the vestibule, a plaque recorded the fact that, 'This coach entered service in May 1977—the Silver Jubilee Year of the Reign of Her Majesty the Queen.' The Queen and Prince Philip were already familiar with the decor, for they had personally selected the furniture and fittings. Sir Hugh Casson, later to become president of the Royal Academy, had advised them.

With what British Rail describes as 'a formal entrance vestibule with double doors' at either end, the Queen's saloon is not unlike an apartment on wheels. There is a lounge (complete with settee, easy chairs, and a desk), a bedroom (the bed is a 3-foot-wide divan with room for luggage underneath), and a bathroom. Adjoining it, more modest accommodation, but still with a bathroom, is provided for the Queen's dresser.

The lighting, by fluorescent tubes, is subdued, but reading lamps provide enough illumination for when Her Majesty wishes to study official documents, or, possibly like less illustrious travellers, settle down with a good book.

Prince Philip's saloon is more masculine in its decoration. Whilst the Queen's saloon has a bath, his has a shower compartment. Unlike Her Majesty's coach, there is an all-electric kitchen capable of providing meals for up to ten people. The idea is that this can be used when the saloon is on its own, rather than being one unit in a complete royal train. As all this may suggest, these are as luxurious a pair of vehicles as ever rode the lines of British Rail.

Once the Queen and the Duke and their party had embarked, the guard blew his whistle and the train—eight carriages long—departed into the night. Glasgow, in terms of time, was now that little bit closer, for the new rolling stock was able to travel at 100mph (160km/h) and thereby to fit in with a system designed for such speeds. Not only would this hasten the royal couple northwards, it would also avoid the uncomfortable possibility (in terms of protocol) of their being passed by a humble member of the permanent way's populace—such as a goods train!

———————————————◆———————————————

When the before-mentioned picture was drawn depicting Queen Victoria

The present royal train came into service on 16 May, 1977, when the Queen and Prince Philip travelled overnight from Euston to Glasgow. The exterior of the coaches is painted in royal claret (easily mistaken for black). As these two illustrations show, the Queen's saloon is a simple but restful essay in mobile luxury. A far cry from the cluttered splendour of Queen Victoria's parlour on wheels. The decor is by Sir Hugh Casson—with royal guidance. (Left and bottom left.)

The Duke of Edinburgh's saloon is more masculine in its colour scheme. Unlike the Queen's saloon, its facilities include a kitchen that can provide meals for up to ten people. (Bottom right.)

and her family at Maiden Lane, British royalty had already been in the habit of making journeys by train for the better part of ten years.

It might be argued that rail travel in the United Kingdom got off to a bad start when no less than a cabinet minister, William Huskisson, former president of the Board of Trade, was run over and killed by Stephenson's *Rocket* at the opening of the Liverpool & Manchester Railway in 1830. By 1842, there had been at least five serious rail disasters. Apparently the greater speed that steam locomotion could offer could not be enjoyed without the possibility of danger.

Despite this, Prince Albert, always anxious to experience the products of mechanical ingenuity, had already made several journeys by train. Queen Victoria was less ready to commit herself to this new and, it sometimes seemed, recklessly swift system. After one of Albert's journeys, he had been compelled to tell a railway official, 'Not so fast next time, Mr Conductor.' As any other traveller, he found the going rough on occasion. The turbulence was partly caused by the fact that, not having progressed very far beyond their horse-drawn equivalents, the carriages had only four wheels apiece. Nor, indeed, was the suspension more than rudimentary.

The emerging railway companies, of which there were many, were obviously eager to carry the Queen. To do so would make their undertaking respectable. It would imply that a mode of transport sufficiently safe to convey the sovereign was safe enough for her subjects.

In the attempt to secure royal patronage, the Great Western Railway had, as the other companies were compelled to admit, nearly everything in its favour. After all, its station at Slough was not far from the Queen's castle at Windsor; from there, the journey to Buckingham Palace could be accomplished in little more than half-an-hour. Since Queen Victoria travelled between her homes in London and Windsor with a frequency approaching that of a latter-day commuter, it could not have been too difficult to persuade her to make a trial trip. After all, as rumours in court circles had it, Prince Albert approved of railways, and had reassured his wife that they did not represent the greatest hazard to health and safety since the invention of the wheel.

To ensure that, when the time came, they would be ready, the directors of the GWR commissioned a well-known London coach-builder named David Davies to build what was described as, 'a splendid railway carriage'. It was 21ft (6.4m) long and divided into three compartments. The central, and most important, was 'a noble saloon' fitted out by Mr Webb, the Old Bond Street upholsterer. There were sofas in the style of Louis XIV, a rosewood table in the centre, and the panelled walls were decorated with paintings said to represent the four elements. At either end of the carriage, there were windows that, in theory, afforded the royal traveller a view of the line ahead or behind. However, as there was a locomotive in front, and some other item of rolling stock at the back, there was little to see, and Mr Davies might have saved himself the trouble of making them.

Albert approved of the carriage. When asked for his views, Lord Melbourne, a previous prime minister, replied in a letter to Victoria that, [he] 'was sure that Your Majesty being *fond of speed*, would be delighted by the railway'. Since Lord Melbourne's experience of his sovereign's love for speed had been confined to an occasional canter in the park, it is difficult to see how he came to this conclusion. Certainly experience was to show that he exaggerated. Queen Victoria would never permit an engine driver to exceed 40mph (65km/h), and, indeed, a later royal saloon had a signalling device constructed on its roof. The object was to enable the Queen to transmit signals to the locomotive cab should she wish to travel more quickly or more slowly.

On 13 June, 1842, the handiwork of Messrs Davies and Webb was completed. A royal waiting room had been added to Slough station, the Queen had agreed to give rail travel a trial. The directors of the GWR were in a furore, combined in equal parts of agony and ecstasy, and the company's latest engine, the *Phlegethon* (completed a month earlier and only just run-in), had steam up. On the footplate were Daniel Gooch, its designer, and Isambard Kingdom Brunel who had built the Great Western Railway.

Considering the comparatively short distance to be covered, the train was an elaborate affair. In addition to the royal saloon, there were two posting carriages for the royal suite, three carriage trucks for the baggage, and a second class brake carriage. Just before noon the Queen and Prince Albert arrived at Slough station from the castle. They were greeted by a director of the GWR and by the company secretary. After a quick inspection of the train, the royal couple climbed aboard. Twenty-two and a half minutes later, *Phlegethon* steamed into the Great Western's London terminus at Bishop's Road, Paddington. Today's Paddington station was not built until 1854, when it was opened by the Prince Consort. The journey had been $18\frac{1}{4}$ miles long (nearly 30km). The average speed of 48.66mph (*c*78km/h) was, perhaps, excessive for a royal train and was certainly not permitted again.

Nevertheless, Victoria had thoroughly enjoyed herself. In a letter to her uncle, Leopold, the first King of Belgium, she enthused, 'We arrived yesterday morning, having come by railroad from Windsor, in half an hour, free from dust and heat, and I am quite charmed by it.'

Elements of the press were less delighted. To subject the monarch

to the perils that attended travel by train seemed a disgrace. The news-paper *Atlas* was particularly incensed. Its leader writer grumbled that if this sort of thing was allowed to continue, there was no calculating the consequences. 'A long regency', he wrote, taking the gloomiest possible view, 'would be so fearful and tremendous an evil that we cannot but desire, in common with many others, that these Royal railway excursions should be, if possible, either wholly abandoned, or only occasionally resorted to.'

It required more than the thunder of a journalist to quench the Queen's liking for such 'excursions'. She had left Windsor Castle just before noon, had arrived at Buckingham Palace in time for lunch—and this had included both the inspection of a guard of honour from the 8th Royal Irish Fusiliers that had been hastily assembled on the platform at Bishop's Road, and the making of suitable laudatory remarks to the officials of the railway company.

Ten days later, she returned to Windsor by the same method, this time taking the infant Prince of Wales with her, and thereby incurring more disapproval in the press. The peppery Colonel Charles Sibthorp, Member for Lincoln, went so far as to ask a question in Parliament. But the colonel was not to be taken too seriously. It seems that he was opposed to almost everything, from catholic emancipation to parliamentary re-form; from free trade to, one must suppose, the Prince Consort. At all events, Sibthorp was responsible for a reduction in Prince Albert's grant from Parliament.

The Queen was undismayed by the critics of royal travel by train, and so were the railway companies. The business of building royal saloons boomed, with each company attempting to outdo the others. The London and Birmingham which, at that moment, offered the only route to the north, made travel history by installing the first heater ever to be used in a railway carriage. Relying on a small boiler concealed beneath the floor, it was the invention of a Mr Perkins. Mr Perkins had been less successful with an earlier invention, when he attempted to produce a gun that un-leashed its projectiles by steam instead of by high explosive.

When Queen Victoria established herself at Osborne on the Isle of Wight, the London and South Western produced a coach with four armchairs and a sofa, and an adjoining room in which to house the royal children or the attendant equerries. A glass door separated the two compartments, which meant that an eye could be kept on the youngsters, or the watchful equerries summoned by a gesture. To reduce the noise, the saloon's ingenious designer, Joseph Beattie, who later turned his

Queen Victoria's parlour on one of her many royal trains. Although, in 1869, a bellows gangway was introduced to connect one coach to another, the Queen resolutely refused to use it—just as she viewed the introduction of electric light with considerable suspicion.

With twin brass bedsteads, and a white quilted ceiling, Queen Victoria's bedroom on wheels was nothing if not luxurious.

talents to the building of locomotives, fitted the vehicle with wooden wheels. The engine that hauled it, no. 119, established a record by remaining in royal service for forty years. It was not its speed nor its reliability that commended it, but its axle loads. They were so light that it was the only member of its species that could steam with safety on to the rickety old railway jetty at Portsmouth—from whence the royal party proceeded to the island by yacht.

When, in 1850, the GWR decided that its original royal saloon was due for replacement, David Davies was again invited to produce the coachwork. Whilst less decorative than a vehicle produced by the South Eastern Railway in the following year (a rococo masterpiece with carvings and gildings galore, a maple table with a marqueterie inlay in the centre, and four couchant lions executed in high relief adorning the outside), it was, in at least one respect, more practical. Possibly at the suggestion of the Prince Consort, its amenities included a lavatory, thus making it the first railway carriage in the world to be so equipped. The GWR's royal saloon was probably a more pleasant conveyance than the South Eastern's elaborate folly, which, despite a flamboyance that even extended to gold-plated door handles, was described by one critic as 'the last work in luxurious discomfort'.

Inevitably, a time would come when the Queen would travel to or from Scotland by train. The occasion was 28 September, 1848, and it was unplanned. Had it not been for unexpectedly bad weather, it might have taken longer to come about.

Victoria and her family had been spending a holiday at Balmoral (to be re-built by that restless architect, Prince Albert, five years later). They had made the journey north in the royal yacht, *Victoria and Albert*, and they had intended to return to London the same way. That afternoon, they set off by road to Aberdeen. The villagers turned out along the route to wave, and one or two had actually erected crude but nonetheless touching triumphal arches. At the entrance to the landing stage at Aberdeen, there was a rather better version illuminated by one thousand lamps. At 7 pm, smartly on cue, the bells of the city pealed a greeting and a detachment from the 93rd Highlands (the Gordons) smartly presented arms. The Lord Provost, the magistrates, the members of parliament for both the city and the county, the Lord Lieutenant and sundry other dignitaries, all bowed. The Queen alighted, followed by Prince Albert and the tiny figures of the Prince of Wales, Prince Alfred and the Princess Royal.

On board the *Victoria and Albert*, Captain Lord Adolphus Fitz-

Clarence met the royal party at the head of the prow. Nearby, the comforting shapes of a squadron of warships stood sentinel. On land, the function was performed by the Highlanders and by Aberdeen's special constabulary. Soon afterwards, the royal family took dinner aboard the yacht.

The idea was that *Victoria and Albert* and her attendant warships should sail at two o'clock next morning. The night was unusually dark and a strong north-wester was blowing. While the Queen slept, Lord Fitz-Clarence conferred with his second-in-command and the navigating officers from the other men-of-war. They were agreed that it was a dirty night, so bad, indeed, that there could be no question of sailing at the appointed time. According to Fitz-Clarence, if the weather did not moderate by noon, 'it would not be altogether safe for Her Majesty to leave harbour'.

Far from moderating, the strength of the wind increased. The sea voyage was abandoned, and the Queen was advised to return to London overland. At 2.30 pm, she and her family disembarked. They were taken to Perth in an ordinary 1st class (compartment-type) carriage belonging to the Aberdeen Railway Company.

In England, nearly every railway company had a royal saloon awaiting the Queen's pleasure. In Scotland, there were no such luxuries. Nor could there be any question of the royal family making the journey non-stop. There would have to be two nights in lodgings. Since six railway companies and two hotels were involved, the result was a masterpiece of extempore arrangement. Admittedly, a message by the electric telegraph preceded whichever train was carrying the royal party, but, nevertheless, the timing was fine.

For example, the management of the George Hotel at Perth heard of its forthcoming role in the royal progress only $1\frac{1}{2}$ hours before the guests arrived. There was little enough opportunity to make ready the best bedrooms; to think up something special for dinner; and generally to prepare for far-from-average visitors.

With the best will in the world, there is a limit to the amount that can be done in ninety minutes. Even when the Aberdeen Railway Company's flier sighed to a halt in Perth station, arrangements at the George were not yet complete. The royals had to wait for half-an-hour in the station waiting-room before a carriage arrived to convey them to the hotel. Her Majesty was full of understanding. The notice had, she agreed, been short; as her demeanour made plain, she was far from displeased.

One can assume that the staff of the George excelled itself for, nowadays, it is called the *Royal* George (author's italics). To judge by the adequately enthusiastic remarks of Egon Ronay and other pundits of the art of gracious innkeeping, the high standards are still maintained.

The inn at which the royal party stayed on its second stop-over, Crewe, was already named *Royal* Hotel, so there was not much scope for regal additions. Nor is it mentioned by Egon Ronay—but then Mr Ronay does not mention *anywhere* in Crewe. All that can be said is that the Queen and her family departed at the uncommonly early hour of six next morning to take the train to London. It was not, one is sure, the result of an uncomfortable night, for, on her arrival at Euston four hours and ten minutes later, neither Victoria nor Albert (in the words of one reporter) 'appeared to be in any degree fatigued by their rapid journey of 500 miles'.

◆

At the Battle of Waterloo, when the minds of most British within the area were marvellously concentrated upon Napoleon's soldiers, not very far from the front line, a Mrs MacKenzie had other things to think about.

Her husband was within earshot, fighting the French. No doubt, had she been otherwise employed, Mrs MacKenzie would have been worrying about his future. As it was, under the circumstances, such thoughts were more or less impossible. While the world's male population was being depleted by the clash of armies, she was giving birth to a son.

The child, who was named Donald, eventually joined the London and North Western Railway, in which, after a suitable initiation, he became a guard, serving on the stretch of line between Bushbury (just north of Wolverhampton) and Carlisle.

As has already been remarked, Queen Victoria liked to see familiar faces about her, and thus it was that Duncan MacKenzie nearly always accompanied royal trains on this part of the journey south. Each of the railway companies had men such as he, an elite of guards, engine-drivers and other leading players, who were quickly withdrawn from their more humdrum duties whenever the occasion demanded.

In the middle of the nineteenth century there was a disturbingly large number of train crashes, and the protests of that leader writer on *Atlas* were not entirely unjustified. However, by putting their best men in charge of royal trains, the companies did their best to ensure the safety of the sovereign, though the precautions did not stop there. Fifteen or twenty minutes before the approach of a royal special, a pilot locomotive steamed on ahead to make sure that the line was clear; that the gates of level crossings were locked; and that everything was in good order. Once it had passed, all other traffic came to a standstill and no shunting was permitted on adjacent lines.

The Queen herself was concerned that the safeguards, so diligently applied to her own transportation, should be extended to all rail passengers. After a succession of accidents in 1873, she took up her seldom still pen and wrote to the Prime Minister, Mr Gladstone. In a letter that contained some of the Queen's most powerful invective, she wrote,

> 'The Queen must again bring most seriously & earnestly before Mr. Gladstone & the Cabinet the vy alarming and serious state of the railways. Every day almost something occurs & every body trembles for their friends & for every one's life. . . . .
>
> 'If some people were punished for manslaughter who neglect their duties—or if a Director was bound to go with the Trains we shld soon see a different state of things! There *must* be fewer Trains, —the speed must be lessened to enable them to be stopped easily in case of danger & they must keep their time. . . .'

Queen Victoria was never involved in an accident. The pilot locomotive, forging ahead somewhat in the manner of a minesweeper, was efficient. And, if the driver of a Great Western engine came near to exceeding the Queen's stipulated limit of 40mph (64km/h), there was the specially mounted signal to wag its admonitory finger at him. She was certainly more fortunate than the Tsar of Russia, Alexander III, who suffered a considerable pile-up in November of 1888. The imperial train came off the rails while hurrying down a steep gradient near Borki (just south of Kharkov) when returning to Moscow from a visit to the Crimea. Twenty-one people were killed. The casualties included the Tsar's

When the Prince of Wales visited St Petersburg in 1874 for the marriage of his brother, Alfred Duke of Edinburgh, to Princess Marie of Russia, he was met at the station by the Emperor Alexander II. For the journey, the prince used a Mann-Nagelmackers 'boudoir car'—and thus travelled in above-average comfort. Assassinated seven years later, Alexander II was succeeded by his son Alexander III, who promptly put an end to his father's reforming policies.

The Khedive of Egypt greets the Prince of Wales at Cairo station. The Egyptian ruler was virtually bankrupt at the time; largely due to overspending on status symbols such as railways.

personal servant and his dog. Alexander, who was in the dining car at the time, received only bruises; the Tsarina was not injured at all.

In 1900, the Prince of Wales (soon to become Edward VII) had a narrow escape when seated in a stationary carriage in Brussels station. He was on his way from London to Copenhagen to visit his in-laws. As he noted afterwards in his diary, 'Arrive at Brussels, 4.50 Walk about station. Just as train is leaving, 5.30, a man fires a pistol at P. of W. through open window of carriage (no harm done).'

The 'man' was, in fact, a 15-year-old student who belonged to an anarchist organisation. When he was arrested, it was discovered that he had discharged only one round from a six-chambered revolver. The Prince of Wales took a lenient view of the matter and suggested that the youth should not be punished too severely. He was not very pleased, however, when the court showed excessive clemency by absolving the youth of all criminal intent on account of his age. The boy was merely placed under police supervision, which cannot have been very strict, as not very long afterwards he defected to France.

Children and youths who go around firing shots at heirs to thrones should, perhaps, be taken more seriously. When, fourteen years later, another student aimed his gun more successfully at the Austrian crown prince at Sarajevo, he started a world war.

———————————◆———————————

In Britain a member of the royal family could ride the rails without fear from the weapons of potential assassins, or inadequate 'permanent way', which, in the Tsar's case, had turned out to be rather less than permanent. Queen Victoria was, of course, cautious; a contradictory character who, in an age that abounded with innovations, mistrusted such things. Her marriage to Prince Albert had a profound effect on her life style and on her character. But she never acquired Albert's passion for technical progress.

During the earlier part of her reign, one problem facing rail travellers had been how to pass from one carriage to another, or, indeed, from one compartment to another. Coaches with corridors had not yet been invented. The result, so far as the Queen was concerned, was that if she required the attention of a lady-in-waiting, she would have to wait until the train reached a station. It would then stop, the attendant would get out and move into the royal saloon.

This was all very well, provided that the station in question had a platform, but some did not. On such occasions, one of the more robust railway officials had to unload the lady-in-waiting from her compartment and hoist her into the royal presence.

In 1869, the London and North Western Railway had the bright idea of building two six-wheel saloons: one of them for use by day, the other to serve as a sleeping car at night. The craftsmen at Wolverton applied their skills to the project, and someone provided the ingenious idea that it would be possible to devise a means of travelling from one saloon to the other. Thus the first-ever bellows gangway in Britain came into being. The Queen was not impressed. She did not consider the gangway safe and refused to use it. As before, the train had to pull up in a station whenever the Queen chose to walk from one saloon to the other. She did, however, appreciate the compartment for a sergeant-footman that was incorporated at one end of the day saloon. The incumbents varied; though, during the latter years of her reign, the adored John Brown occupied it almost to the exclusion of anyone else. As for the sleeper, it was equipped with two tolerably large beds. There was a long compartment for the Queen's dresses, and, to deaden the sound of wheels rattling over the rails, there was a double floor, with cork between the two layers, topped by a thick felt overlay and a deep pile carpet.

Initially, lighting was provided by oil lamps that were lowered through holes in the roof. Later, gas was used and later still electricity. But, just as it had required the advice of her occulist to persuade her to use the electric lights aboard the royal yacht, so did she mistrust their use on the royal train. In this case, nothing could overcome her prejudice and she never dared to switch them on.

So far as meals on trains were concerned, Queen Victoria's attitude was curiously ambivalent. On the mainland of Europe, by all accounts, she enjoyed hearty luncheons and dinners in one of the dining cars operated by *Le Compagnie Internationale des Wagons-Lit*. In Britain, on the other hand, she refused to take food while travelling. When she was at Windsor, she was driven by coach to Farnborough, where the London and South Western Railway's royal train took her to Gosport *en route* to Osborne. Since the journey was a short one, it was unnecessary to give any thought to Her Majesty's nourishment.

Journeys to Scotland were more difficult. Until the death of Prince Albert in 1861, the royal family sometimes patronised the west coast route; which means to say that part of the trip was accomplished by the London and North Western. Further north, the Caledonian Railway took over, and then, beyond the tree line, the Great North of Scotland Railways became responsible. On the east coast route, the Great Northern took charge of the royal travellers. After Albert's death, the Queen seldom used it.

The procedure was, of course, governed by the fact that some provision had to be made for refreshment. In London, the Queen embarked in her saloon either at Euston or (after it had been built) at King's Cross, for the Great Northern. When she was at Windsor, it followed almost automatically that she would take the west coast route, for it was an easy drive by coach to Watford junction, where the services of the LNW awaited her. The railway company had even taken the trouble to build a special royal waiting-room.

Everybody ate luncheon before setting off for the station. At Banbury, the royal train stopped, and the Queen and her party consumed high tea at one of the hotels, while the engine and rolling stock were given a quick once-over in readiness for the long haul ahead. Back on board, the sovereign and her party prepared themselves for sleep. The next stop would be Perth, where the directors of the Scottish railway companies would be waiting to welcome her and provide her with an agreeably substantial breakfast in the Great North of Scotland's boardroom.

After Perth, the Queen's spirits always seemed to improve. What began as a rather formal royal progress seemed to relax and become more of a holiday outing. The villagers along the route turned out in full strength, waving their small Union Jacks and uttering cheers that, alas, were seldom heard above the rattle of the rolling stock.

So far as European journeys were concerned, a special royal saloon used to be kept at Calais. It seemed to have been designed by a boat-builder rather than by a train-maker! The sofas were converted into beds at night, ships' lamps provided the lighting, and the clerestory roof put many people in mind of the coach roof of a yacht. With a Wagon-Lit diner attached, it set off for the south of France and Victoria's villa at

Cimiez (near Cannes).

During her later years, the system was changed, and a royal saloon was based at Cherbourg. It was simply attached to *Le Train Bleu*, which took it to Nice. But by this time, the Queen had become less restricted in her habits. The great impressario of luxury rail travel, exotic meals, and sumptuous hotels, Georges Nagelmackers, had just opened the Riviera Palace at Nice. Determined that 'Palace' should be more than a mere figure of speech, he suggested that the monarch should give up her villa and take over a special apartment in the hotel. The Queen agreed. Possibly it had not escaped her notice that Nagelmackers had used his guile to induce Leopold II (Uncle Leopold's successor as King of Belgium) to support his fledgling Wagons-Lit company.

On these occasions, the Queen broke her rule; she dined well and, next day, enjoyed what has been described as a 'substantial lunch' on the train. On arriving at Nice at 9 pm she always seemed to be fresh despite a trip that had lasted 20 hours. By arrangement, formalities at Nice were kept to a minimum. The mayor and the prefect made brief speeches of welcome, then a landau carried her to the Riviera Palace, where she went immediately to her apartment. Once she had sat down, her first action was invariably to ask to see the dinner menu.

But this, according to a correspondent of the American magazine *American Society* (quoted in Martin Page's *The Lost Pleasures of the Great Trains*), was a different queen to the one her people knew. 'It should be understood,' wrote the reporter, 'that when the Queen is on her travels considerably less ceremonial is observed than when the Court is in England or Scotland.' Lack of ceremonial included the rather homely touch of a copper kettle—an essential item in the royal baggage, for it guaranteed Her Majesty a decent cup of tea on the train journey.

◆

On routine journeys, the locomotives that hauled the Victorian royal trains went about their business unadorned. On ceremonial occasions, such as a jubilee, or when collecting a royal relative, or a visiting head of state, from one of the ports, they were decked out in ceremonial finery. The embellishments included the flying of whatever flags fitted the occasion, coats of arms either on the front platform just above the buffers or else on each side of the smoke box, and decorations on the splashers that encased the upper portions of the driving wheels. The possibilities were endless.

The ultimate in engine decor was probably reached by a rather small company named 'The London, Tilbury and Southend Railway', when it prepared to celebrate the coronations of Edward VII and George V. On both occasions busts of the newly enthroned king and queen were installed on pedestals, one above each front buffer. Between them, a fountain merrily played in celebration. As for the remainder of the chosen locomotives, their parts were garlanded with flags and replicas of the royal coat of arms.

In 1895, the two six-wheelers that had been built at Wolverton in 1869 were united on to a twelve-wheel chassis. The LNWR directors, feeling, perhaps, that after 26 years' service, these items of rolling stock were due for replacement, offered to build an entirely new coach. The Queen refused; she was adamant. She liked the existing saloons; she used them regularly for her journeys to Ballater *en route* for Balmoral; and she was in no mood for extravagant changes. The fusion of the two units into one was as far as she would go—though she agreed to the installation of an enormous electric bell to summon members of her staff. Like the sovereign herself, it was imperious. Once she had pressed the button, it kept on ringing until somebody switched it off and hastened to do the royal bidding.

A similar reaction was received by the well-meaning directors of the GWR in 1897. Since that year marked the Queen's Diamond Jubilee, it would, they felt, be an appropriate moment to build a brand-new royal train. This would have corridors throughout, electric light and all the most modern advances of rail travel. The proposition was put to the Queen, who replied that they could do what they liked with the rest of the train so long as they retained the existing royal saloon. Built in 1874, its ceiling was shaped rather like the interior of a dome, lighting was still by oil lamps, and some might have regarded its furnishings as hideous. But Queen Victoria loved it, and, as anyone who travelled in it had to agree, it was *very* comfortable.

The directors had to abandon their idea. The old coach was treated to new bogies and vestibule gangways. Other than that, there were no changes.

For her trip to Scotland that year, the three companies involved took pains to ensure that the first section of the journey was made with a red locomotive hauling the train; the second with a white locomotive; the third with a blue. This may seem a rather cumbersome expression of patriotic fervour, but it was a reasonably sober indulgence of the imagination compared with the manic instructions issued by the directors of the London Brighton and South Coast Railway on the occasion of a visit by the President of France to Edward VII. The locomotive was renamed *La France* and decorated with French tricolor flags, which may not be remarkable, but for some reason that surpasses all understanding, the coal in the tender was given a coat of whitewash.

In January 1901 Queen Victoria made her final journey, in her cherished Great Western saloon of 1874 vintage, when it served as the funeral car to take her body from Paddington to Windsor for interment at Frogmore. Earlier that day, the locomotive responsible for taking the dead queen and the chief mourners from Portsmouth to London travelled at a speed that, had she been alive, Victoria would never have tolerated. On arrival two minutes early, the Kaiser, who noticed these things, was so pleased that he sent an equerry to congratulate the driver.

----------------------◆----------------------

Edward VII had none of his mother's prejudices against high speeds. His experiences as a rail traveller had been rather more cosmopolitan. Among the visitors to London in the mid-nineteenth century was a former colonel in the United States cavalry named William d'Alton Mann. He set himself up in the Langham Hotel, where, with the advertising acumen particular to Americans, he went about promoting his 'Mann Boudoir Sleeping Car Company'. It was an essay in railroad luxury that, the ebullient colonel believed, would out-do the products of his business rival, George Mortimer Pullman.

Georges Nagelmackers was going through a bad economic patch with his Wagons-Lit company, and it seemed only natural that he and Mann should merge their projects. Mann bought an empty factory at Oldham, Lancs. Before very long, the first boudoir cars could be seen on the rails of Europe.

There was no denying that Colonel Mann's business methods were questionable, but there was also no gainsaying his ability to create publicity. His greatest scoop, apart, perhaps, from building a special rail car for Lillie Langtry, was to ingratiate himself with the Prince of Wales. Miss Langtry is generally given credit for the introduction, but this is impossible. She and the future Edward VII did not meet until 1877. But no matter; when, in January 1874, the Prince of Wales travelled to St Petersburg for the marriage of his brother Alfred, Duke of Edinburgh, to Princess Marie of Russia, he travelled in a Mann-Nagelmackers boudoir car and the future sovereign enjoyed himself. (Georges Nagelmackers eventually bought out Colonel Mann.)

Among the trains that grew out of this enterprising if short-lived business association was the Orient Express. The Prince of Wales used it on several occasions. Often it took him to Marienbad where, under the not altogether inaccurate alias of Duke of Lancaster, he professed to undergo treatment for his obesity. In fact, it was the social life of the spa that appealed to him.

The Prince of Wales liked speed. On his accession, he saw no reason why the royal trains should be confined to a miserable 40mph (64km/h). On a trip up the east coast route to Scotland, he was told that the latest Atlantic locomotive was hauling the carriages. 'Well', said Edward, 'show me what it can do.' The driver obliged. As a result, the royal traveller reached Edinburgh ten minutes ahead of schedule—to the discomfort of the reception committee, which had not yet arrived at the station.

Royal trains, unlike royal motor cars, do not belong to the sovereign; they are the property of the railway. It is by no means clear whether, in 1902, the LNWR directors (sensing, perhaps, Edward VII's resolve to clear away any remaining vestige of the nineteenth century) offered the new monarch a fresh collection of rolling stock, or whether he demanded it. The question, in any case, is unimportant. Edward never required much persuasion to adopt anything that might improve his comfort. It is, certain, however, that when they asked him whether he had any preferences about the design of a new saloon, he replied somewhat vaguely, 'Make it like a yacht.'

When the result emerged from Wolverton in the following year, it required rather a lot of imagination to detect a resemblance to anything that floated. The 'yachtlike' effect of his new saloon, if it can so be des-

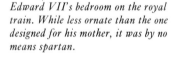

Edward VII's bedroom on the royal train. While less ornate than the one designed for his mother, it was by no means spartan.

cribed, was achieved by a coat of white enamel.

In fact, there were two new twelve-wheeler coaches; one for the King and one for the Queen, plus a dining car (Edward had none of his mother's prejudices about not eating on British rails). Each saloon was equipped with a silver-plated bedstead, large over-stuffed chairs and highly polished tables. Less obvious to the admiring eye was the sturdiness of the two coaches. They formed the basis of regal rail travel for the next forty years.

Doubtless, the LNWR had seized the initiative, as their's had been Queen Victoria's preferred route to Balmoral. But the companies on the eastern side of the country were not to be outdone. This surely, was an opportunity for a return to royal favour. In 1908, they, too, produced a magnificent pair of twelve-wheelers, again, one for the King and one for the Queen. Not only were they luxurious, they *lasted*. Both remained in service until the late 1970s, though they had been retired from overnight journeys some while before the outbreak of World War 2. Consequently they had not been used so often as the hard-worked Wolverton rolling stock. For this reason, they were regarded as less vulnerable to the ailments that can affect even units built for a king.

Despite this updating of royal trains, when Edward VII died in 1910, the antique coach that had taken Queen Victoria to her resting place in the Frogmore mausoleum was again taken out of store. For the coach as well as for its passenger, it was the last journey.

The funeral train was made up of ten vehicles; the locomotive decorated with the royal arms on either side of its smoke box, which was suitably draped in purple.

◆

Just as the profusion of railway companies that multiplied in the middle of the nineteenth century had been pruned by mergers and bankruptcies, so had the royal train situation become rather more rational. George V took over his father's supposedly yacht-like rolling stock when he came to the throne. He too had no objection to a driver giving the engine its head. When he and his wife accompanied Edward VII on a journey from Paddington to Plymouth in July 1903, the *City of Bath* (which hauled the train) covered the $246\frac{3}{8}$ miles in $233\frac{1}{2}$ minutes—an average speed of 63.14mph (*c* 395km at about 102km/h).

Whilst George V may have shared his father's taste for a quick journey by train, he did not share his flamboyant theory that a royal railway carriage should look as far as possible like a royal yacht. He much preferred the distinctive livery of the LNWR, which not only suggested good taste, but also sweet reasonableness. After all, they belonged to that

The ultimate boat-train! When King George V and Queen Mary travelled to India in 1911 for the coronation durbar, the latest P&O liner Medina *was chartered for the trip and assumed the role of a massive royal yacht. With 733 people on board, the extra space was badly needed.*

company and it was only fair that they should wear its colours.

At the time of George V's accession, there were no fewer than four royal trains available for services on the main lines that radiated from London. In addition to this, a few royal saloons were available on other, lesser routes. When World War 1 broke out in 1914, the situation became less elaborate, until finally the bulk of the King and Queen's travel was confined to one set of rolling stock—the LNWR's.

It quickly became clear that as the King and Queen would spend much more time going about the country, reviewing troops, visiting factories and generally encouraging the war effort, the role of the royal train would become very much more of a roving commission. There would be times when it would virtually become the royal home. It would be necessary to shunt it into remote sidings where, anchored for the night, the sovereign would be able to enjoy a reasonably good sleep. It would also be necessary to provide rather more elaborate toilet arrangements.

Another step forward was achieved. The interior of the LNWR sleeping saloon was modified, and a couple of baths were installed. As befitted instruments of royal ablution, each was silver-plated and encased in polished wood.

George V's heir, Edward VIII, was not impressed by his family's excursion into railway carriage design. For most of his brief reign he borrowed the official saloon that was normally used by Sir Josiah Stamp, the head of the London Midland and Scottish Railway. It was rather like a small apartment on wheels, complete with a kitchen and bathroom.

During his visit to Canada in 1919, the Prince of Wales looked in to see the driver of the giant Canadian Pacific Railway's locomotive that hauled his train across the Rockies.

For shorter trips, he travelled in Pullman cars and, occasionally, in ordinary first-class carriages.

He, like his grandfather, was familiar with the ways of the Orient Express. As Prince of Wales, he had made several trips to Vienna— ostensibly to receive treatment by a specialist for some chronic ear complaint; in fact, again after the fashion of his grandfather, he went to enjoy the richness of the Austrian capital's social life.

But his most spectacular journey in this legendary train took place after he had become king. Among the countries traversed by the Orient Express was Bulgaria. King Boris of Bulgaria, like his father King

On a rather smaller scale, the Prince of Wales found time to study the driver's compartment of a London underground train.

Ferdinand, had an inordinate love of railways. One of his favourite pastimes was to put on an immaculately tailored boiler suit and mount the footplate—where he would drive the locomotive as it sped through his realm. On one occasion, in an attempt (successful) to make up lost time on the stretch leading to Sofia, he misjudged the furnace's capacity for coal. The result was that draught blew back the flames and the fireman was burned to death.

On the occasion of Edward and Mrs Simpson's train journey through Bulgaria from Istanbul (to which the yacht *Nahlin* had taken them on a supposedly state visit to Kemal Ataturk), King Boris invited the English sovereign to join him at the controls. Edward was not required to shovel coal, but was allowed to blow the whistle at the approaches to level-crossings.

———————————————◆———————————————

Edward VII's saloons were still in royal service at the outbreak of World War 2. As in the previous clash of arms, the sovereign was required to travel the land, encouraging and exhorting his people, and being seen in the right places. The addition of bathrooms had done much to improve their amenities as mobile palaces, but King George VI faced a hazard that had not troubled his father. Combat aircraft had developed considerably since 1918; now they were able to shoot up trains.

In 1923, the LNWR had become part of the London Midland and Scottish with the result that its rolling stock had been repainted in crimson lake. The exceptions were those two 1903 saloons which, in accordance with George V's wishes, had retained the old livery. Beneath the waist, they were claret-coloured and adorned with the royal cypher; above it, elegant white panels were picked out in gold. It was nothing if not regal: unfortunately it was also extremely conspicuous and almost certain to catch the eye of any German pilot who might be flying overhead.

To remedy the situation, the saloons were quickly re-painted in the LMS colour scheme. Soon afterwards, in 1941, work began at Wolverton on replacement units. When they came into service, not a word was published about them. In many respects they resembled the old coaches, though there was one vital difference; they were completely armour-plated. Even the windows were protected by splinter-proof shutters. As a result, each carriage weighed 57 tons—against 32 tons for an ordinary passenger carriage. They were also air-conditioned, though the system, which depended on ice-boxes, could not be described as sophisticated.

◆

As the railway companies became nationalised, and the age of steam gradually yielded to diesel engines and to electric, whatever financial criticisms might be levelled against the royal family by aspiring republicans, nobody could accuse them of being wasteful in matters of transportation. Edward VII's saloons had lasted a very long time, and George VI's were only moderately less durable.

There had been some modest refurbishing of the royal rolling stock after the war. Two new saloons—described as 'semi-royal'—were built by the Great Western in 1945. Towards the end of their lives, these were used by the present Queen Mother. In the 1950s British Rail constructed three vehicles to replace the old LNWR coaches used by the household and train staff, which was only reasonable, as the others were now very old indeed. But the royal saloons, stripped of their armour plate, were required to soldier on, while less illustrious passengers were able to enjoy the high speeds and allegedly greater comfort of Inter-City trains. The royal coaches were, admittedly, far from primitive, but the fact that they could not safely exceed 70mph (112km/h) was a decided disadvantage. Not least, it made things difficult for those who had to plan their movements.

The bodies of the present day royal saloons were built in 1972. They were produced as prototypes of the latest standard Inter-City passenger coaches—meaning that they would be used in the 125 series of high speed trains—and the beautifully designed fitting-out for their royal occupants began two years later in 1974.

A spokesman for British Rail said that, 'I think it is worth emphasising that there is no "Royal Train" as such. There is a pool of a dozen vehicles from which the required ones are used to make up a train. This will vary from journey to journey, taking into account such things as whether sleeping accommodation is required, whether meals will be served—and, of course, how many (and which) members of the royal family are travelling.'

Included in the 'dozen' are a coach that was originally built in 1955 to provide accommodation for the royal children. Since then, it has been brought up to date by the provision of air brakes, a new electrical system, and B4 bogies that enable it to travel at 100mph (160km/h).

Various other more elderly items of rolling stock also appear on the list—though all of them have been modernised in the manner of the former nursery on wheels. A dining car for the royal travellers dates back to 1956 and a standard restaurant car (for members of the household) is of 1962 vintage. The oldest vehicle is a saloon that was originally constructed in 1920 for the chairman of the London and North Western Railway. In 1967, the body was taken from its original frame and mounted on an up-to-date version, with the B4 bogies essential for more ambitious speeds.

The days when the royal train was preceded by a pilot locomotive are long past. If, however, the driver is required to operate on unfamiliar stretches of track, he is provided with a 'pilot' in the shipping sense, to warn him of whatever may lie ahead. There are also at least two support vehicles, each of which has a diesel-driven generator, a telephone exchange, a radio station—operating on frequencies used by the police—and a repair crew.

After every trip, any comments or complaints (usually made verbally) are considered carefully by British Rail. Predictably, the locomotive and rolling stock are serviced before and after each journey. From the point of view of the staff at Wolverton, the higher speeds made possible by innovations are a mixed blessing; trains travelling at 100mph (160km/h) require double the amount of maintenance needed by those that never ventured beyond the more cautious 70mph (112km/h).

There used to be an elite of drivers and guards ear-marked for service with the royal trains. Nowadays, the arrangement is less formal, but the driver will certainly be what British Rail describes as a 'top link' man; which means to say that he is very experienced. More often than not, he receives no warning of the nature of his passengers. For example, he'll be told to, 'take out special number . . .' and discover, almost at the last moment, that it is carrying the Queen. Sometimes a railway employee is caught unprepared. There was the guard who, unaware of his exalted passengers, turned up at Euston wearing a crumpled pair of trousers and a shirt that was overdue for a session in a washing machine. The alert eye of the more suitably top-hatted station master spotted him at once. Clearly, this would not do. The luckless railway worker was hustled into a luggage van and instructed to remain there until the train stopped at Crewe. He would then be given the opportunity, and the necessary garments, to change into something more suitable.

Princess Elizabeth (as she then was) and the Duke of Edinburgh during their 1951 tour of Canada.

The royal travellers take members of their personal staff with them, though everything to do with the train is handled by British Rail—and this includes the catering. All who have ever served in these surroundings, or who have had any other connection with them, have a considerable sense of loyalty. For fairly obvious reasons they are reluctant (*unwilling* in many cases) to speak to the media.

Nevertheless, by conscientiously delving, it was possible to discover that, somewhere in the Royal Trains store at Wolverton, there is a much cleaned piece of carpet, used on appropriate journeys for the convenience of the Queen's corgis!

Cases of mistaken identity are rare, so far as the royal family is concerned. There was, however, the case of the signalman and a stationary train carrying the Duke of Edinburgh to some destination long since forgotten. When time allows, the royal saloon is shunted into a quiet siding for the night—instead of hurtling over the tracks, which does not afford a good night's sleep. Early next morning, the Duke decided to take a short stroll before continuing his journey. Climbing down on to the track he wandered over to a nearby signal box—doubtless with the idea of looking around and wishing its occupant a pleasant day.

Perhaps the light was not very good; perhaps the signalman had other things on his mind. At all events, he did not recognise the man climbing the stairs to his box. Recalling the collection of rolling stock that was parked a few yards away, the signalman recoiled in horror. 'It's as much as my job's worth,' he said, 'to let you in here with all that lot down below. Just you get to hell out of it.'

Mistakes, it seems, can occur—even to the most illustrious train in the realm.

———————————————◆———————————————

In Britain, the royal train is a commonplace of royal travel; a permanent collection of rolling stock that can, so to speak, be taken out of store and used whenever it is needed. Nor are the distances particularly long, which simplifies the requirements. The situation overseas is more complicated. In places such as Canada and (before it became a republic) South Africa, a visit by the sovereign produced by no means small problems. For one thing, it would clearly be absurd to set aside a number of specially fitted-out carriages, standing idle for year after year, in the hope that, one day, they might come in useful.

During February, 1946, the authorities in South Africa received the first intimation that, early in the following year, the King and Queen, and their two daughters, Elizabeth and Margaret, intended to make a tour that would take them from Cape Town to Bulawayo in what was then

During their visits to Canada, the Queen and Prince Philip travelled in a narrow-gauge train from Whitehorse in the Yukon to McCrea—a tiny village a few miles away. The train had been built in the late 1890s to carry the sudden flood of 'gold rush' prospectors.

The scene Waterloo Station; the time, a few hours after the marriage of Charles, Prince of Wales to Lady Diana Spencer. A platform, which at that time of day was normally thronged with commuters, was cleared for the couple's departure to Broadlands, the late Lord Mountbatten's house near Romsey in Hampshire, on the first stage of their honeymoon journey. Later, they flew to Gibraltar to join the royal yacht Britannia for a Mediterranean cruise.

Rhodesia, stopping at innumerable places in between.

A train, obviously, would be needed; but *what* train? The governor general of what was then a dominion had his own, which was known as 'the White Train'. Perhaps this would do? It was decided fairly quickly that it would not be suitable. As a result, a dozen new coaches were ordered from the Metropolitan-Cammell Carriage & Wagon Co Ltd near Birmingham in England. The specifications were daunting; this was to be more than a mere railway train adapted to the needs of a king and his family. It was, and this is no exaggeration, virtually a palace on wheels, or, at the very least, a luxury hotel crammed into ridiculous dimensions.

Furthermore, it was to include one comfort that the white train did not afford—complete air-conditioning.

Before the war that had just come to an end, two years would have been regarded as a reasonable time for the completion of such an assignment. This was out of the question. The time must be reduced to about one-third of what was considered normal. Metro-Cammell and its subcontractors applied themselves to the project with amazing speed. The order was received in March, 1946, by 21 November, the royal-train-to-be was ready for inspection, and when King George VI and his family disembarked from the battleship, HMS *Vanguard*, at Cape Town on 17 February of the following year, it was waiting for them on the quayside.

The King and the Queen had coaches of their own, and the princesses shared a third. Within the King's coach there was a study and a 'stateroom' (in the ocean liner sense; it was really a bedroom) with an adjoining bathroom. A workroom was provided for his valet and there was also accommodation for an equerry and for the sovereign's physician. The walls of the stateroom were veneered with finely figured English chestnut; the furniture was made from English walnut. A plain beige carpet covered the floor. The windows were fitted with art-silk curtains and pelmets, net curtains and roller blinds. A similar scheme was used in the study, which had a telephone and a loudspeaker unit connected with the train's central receiving set.

Radio was, indeed, an important feature of the train. According to one estimate, the operator transmitted between 20,000 and 30,000 words a day.

The Queen's coach included a very comfortable lounge for the royal family, panelled in walnut and equipped with such pleasant ways of passing the time as a radiogram—complete with a small cabinet for records.

Before embarking on the tour, the King had insisted that, to quote from the January 1947 issue of *South African Railways and Harbours Magazine*, he was determined 'to abide by all South Africa's food

regulations'. All the menus were inspected by the Queen, and she was a ruthless editor. From a fairly typical example, we see fruit cocktail, soup, lamb cutlets and peach flan deleted. Thus, at luncheon that day, the royal family was able to choose from: Omelette Rossini, Pigeons en casserole Paysanne, baked beans, green peas, boiled rice and chateau potatoes. Cold dishes with assorted salads were also available. For pudding, once the peach flan had been removed, there was only one option—vanilla ice cream.

Another section of the underground; another Prince of Wales. The date was 30 April, 1979, when Prince Charles opened the Jubilee line.

In fact, of the five thousand miles covered by the royal family on the tour, only five hundred were made by train. For the remainder, Viking aircraft, which had recently been added to the King's Flight, were used. Nevertheless, South African Railways were well content with their achievement. As the editor of their magazine proudly announced in a headline, *Our Royal Guests Will Travel In A TRAIN FIT FOR A KING*. And so it was; nor did he exaggerate when, in a sub-heading, he referred to 'South Africa's "Palace-on-Wheels"'.

As this may suggest, making arrangements for a royal visit to an overseas country is a complex and expensive business. Admittedly, after the tour of South Africa, the royal train's rolling stock was absorbed into South African Railways' system and employed on lesser duties.

However, as an example of weaving a pattern from pretty well all forms of transport, it pales into insignificance beside the trip to Canada made by Queen Elizabeth II and the Duke of Edinburgh between 18 June, 1959—when a BOAC aircraft deposited them at St John's Newfoundland, and their departure from Halifax on 1 August. They travelled in the royal yacht *Britannia*, in cars, in an assortment of aircraft including sea-planes, and in the royal barge. But the greater part of the time was spent in a royal train, eight coaches long that travelled over the tracks of the Canadian National Railway and the Canadian Pacific. This, indeed, was also a kind of mobile administrative centre for the tour. It was here—at Calgary, Kamloops, Vancouver and Edmonton—that the laundry was collected and delivered and to here that, three times a week, a courier service, flown by pilots of the RCAF, delivered the diplomatic boxes. Mostly they used jet planes, but, when suitable landing facilities were not available, what were described as 'conventional aircraft' were employed.

The Queen and Prince Philip had a coach to themselves; the other vehicles were occupied by members of their household, their staff (including six footmen, the Queen's hairdresser and the Queen's page) and, in the last carriage, thirteen members of the Royal Canadian Mounted Police. The Queen's private secretary, Sir Michael Adeane, had a car of his own—which also served as an office. There was another office in coach number six, from which a Mrs Corbet, secretary of the programme committee for the royal tour, operated. This also seems to have been a communications centre. In the *Arrangements* for the royal tour, we read that the letter box in car 6 should 'come under control of the confidential clerk who will co-ordinate mail arrangements'.

Little more than a century separated this visit to Canada from Queen Victoria's first journey by rail between Slough and Paddington. But, in the realm of royal travel, that century had seen more changes than all the others put together.

5
KINGS, QUEENS AND MOTOR CARS

One of the less fruitful journeys in the longish and chequered history of motoring was accomplished on a day in 1895, when the Hon. Evelyn Ellis clattered down to Windsor Castle on his Daimler. One uses the word *on* advisedly; in those days, the driver did not sit inside the vehicle but, rather, he perched on top of its rickety frame. Mr Ellis's purpose was to obtain an audience with the Queen. A considerable horseless-carriage enthusiast himself, he felt it his duty to introduce Her Majesty to the latest marvel of the machine age.

As many could have told him (and should have done), it was a fool's errand. Queen Victoria, as already noted, did not take particularly kindly to mechanical innovations. Now, at the advanced age of 76, she had no intention of trying to come to terms with yet another new-fangled product of the march of progress. She had, admittedly, put her name to acts of parliament regulating the conduct of those who had charge of such contraptions, but her interest went no farther; in any case, she was fond of horses.

No doubt politely—he was, after all, an hon.—an official told Mr Ellis that Her Majesty was not available. Ruefully, he turned his Daimler round and chugged off whence he had come.

The Queen's son, the future Edward VII, was more receptive to new ideas, although like his mother, he had no great understanding of technical matters; he never managed to accept the fountain pen as a suitable instrument for writing letters, nor was he at ease when speaking into a telephone. However, when, in 1860, as a lad of 18, he heard about a light steam-carriage built by a Mr Thomas Rickett of Buckingham, he actually asked to see it. No doubt prudently, he did not take a ride on it.

Precisely when the Prince of Wales first made the acquaintance of a motor car is a matter of conjecture. It may have been on one of his visits to the South of France. It may equally well have been at an exhibition held at the Imperial Institute, London, in 1896. The occasion was partly to show what a wonder the fledgling horseless carriage was, and partly to

Edward VII's first real experience of a motor trip occurred when he was Prince of Wales. He was staying at Highcliffe, near Christchurch, when John Scott-Montagu took him for a spin in his new 12hp Daimler. The Prince was delighted and soon afterwards bought a car of his own.

persuade those in authority to take a less severe view when it came to framing laws for its behaviour. To encourage this, members of both houses of parliament were invited—as was the heir to the throne. It was successful to the extent that it helped produce the so-called Emancipation Act of 1896, which was not really an 'emancipation act' at all. Nevertheless, it has since been celebrated, on innumerable occasions, by a November pilgrimage to Brighton in which veteran cars, growing ever longer in the tooth, take part.

If he could stand the smell and the noise of a largely indoor display, there was much to impress the visitor. An ingenious system of wooden roads and ramps (representing hills) had been laid down, and some of the vehicles ventured outside to the institute's grounds. This time, the Prince did more than play the passive spectator; he heaved his portly body on to one of the Daimlers and allowed himself to be driven. He also asked a good many questions. The general impression was that, if not yet an enthusiast, he was at least interested.

Next year, when he was staying at Warwick Castle, he agreed to make a short journey along a road, and in 1898, royal progress took another step nearer the steering wheel. This time, the Prince was a guest at Highcliffe Castle near Christchurch. One day, the Hon. John Scott-Montagu drove over to lunch on his 12 hp Daimler. Afterwards, he suggested an outing. Edward said that, as it was a fine afternoon, it might be quite pleasant. Two ladies accompanied them; Montagu, whose enthusiasm was no less than that of Evelyn Ellis, drove with zest to a point not far short of Southampton. On the way back, breaking just about every law of the land, he speeded up the motor car to a breath-taking 40mph (64km/h). His royal passenger chortled, and suggested to the ladies that, if this sort of thing continued, they'd have to think about buying more suitable hats. When the Daimler had been brought to a stop outside Highcliffe Castle, the local schoolmaster—who seems also to have been the local photographer—was summoned. He took pictures of everyone, including the car.

For his first Daimler, Edward invested in a 6hp model. His equerry was not confident that it would be sufficiently powerful, and he was right. Later that year (1900), it was replaced by two 12hp versions of what, for many years, was to become the marque preferred by the royal family.

Quite obviously that journey planted the beginning of an idea in the Prince's mind. A few weeks later, John Scott-Montagu was invited to call at Marlborough House (where the Prince of Wales was living), bringing with him his motor car. The vehicle remained there for a week. The Prince and many others examined it; this time his curiosity was insatiable. Those who knew him well could see that he was impressed, and it came as no great surprise when, not long afterwards, he decided that he must have a car of his own and that it should be a Daimler.

Mr Rolls had not yet met Mr Royce, and a Daimler was generally considered to be the best of the automotive breed.

Many years earlier, the firm of Cadbury had dared to involve the sovereign in its advertising. A drawing showed a rather bilious-looking Queen Victoria sipping at a mug of cocoa in the dining car of a train. Windsor Castle was visible through one of the windows. It was not only inaccurate; it was unpardonable. Edward had no intention of affording the car-makers any publicity—even of a more restrained nature.

As his equerry, Major-General Sir Arthur Ellis, wrote to Frederick Simms (the man who introduced the Daimler Patent Petrol Motor to Britain, and who became the first secretary of the society of motor manufacturers and traders), 'H.R.H. has the greatest possible objection to being made the vehicle of advertising of any sort and I cannot sufficiently advise you to do your utmost to keep his name out of the newspapers.'

Sir Arthur suggested that, if the Prince *did* order a car, he would choose the '12hp rather than 6hp' model 'in view of steep hills near Sandringham'. This suggests an unaccountable flaw in his knowledge of Norfolk geography. As Noel Coward pointed out with more exactitude in *Private Lives*, the county is 'very flat'.

Despite Arthur Ellis's warning to Mr Simms, the news did leak out.

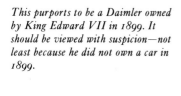

This purports to be a Daimler owned by King Edward VII in 1899. It should be viewed with suspicion—not least because he did not own a car in 1899.

In its issue dated 24 February, 1900, the magazine *Autocar* told its readers that the Prince was about to become a car-owner. Contrary to the equerry's prediction, he did select a 6hp model. It was an open four-seater standard model. The engine was fitted with burners as well as with electrical ignition in case anything went wrong. Steering was by means of an inclined wheel. There were four forward gears and a reverse—acceleration was controlled by a foot pedal, which was something of a novelty. Hitherto, a hand lever had been employed for this purpose. There were pneumatic tyres and wider-than-usual leather mudguards, and its phaeton body was painted in chocolate and black, picked out in red. The Prince's crest, displayed on a panel behind the nearside head-lamp, was the only indication of royal ownership.

The colour scheme is something of a mystery. Traditionally, the royal road vehicles had been decorated in claret and black, so why brown? In this respect, the first car was unique; thereafter, the time-honoured claret was used. Nor, despite the fact that the area around Sandringham can hardly be described as mountainous, does the 6hp engine appear to have been an unqualified success. Later in 1900, as Sir Arthur had predicted, Edward sold the vehicle and invested in two 12hp models. One was a car, the other a small 14-seater bus intended for the use of beaters on the royal shoots.

Having acquired a car, Edward's next preoccupation was that of learning to drive it. A former Daimler mechanic named David Letzer was installed to maintain the vehicle in good condition. To master the skill required to coax it along in a reasonably straight line, the services of a Londoner named Oliver Stanton were sought.

Mr Stanton, who smoked cigarettes in a long holder, was an American by origin. He had a thriving business, giving bicycle-riding lessons in Battersea Park. Doubtless his shrewd eye told him that the advent of the motor car was liable to bring people trouble as well as convenience. At any rate, he was quick to start up a sideline selling insurance policies on a commission basis.

This expert (now on four-wheeled locomotion as well as on two) was called to Sandringham, where, for many an hour, he tutored Edward on journeys up and down the drive, on excursions round the bends of the shrubbery and on quick trips along the terrace. The royal pupil, it seems, mastered the art of motion in second gear tolerably quickly. The other gears, one imagines, followed in due course—though not a lot has been recorded about this part of his education. Nor, as time was to show, did he become an enthusiastic driver. He was content to be driven—on his own terms.

His Queen (for it was now 1901) was, perhaps, more eager to take the wheel. Like her husband, she enjoyed speed. Her performance at the reins of a pony cart on the Sandringham estate was little short of terrifying. Describing a motor journey in a letter to her son, the future George V, she remarked on how much pleasure she had experienced in being 'driven about in the cool of the evening at *fifty miles!!*' She did, however, admit that she was apt to poke the chauffeur 'violently in the back at every *corner* to go gently and whenever a *dog, child* or anything comes in our way'.

To satisfy her wishes to take an active rather than a passive role in motoring, Edward spent £1,000 on an electric vehicle for her use on the estate. It was a Columbia, supplied by the Electric Vehicle Co of Hertford, Connecticut. Its 2hp motor was mounted on the rear axle and powered by 48 two-volt cells, giving it a top speed of 25mph (40km/h)— more than sufficient in these circumstances. There was a footbrake and a tiller enabling it to be steered. The wheels were of wood and the tyres were solid.

Queen Alexandra made history of a kind in 1901 when she acquired a 2hp Columbia for use at Sandringham. Powered by electricity, its range was rather limited, and so was its speed.

It is greatly to Alexandra's credit that she managed to manoeuvre the vehicle. Tiller steering was by no means easy, and the gawky shape suggests a flaw in determining its centre of gravity. One feels that it must have been easy prey for even the most moderate puff of wind, that might, quite easily, have pushed it over on to its side.

King Edward VII was a man of enthusiasms, and motoring was now one of them. His fleet of horseless carriages multiplied until, towards the end of his reign, his collection included a Daimler, two large Mercedes and a small Renault. He preferred the German cars and was more inclined to use them on private journeys. Officially, of course, he was bound to favour the home-grown Daimler, which, despite its teutonic origins, was now being manufactured at Coventry.

Once, during a visit to Homburg, the King seems to have toyed with the notion of investing in a French steam-driven conveyance named a Serpollet. Monsieur Serpollet, himself, turned up at the spa and invited the King to sample his wares. He had, as he was quick to point out, already sold one of them to the Shah of Persia.

King Edward was due to take luncheon with the Grand Duke Michael of Russia at a village named Langenschwalback, about six miles (10km) down the road. M Serpollet might, if he cared, drive him there and collect him afterwards. The trip seems to have been a success. At any rate, Serpollet was invited to come again the next day. On this occasion, the King wisely visited an occulist beforehand, where he bought a pair of goggles. With the French car-maker at the controls, they travelled 31 miles (50km) to Frankfurt-am-Main. No sale resulted from these excursions, though the sovereign expressed his gratitude by presenting Serpollet with a scarf pin that sparkled with brilliants.

By 1905, his use of cars had become so considerable that the services of the mechanic Letzer were not enough. What he needed, he decided, was a sort of consulting engineer, who would advise him on his purchases, supervise their welfare, and accompany him on his journeys. A man named C W Stamper seemed suitably qualified; he was added to the strength of the royal household as the expert in charge of horseless carriages.

Edward's nephew, Kaiser Wilhelm II of Germany, was another automobile enthusiast. In order to reconcile German farmers to the new mechanical beast, the noise and appearance of which might frighten their horses, Whilhelm made an attempt to propel his vehicles with potato alcohol (and thereby increase the demand for these vegetables). He tried to persuade Edward to do likewise, but the British sovereign refused. Unfortunately, as experience was to show the Kaiser, the produce of the Fatherland's soil was not accepted by the automobile as a substitute for motor spirit. Fed on this homely diet, there was no zip to its performance, and its engine knocked in passable imitation of a squad of Prussian drummers.

The Kaiser did, however, have one motoring accessory that his uncle coveted. It was a horn manufactured by an ingenious craftsman of such instruments, and it played a little tune. If you had a talent for fitting words to music, you could interpret its melody as chanting *Der Kai-ser Kommt*. It was a warning to lesser road users that the All Highest was approaching; and that they should either stand to attention or get smartly out of the way!

Whenever King Edward journeyed to Biarritz or Marienbad, Stamper was sent on ahead with three of the cars. On one of the Biarritz trips, the industrious car manager discovered a similar device that could be blown somewhat in the manner of a trumpet. The sovereign loved it. Like Stamper, it became his constant motoring companion.

Another item that accompanied the sovereign whenever he travelled by car was a footstool that had been a present from somebody. Inside it, a silver-plated first-aid box contained such basic essentials as bandages, scissors and a sealed bottle of brandy.

◆

The laws of the land—that is to say, of Britain—did little to make the motorist's lot an easy one. Doubtless with the best of intentions, the roads abounded with speed traps mounted by sharp-eyed policemen ready to prosecute any driver who exceeded 20mph (32km/h) over a measured furlong. To make sure that malefactors could not escape unidentified, each car had to be fitted with an individual set of number plates.

In the world of motoring, the sovereign was above the law. The King was not required to display number plates on his vehicle, nor was he compelled to conform to the speed limits. This was perhaps just as well— for the peace of mind of the magistrates if not for the other road users. Having experienced the delights of travelling quickly, Edward took a fierce delight in exhorting his chauffeur to race along trap-littered highways at speeds which sometimes reached 60mph (96km/h). Nor did he take kindly to any vehicle that blocked his progress. Whilst not actually encouraging his driver to force the offender into the ditch, he urged him to overtake without unduly counting the possible cost.

One magazine writer tactfully informed his readers that the King, whilst 'no friend of furious driving' was 'scarcely content to drive behind hay motors'. The Crown Equerry, who had added the royal cars to his responsibility for the horses and other means of transport, took a more serious view. This sort of thing, surely, could not be allowed to continue. Sooner or later, there would be a crash. He referred the matter to Stamper, and suggested that his master might be persuaded to impose a limit of, say, 30mph (48km/h) upon himself. The 'private motoring expert', as he now called himself, shook his head. 'He'd never agree,' he said.

Now and again, there were small complications—though none of

The spring of 1905 found King Edward VII and Queen Alexandra, seen here in the gorge of Chabet-el-Akra, on a tour of North Africa. France and Germany were at loggerheads over the Kaiser's desire to obtain a port on the Atlantic coast of Morocco. At Algiers, Edward VII took the unusual step of sending a telegram of support to the French foreign minister. (Opposite.)

In 1909, King George V (then Prince of Wales) treated himself to a shooting brake.

them serious. On one occasion a royal car without the sovereign on board was apprehended by a constable for its lack of number plates. On another, the King and a party of friends had been attending a race meeting at New-market. On the trip back to London, Edward and his chauffeur were racing along with their customary disregard for the limits. Thinking that, if they kept sufficiently close to the royal car, the law might consider them exempt, his companions followed hot on the Daimler's trail. The constabulary was not impressed. All but two of the drivers were stopped and, subsequently, fined.

In 1907, the royal fleet of cars reached some sort of pinnacle with the delivery of a 35hp Daimler Landaulette. Inside the passenger com-partment, there were such refinements as a table, a clock, a speaking tube, electric light, and a duplicate speedometer. If the last of these suggested that the car's rate of progress was too moderate, the speaking tube was quickly brought into action and the sovereign's voice, gutteral with the vestige of a German accent and rough from excessive smoking, barked the appropriate orders.

Two other events that occurred during that year were, perhaps, of greater importance. The King made public his enthusiasm for motoring by allowing the Automobile Club to add the prefix 'Royal' to its name (in the following year, his daughter-in-law's brother, Prince Francis of Teck, became chairman of the club and remained in office until his death in 1910). The King also carried out the first-ever official royal tour by car (of Wales, in this instance).

On all his journeys, he was accompanied by a back-up vehicle in

case anything broke down. Mr Stamper recalled the punctures to which
royal tyres were just as prone, and how, when this occurred, his master
used to shout 'Another tyre, Stamper!' In more recent times, a chauffeur,
who began his career in a garage beside the Brighton Road at Crawley,
remembered that his boss was not infrequently called out to minister to
a royal vehicle that had fallen sick beside the highway. But, whenever he
went on such errands, the King was never there. He had been quickly
transferred to the other car and swept on towards his destination.

Brighton was a resort that appealed to Edward; the air, he believed,
did him good. He used to stay with his friend, Arthur Sassoon, who had
a house in the exclusive and appropriately named King's Gardens. On
these occasions, he tried to indulge his fondness for travelling incognito.

It did not always work. When he was nearing the end of his life, he
was staying with the Sassoons and decided to drive over to Worthing. It
was on 9 February, 1910. The morning was sunny and, for the season,
pleasantly warm. Believing himself to be unobserved, King Edward
ordered his car to be parked by the pier, then seated in a deckchair, he
glanced through the day's newspaper and dozed off.

While he slept, someone noticed the unmistakable black and
claret-coloured vehicle. Word spread quickly and a crowd assembled. It
required the local police to disperse the people and convey the ailing
King safely back to his automobile. It was, perhaps, surprising that he
could have hoped for anonymity. His appearance was nothing if not
distinctive, and a motor car that had no registration plates and was painted
black accompanied by that shade of maroon which would not disgrace a
good wine from Bordeaux, was bound to attract popular attention.

♦

That was almost the last of King Edward's motoring excursions. Less
than three months later, on 6 May, he died. His son, George V, did not
share his enthusiasm for motor cars and was much more moderate in his
ideas about the definition of 'fast'.

The new King had acquired his first car a few years earlier and it
seldom strayed far from its home at Sandringham, which was not really
surprising. It was a four-seater phaeton, propelled by an electric motor
that produced a top speed of 25mph (40km/h), but which could travel for
no more than nine miles before its batteries ran out. Later, following what
had now become a royal tradition, he bought a Daimler. The royal family
was commendably loyal. The Hon. Charles Stewart Rolls had by now
been acquainted with Henry Royce for some years; indeed, the former,
having made the first two-way flight across the English Channel, was not
long in following Edward VII to the grave, when he perished in an air

This 57hp Daimler is one of the first in a long line of these cars owned by George V. Midway in the rear compartment, you can just make out the tops of the two armchairs in which the King and Queen travelled. Behind them sat two police officers.

disaster. Fortunately, the engineering genius of the partnership was Mr Royce and he was already producing what were possibly the best cars in the world. Nevertheless, the royal family had begun with Daimlers and it stuck to the marque through the reigns of four sovereigns—during which its members owned, at one time or another, no fewer than fifty.

George V was very much a Daimler enthusiast whose views on motor cars were less cosmopolitan than his father's. About the only occasion when he permitted himself to be driven in anything else was during World War 1. Vauxhalls were used as staff cars almost to the exclusion of any other make. Consequently, when he visited his troops, the King rode as his generals rode—in the back of an open Vauxhall.

He did once try out a Rolls-Royce, but was not impressed. The occasion was a visit to Sandringham by his sister, Princess Victoria, who had just taken delivery of one of these cars. On the journey to Norfolk, she asked her chauffeur, 'Have you never driven King George?' When he replied that he had not, she asked him whether he would like to remedy this gap in his experience. Yes, he said, he would like that very much. 'Very well,' said the Princess, 'we shall get him into the car.'

They stopped at the sovereign's entrance, and the King himself came out. What, Princess Victoria asked, did he think of her new car? The monarch muttered something to the effect that yes, yes indeed, it was quite nice. To a discerning observer, his attitude must have appeared polite rather than interested.

Nevertheless, after a few minutes' conversation, the Princess persuaded him to make a very short trip to the nearest village and back. When it was over, she asked him again for his opinion. 'It is,' said the King, 'just like getting out of a rabbit hutch.'

Everyone has his or her preferences so far as motor cars are concerned. One of George V's was that he should be able to enter the vehicle without having to bend down. Daimler's (or, to be more accurate, Hooper's—the firm that built the bodies for the royal cars) coped admirably by producing high doors and high interiors. Amidships, as it were, there was a pair of armchairs in which the King and Queen sat; behind them, a rear seat was occupied by police officers. It was all enormously comfortable; rather like a small room on wheels.

Queen Mary's introduction to motoring had not got off to the best of starts. While spending a holiday at Mentone in 1898, she had written to her Aunt Augusta, the Grand Duchess of Mecklenburg-Strelitz, that an excursion in a horse-drawn vehicle had been 'somewhat disturbed by an odious motor car which kept on passing us and then slowing down, it smelt so nasty and made such a noise.'

As time went by, however, her views became more moderate until, eventually, she actually became fond of the things. For example, at Interlaken in 1903, she wrote to her husband, 'Do you know that the roads are so good here that it would have been rather fun to have a motor car to go about—two people in the hotel have their own.' And, later, to Aunt Augusta, 'Only think what George and I did this afternoon, we went in Lord Shrewsbury's *motor car* (driven by him) down to Hampton

Court which George had never seen. I really enjoyed the drive very much and we flew . . . [we] have just returned at *7.15*, it took us *38* minutes to get back—I feel you will nearly have a fit at me going in a car.'

She was quite right; Aunt Augusta was indeed disturbed by her news. That formidable lady replied with alacrity, 'And now to your drive in a motor car! yes, I very nearly had a fit and quite screamed out to myself . . . oh! dearest child, how could you?'

Undaunted, the Princess of Wales (as she then was) made more such journeys. A few months later, she and her husband were in Cornwall making long drives in their own Daimler. As for Aunt Augusta, she never came to terms with cars. She variously described them as 'horrible', 'dangerous', and 'so un-royal'. Which would doubtless have been Queen Victoria's opinion too.

Much as she grew to enjoy motoring, there was one feature of travel with the King that Queen Mary found hard to endure. She could not abide the smell of tobacco smoke. George V, like his father, was a heavy smoker and it was asking too much to expect him to forego cigarettes on a long journey. The problem was put to the craftsmen at Hooper's, who devised a form of air-conditioning. It amounted to an arrangement of ducts through which the tainted air could make its escape, and into which fresh air would pour. The one consideration was, the Queen insisted, it should not blow a cold draught of air on to her husband's head.

Before delivery, the car in question was tested by a member of the Hooper management, who sat in the back puffing his pipe for all he was worth and, simultaneously, burning strips of smouldering brown paper. When the vehicle was at a standstill, it seemed to work very well. Out on the road, however, things went wrong. The back pressure created by a following wind forced the exhaust fumes into the ducts and well nigh gassed the unfortunate passenger. Eventually, the problem was solved by fitting a flap over the tail piece of the exhaust.

When the royal family travelled to or from Balmoral, the royal yacht (or, possibly, a royal train) was the more usual means of transport. However, this peaceful pattern of conveyance was to be interrupted at the end of April, 1926. The King and the Queen were in their Scottish castle, no doubt enjoying the spring that had come late to the Highlands, when, in darker parts of Britain, the coal miners walked out of the pits. This was the brief prelude to the General Strike that began on 4 May, and caused a large slice of society to down its tools.

Since then, the world has become so experienced in the results of industrial unrest, that one might imagine George V glancing at his newspaper, remarking to Queen Mary that, 'I see the miners are coming out', and then turning the conversation to lighter matters. In 1926,

however, the possibility of a general strike (anti-climactic though it turned out to be) was regarded with a good deal of alarm. There were visions of mobs storming the barricades; even, conceivably, of civil war. As King George told himself, the place for the monarch was in his capital and not on some Aberdeenshire hillside. He ordered one of the Daimlers to be loaded up, eased himself into his armchair amidships, and was driven non-stop to London.

King George V leaving Buckingham Palace in a classic example of the royal Daimler. King George VI was the last sovereign to order one of these cars. Nowadays, they have been replaced by Rolls-Royces.

In 1931, the King did his best in a smallish way to relieve the suffering of the depression that had Britain in thrall. Hooper and Daimler had given the royal family such good service, that he was concerned to do something, *anything*, that would keep as many workers as possible employed during what threatened to be a very unhappy winter. The only way was to buy cars. Several members of his fleet were old vehicles; the time was perhaps ripe to have them replaced.

But economy, even for royalty, was a matter of importance. Rather than dip into the privy purse, he paid for the newcomers out of his own pocket.

◆

King George's health was less than good. In 1928, he fell seriously ill.

Afterwards, his doctors advised a period of convalescence, ideally by the seaside. Craigwell House at Bognor was put at his disposal; one of the Daimlers was converted into an ambulance for the 65 mile journey from London. As it purred sedately along the highway, no vehicle was allowed to overtake it.

The Bognor air and the skill of his physicians restored the King's health to something approaching its previous condition, though he would never be completely fit again. In any case, he was now 63 years old. He had enjoyed tramping over the grouse moors with his gun. Now such tolerably strenuous exercise was out of the question, though his enthusiasm for the sport had not diminished. If he could no longer walk, was there some other method of locomotion?

Hooper and Crossley (a car maker of not inconsiderable repute until it went out of business in 1937) produced the solution. It was a six-wheeler that was able to travel over rough country. To increase the amount of space inside, the front seat was so constructed that it could be folded up and concealed beneath the dashboard. The vehicle provided not only transport, but also shelter. If he had a mind, the King could exercise his marksmanship from the comfort of its interior.

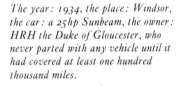

The year: 1934, the place: Windsor, the car: a 25hp Sunbeam, the owner: HRH the Duke of Gloucester, who never parted with any vehicle until it had covered at least one hundred thousand miles.

Edward VIII, who succeeded to the throne in 1936, had bought his first car (predictably a Daimler) when he was up at Oxford. Before concluding the deal, he asked his father for permission. King George was not entirely happy about the idea. As he saw things, royalty should be driven but should not drive. The Prince of Wales, he suggested, could not hope to manoeuvre his vehicle so well as an 'expert who does it every day of his life'. Furthermore, if the Prince were involved in an accident, the details would be 'exaggerated in every paper in Europe'. Nevertheless, his son's plea must have been sufficiently eloquent. Albeit reluctantly, the King gave his consent.

The Prince kept his car in an Oxford garage run by William Morris. Morris had obviously looked after the Prince's Daimler well; for the two men became friendly and quite often played a round of golf together at Huntercombe. One result of their conversations on the links was that, at the Prince's suggestion, Morris gave the university £10,000 to endow the King Alfonso Chair in Spanish.

Despite his eagerness to invest in a Daimler when he was an undergraduate, the Prince was not a particularly enthusiastic motorist—unlike his brother, the Duke of Kent, who treated himself to an 8-litre Bentley. Nevertheless, the future Edward VIII briefly owned what must have been the most unconventional car ever bought by a member of the royal family. The vehicle was known as a Burney after its creator, Sir Dennistoun Burney, who introduced it to the market in 1930 (the Prince purchased his in 1931). Sir Dennistoun had distinguished himself as an airship designer. From his drawingboard had come the plans for the R100—a dirigible built by private enterprise to rival the government-backed R101. Unlike the R101, which crashed in France on its maiden flight and caused the death of all but six of the 54 people on board, it gave promise of success. But, after the R101 disaster, the idea of these monsters as a means of transport was abandoned. Sir Dennistoun turned his talents to other matters.

The Burney reflected its begetter's background. It looked rather like an aeroplane without wings; or, perhaps, the engine pod of an airship. The very powerful motor was situated at the rear (very unusual in those days), and its shape suggested that it was probably the fastest thing on four wheels. Unfortunately, its handling was almost impossible, and, at £1,000 each, the public were in no mood to experiment with such a freakish member of the automotive species. In 1933, Crossley took the Burney over, but failed to make a success of it. It seems doubtful whether, once he had acquired this novelty, the Prince ever drove it.

As King, Edward VIII added one more unit to the royal family of Daimlers. He also bought two Buicks, which were similar though not identical. One was for himself; the other was registered in the name of Ernest Aldrich Simpson. In fact, it was a gift to Mr Simpson's wife.

While King Edward VII may have purchased a couple of Mercedes and a small Renault, the royal family since then had traditionally supported home-grown products to exclusion of everything else. At first glance, his grandson's choice of an American car was unfortunate. But anyone who delved sufficiently into the matter would have discovered that the two vehicles had been manufactured at the company's Canadian plant. In any case, the firm's founder, David Dunbar Buick, was a man of Scottish extraction who had begun his career by manufacturing enamel bathtubs.

On a dark night it was hard to tell the two Buicks apart. This resemblance served the future Duke and Duchess of Windsor well one November night in 1936 when, unable to remain in Britain any longer, Mrs Simpson fled to France. She made her departure from Fort Belvedere in her Buick. Inevitably, the hounds of the press would take up the chase unless something was done to mislead them. The King's Buick was accordingly used as a decoy with considerable success. Mrs Simpson reached Newhaven without let or hindrance, and a number of newsmen wasted a great deal of time tailing the wrong car around much of the home counties.

◆

Although they were carefully built to the requirements of the reigning monarch, the purchases of the royal cars were carried out in a manner very similar to that of an ordinary motorist. There was even a dealer involved— in this case, a firm named Stratton Instone Ltd, who, in due course, merged the *strat* and the *stone* into Stratstone. One of the more aged members of the King's mechanical tribe was traded in; a new one was commissioned. For example, a negotiation carried out in 1936 looked like this:

A special straight-8 chassis from Daimler . . . . £ 900
A Hooper enclosed-drive limousine body . . . . £ 675
                                                                                          —————
                                                                                          £1,575

—minus an allowance of £475 for a 30/40 Daimler that was taken in part exchange.

Three months were required to build a royal car in the days before World War 2. Nowadays five or even six months would be needed. This is partly because the men on the production line enjoy shorter working hours, but largely because the modern vehicles are more complex. Those old Daimlers were, when one thinks about them, rather boxlike, not, perhaps, the kind of thing to which today's leading designers would be proud to put their names.

In the 1930s a Daimler's life with the royal family was reckoned to be about four years, during which it gave very little trouble. For example, a car bought by Queen Mary in 1931 had only twice given cause for complaint when she parted with it in 1935. On one occasion, there was a stoppage in the fuel pipe; on the other, its radiator over-heated on a particularly warm summer day.

Once it passed out of the sovereign's possession, a vehicle was stripped of anything that might betray its distinguished past, such as the police lamp on the roof, gadgets for the display of royal insignia and so on. Its body was also repainted to remove as much as possible of the traces of that distinctive claret. From this moment onward, its social path was downward. The next step might either be into the garage of a mayor or (before the last war) to India. Shortly after that country's independence, a onetime royal Daimler was discovered abandoned on an Indian airfield.

But the descent from the Royal Mews at Buckingham Palace did not end there. The second and probably final plunge of a royal Daimler was usually into the hands of a car-hire firm or an undertaker. Thereafter it disappeared without trace.

King George VI before he came to the throne had been a Lanchester enthusiast. It was, perhaps, a suitable initiation into the Daimler tradition, for the firm joined Daimler in the BSA group of companies in 1931. Mechanically, the two had so much in common that, in the second half of the 1930s, the only difference was the radiator grille. Even after his accession, the new sovereign continued to prefer Lanchesters for his private use; his last was delivered shortly after the outbreak of war.

For ceremonial and official occasions, the Daimler remained the royal vehicle. The last to be built with the armchairs in the centre was delivered in 1935. With two young daughters, the new monarch had other motoring requirements. The public wanted not only to see the King and Queen, it was equally anxious to set eyes on the little princesses. To make this possible, certain modifications were needed. Their Majesties sat on the back seat, the police officer was moved up front beside the chauffeur, and the princesses were accommodated on two collapsible seats in more or less the positions where once armchairs had been. The view of the royal occupants was improved by more generous use of glass. Shortly after, on the King's insistence, a pane of glass was inserted in the roof. It was covered by a sliding panel operated, initially, by a hand mechanism. Later, an electric motor did the work.

As if to celebrate his accession (if 'celebrate' is a suitable word for a situation not of his seeking), the new King ordered a shooting brake. Again, it was manufactured by Daimler, and its accommodation was nothing if not roomy. Externally, much of the metal work was painted and grained to give a very passable imitation of wood. Inside, there was a rack for six guns on the partition behind the driver, and a sufficiently large table to enable the royal family to take luncheon aboard, on days when the weather was bad.

When Edward VIII was Prince of Wales, an American car manufacturer had attempted to cash in on the royal image by naming a car 'The Prince of Windsor'. It was as far as anyone dare go, and even this by-no-means-accurate venture received nothing but dark looks from the purlieus of Buckingham Palace. King George VI was adamant that publicity in the matter of vehicles should be kept to a minimum. There was, for example, a row in January 1939, when a new royal Daimler was due to be delivered. Without waiting for his sovereign's approval, some hapless advertising man at the factory issued a photograph to the press. The King was furious; as he pointed out, he had not yet even *seen* the vehicle. An edict was immediately issued to the effect that, in future, written approval to take a picture—let alone to distribute it to the press— must first be obtained from Buckingham Palace. Then, and then only, could the vehicle be exposed to the inquisitive eye of a camera.

As soon as World War 2 broke out, the King gave instructions that no more royal cars were to be built for the duration. The years of hostility,

As a subaltern Princess Elizabeth learned a great deal about motor transport when she served in the ATS. Her daughter, Princess Anne, shows a similar aptitude: she is one of the relatively few women to hold a heavy goods vehicle licence.

though dramatic enough in other ways, were dull so far as the royal
motoring scene was concerned. The only drama occurred in September
1940, when an anti-aircraft shell, instead of exploding in the sky, fell to
earth in the Royal Mews and went off near the cars. Three of the vehicles
were damaged, though not seriously. Some glass was broken, and small
holes marred the bodywork. The bill for repairs came to £215.

George VI had made modifications to the Daimler design. Quite
soon in his reign, he introduced the idea of an armrest to be installed in
the middle of the rear seat. It contained pencils, a notepad and a box to
contain a supply of cigarettes. He also insisted on reading lamps with
adjustable shades so that, on a long journey, he could work at night.

For some time, his family had been urging him to fit a radio set. For
reasons that are not entirely clear, he opposed the idea. However, he
eventually capitulated—but upon certain conditions. There must, he
ruled, be nothing that any eye could see to betray the fact that it was there.

This, you must realise, was many years before the transistor became
common radio hardware, and anyone could, for a few pounds, buy a set
small enough to slip into a carrier bag. However, small radios were
available, and the firm entrusted with the commission used one to
admirable effect. The set itself was sufficiently small to be put into the
armrest. Two loudspeakers were cunningly concealed in the bodywork
behind the driver, and the aerial was hidden beneath the running board.
Reception is said to have been poor when the car was in the neighbourhood
of Balmoral. Elsewhere, it was perfectly adequate.

Daimlers did not slide from royal favour; they simply changed their
shapes. The postwar versions were lower; more sporty than those stolid
conveyances that had served the royal household so well and for so many
years. As most people had to agree, even though the new cars reflected a
better sense of 'design', they were not the sort of cars that lent themselves
to ceremonial occasions.

Rolls-Royce had been waiting patiently in the wings for a great many
years. Now its moment was at hand. It came in 1950, when the first
product of the Crewe factory whispered onto the scene as a wedding
present for Princess Elizabeth and the Duke of Edinburgh from the
Royal Air Force. Four years later, its owner (now Queen Elizabeth II)
bought a Phantom IV landaulette (second hand), which for the uninitiated
means a car with a hood at the back that lets down. In 1960 and 1961 two
Phantom Vs were acquired. In each of these cases, the rear section was
made from one piece of moulded Perspex. When not being used for
ceremonial occasions, it is enclosed within a folding metal panel. They

In one or two Commonwealth
countries, the Daimler refused to die
as a means of royal transport. When
Queen Elizabeth II visited Australia
and New Zealand during the
coronation tour of 1953 and 1954, a
Daimler was put at her disposal for
ceremonial occasions.

During their visit to Nepal in
February, 1961, her Majesty and the
Duke of Edinburgh were conveyed in a
Nepalese royal Cadillac on a
sightseeing tour through the streets of
Patan, a village near Kathmandu. If
the British motor industry had unkind
things to say about the choice of an
American vehicle, they prudently kept
their remarks to themselves.

are variously known as the 'Canberras' or, when the Queen is enclosed in what might be mistaken for a giant goldfish bowl, as the 'bubble-cars'! They are fitted with fluorescent lighting inside; radio sets are concealed in the armrests; and they are powered by big V8 engines. During a procession, they tend to travel in second gear.

The final member of this royal Rolls-Royce quintet is a Phantom VI that was presented to the Queen in March 1978 as a Silver Jubilee present (a year late, but never mind) by the Motor Industry in Britain. It has a transparent rear roof, and a rear seat that can be elevated—the better for Her Majesty to be seen.

In addition to these which are, so to speak, the capital ships of the official royal car fleet, there are a couple of Austin Princesses (of 1962 and 1972 vintage) that are available if needed. Either can be decked out for a ceremonial occasion, though, while one is in the familiar claret and black, the other is black only.

Whenever the Queen is on an official engagement, the car concerned carries on its roof a shield bearing the royal arms. On a particularly important occasion, especially when troops are lining the route, the royal standard is also flown. But the standard never flies alone—without the accompanying shield. Unlike the royal family's private cars, none of the official vehicles are required to carry number plates. They are, however, fully insured to meet the requirements of the law.

When not occupied by the Queen, the black and claret Rolls-Royces sport the traditional 'flying lady' on their radiator grilles. When the sovereign is aboard, this is replaced by her own mascot. Made from silver, it portrays a naked Saint George on a horse with a dead dragon underneath. The device, which was designed by Edward Seago, was first executed in sugar, and appeared on top of the royal wedding cake in 1947.

The official cars are durable (after all, the oldest Rolls-Royce is now 32 years old), but the Queen also makes her personal vehicles last a long time. A dark green 3 litre Rover bought in March 1961 took her about her private business for ten years before it passed on to another owner. Her present Rover, a 3.5 litre saloon (also painted dark green and, like its predecessors, displaying the AA and RAC badges), was purchased in 1974. These vehicles are licensed and carry number plates—just like any other vehicle.

Lists of cars are boring, even when their owners are members of the royal family. It is sufficient to say that the Duke of Edinburgh, the Prince of Wales and Prince Andrew change their vehicles more frequently than the Queen.

The Duke, whose mascot is an heraldic lion wearing a crown (an item from his coat of arms), has had a preference for Range Rovers ever

Occupants of the mews at Buckingham Palace include carriages, motor cars and a sledge Prince Albert designed for his wife. KUV 1 shown on the Zephyer in this photograph, taken in 1968, has been retained by the Palace and is now used on a carriage-transporter cum *horse-box.*

since the Sultan of Brunei made him a present of one in 1972. Prince Charles's first car was a cobalt blue MGC GT that was bought in January 1968. More recently, he has developed a taste for the Aston Martin range, but, like his father, he also owns a Range Rover.

Princess Anne's vehicles—in the first and second instances, at any rate—were birthday presents (a Rover 2000TC on her 18th from her parents; a Reliant Scimitar GTE as a joint Christmas and 20th birthday

present from the Queen, the Duke of Edinburgh and Prince Charles). She still has a Scimitar, and its number plate is a matter of interest.

Her Royal Highness is Colonel-in-Chief of the 14th/20th King's Hussars. The officers of that regiment decided that it might be rather nice if her comings and goings by car gave evidence of the fact. After a fairly exhaustive hunt, they eventually tracked down a milk float in Ealing. Its registration number was 1420H. Nothing could have been more appropriate; they bought the plate and presented it to her when she visited them at Paderborn in Germany one day in November, 1969.

Independent and strong-willed, Princess Anne is an enthusiastic driver and is not inclined to 'hang about' on the road. Out of London, she is often to be found behind the wheel of a Range Rover—as becomes a country woman with a particular interest in horses.

The responsibility for the care and nourishment of the royal cars belongs to the Royal Mews at Buckingham Palace. Ten chauffeurs are numbered among its population of fifty families; the motor vehicles, the horses, the coaches and the carriages—all come under the control of the Crown Equerry, Lieut-Col Sir John Miller, KCVO, DSO, MC. But, before the purchase of anything new, its future owners like to become involved.

A former Army officer who, after retiring from the service, held an executive position with a leading British car manufacturer, recalled the occasion when he visited the Royal Mews to demonstrate a new station wagon. Since it had been designed for use overseas by oil companies, there was no model available with a right-hand drive.

'A colleague of mine was ill, and he persuaded me to take the vehicle down to the Royal Mews as they were looking for something of the kind for each of the royal residences. After an early lunch, I collected my bowler hat and brolly and went to pick up the wagon—complete with a sheaf of papers that authorised me to drive in a royal park with a trade vehicle.

Without thinking out any special route, and after checking that everything worked and was clean, I drove off towards the Palace, going from Hyde Park Corner down Constitution Hill. I had not gone a couple of hundred yards before a copper leapt out from behind a bush and stopped me. He inquired none too civilly why I was in a royal park with a commercial vehicle. I replied that I was on my way to the Palace to see the Queen. After some hesitation, while he hitched up his belt and pondered over my answer, I showed him the right pass and he let me proceed with the remark, "I did not think anyone would give THAT as a reason for being here!"

'At the Royal Mews, I met the Duke of Beaufort (then Master of the Queen's Horse) who bought all the royal vehicles. After a good look round, he asked if the Duke of Edinburgh might have a look at it. Naturally I agreed and, a few minutes later, Prince Philip appeared. After a slight passage of arms because the vehicle was non-automatic—I had to explain that this machine was for use in oilfields and places where it was essential to be able to push-start, something you couldn't do with an automatic gearbox—he asked if he might drive it round the Palace grounds as he had never driven a left-hand-drive car. Off we went round the inner road, going round several times. He then asked, 'May I ask the Queen to have a look-see?' After some telephone calls, she appeared.

'She, too, was intrigued by the left-hand drive, and I gave her a run round. She then asked if she could drive it, having been told that Prince Philip had already done so. I was then driven round and round several times, and the story ends with an order for four of these monsters—which is how I know how difficult it is to get the right shade of maroon for royal cars and trains.'

Royal motoring comes in three different varieties—official journeys and ceremonial occasions on which the Rolls-Royces are used, ordinary journeys from A to B that are no different from those made by anyone else (Prince Charles has been involved in a minor collision and Princess Anne has been fined for speeding), and trips across country or on private roads on the royal estates.

In the Rolls-Royces, the police officer still rides in a front seat beside the driver; on other occasions, such as when the Queen is driving and Prince Philip is with her, the police officer is more likely to be found on the rear seat.

When making a journey, the Queen prefers to inconvenience other road users as little as possible. If a strict programme has to be followed, for example, a trip to London Airport, then Scotland Yard is warned beforehand. The traffic lights are adjusted to give the royal car a clear run. Dangerous crossroads are manned by policemen. But even on these occasions, over-zealous officers, who hold up the traffic for five minutes or so before the car is due, are frowned upon. There are no police outriders, no blaring sirens, and no question of indulging in such small motoring weaknesses as jumping the lights.

Edward VII, who started it all, put himself beyond the law—at any rate as a road user. Of course, since then, the law has become more moderate in this respect. The Queen learned to drive in the ATS during the war and is a good driver. Unlike her impatient great grandfather, she has a very sensible regard for the rules that govern motoring. One cannot imagine her heralding her approach by some special horn, or virtually pushing everyone else out of the way (though, in this matter, the Prince of Wales still uses a bull horn that was installed in his first MG). Nor, indeed, would those responsible for royal security smile on such flamboyance. As an abortive attempt by a mentally-deranged youth to kidnap Princess Anne at the approaches to the Palace once confirmed, you cannot be too careful.

Nor, if one disregards Prince Charles's Aston Martin DB6 with wire wheels, adorned in Seychelles blue, is flamboyance very much part of the royal image. One has to remember that the most humble of cars, the

This Phantom VI was presented to the Queen in March, 1978, by the motor industry in Britain, to celebrate her Silver Jubilee. For her private motoring, the Queen has a Rover.

Mini, became popular when Princess Margaret and the Earl of Snowdon bought one. As Lord Montagu remarked in *Royalty on the Road*, 'all sorts of people were happy to "keep up with the Armstrong-Joneses." Cars were now a common denominator, and the cars that royalty drove in private enabled them to be like everyone else!'

King Edward VII would have detested the idea.

6
PURPLE AIR SPACE

One day in 1909, when Edward VII was staying at Biarritz, he motored over to Pau in the Pyrénées. On a field a few miles from the town, he examined a heavier-than-air machine manufactured by Wilbur Wright. The weather was bad, and it seemed prudent to remain on the ground. But the intrepid birdman was undeterred. For the royal benefit he made a short solo flight. Then, by way of an encore, he went up again—this time taking his sister Katherine as passenger.

King Edward was delighted. The novelty of the occasion was just the kind of thing he enjoyed. It may have occurred to him to see Mr Wright's invention as a possible weapon of war—thereby disagreeing with his senior Army officers, who protested that it would 'never replace the Cavalry'. But he also noticed that it was a dangerous undertaking. Since one of the duties of a sovereign is to survive, he contented himself with remaining a spectator. In any case, it would have been ignominious if the King's considerable weight made it impossible for the flimsy aeroplane to take off.

It is unlikely to have occurred to the King that, within less than four decades the aeroplane would become a commonplace of royal travel: a necessity without which the royal family would be unable to fulfil its tightly-packed and wide-ranging programme of engagements. It was left to his grandson, Edward VIII to appreciate its possibilities and to establish the King's Flight.

The headquarters of this elite unit of the RAF (now, for obvious reasons, known as the Queen's Flight) is at Benson in Oxfordshire. The cleanliness of its hangar has been compared with that of an operating theatre. The aircraft themselves are scrubbed and polished and generally maintained with the loving care that, on a rather smaller scale, chauffeurs lavish upon Rolls-Royces. All this is no doubt an expression of the Royal Air Force's concern for the comfort and safety of its passengers. Apart from their engines, however, which are Rolls-Royce Darts, these elderly aeroplanes are at some remove from the aeronautical equivalent of what claims with some justification to be 'the best car in the world'.

Nowadays, the Queen's Flight employs 20 officers, 156 other ranks and three civilians. It has three Andovers, each of which is about 20 years old. This has prompted one MP to suggest that 'fitness for a Queen does not have to be fitness for the RAF Museum.' When they are all present—which is seldom, especially in summer—the trio share the hangar with two Wessex helicopters.

From time to time the question of the Andovers, their age and their capabilities, crops up in the House of Commons. It is pointed out that Prince Charles and his father both have jet ratings and might be glad of the opportunity to fly something rather faster. After all, the Andover (seating capacity in less illustrious versions—36) was first flown in 1960. Its normal cruising altitude, which it takes half-an-hour to reach, is only 15,000ft (4,570m), and its speed by today's standards is slow. 'Isn't it time,' the Andovers' critics protest, 'that the Queen's flying machines were brought up-to-date?'

The BAC 111 is invariably suggested as an alternative. With extra fuel tanks installed beneath the floor, its range could be extended to about 2,400 miles (3,870km), which would make it superior to the elderly turbo-prop machines in almost every respect.

Money, of course, is involved. A 111 would cost about £6 million, whilst a royal Andover, sold in America, would probably fetch about £1 million—for prestige rather than performance. 'Prestige', indeed, is a word that occurs whenever the matter is raised. Back in 1958, the Flight was largely made up of de Havilland Herons. When, in that year, the Queen was due to make a state visit to the Netherlands, she was advised not to use them. They were, her mentors suggested, neither large enough nor sufficiently modern. In 1962, they were replaced by the Andovers (the RAF version of the British Aerospace 748 airliner). But, before that, the question of investing in the BAC 111 had already been considered—and rejected.

Prince Charles and the Duke of Edinburgh used to enjoy flying the Andovers; their leisurely progress through the air, far from being a snag, provided them with a respite between engagements.

Nowadays, however, their limitations are painfully apparent. So far as overseas tours are concerned, the royal family's busy schedules compel the authorities to look elsewhere—often to commercial airlines—for transport. Writing in the *Daily Mail*, Nigel Dempster described the Flight as an 'antiquated airline which would disgrace a banana republic'—which may be putting it rather too strongly. Nevertheless, another critic has remarked of the Flight's aircraft, 'What a disgrace for a country which pioneered the jet engine!'

On the other hand, faster journeys would produce some kind of vacuum in the royal schedule. Local authorities, good causes, industry, the services, whatever—they all, like nature, abhor such a thing. Other engagements would be squeezed into an already rigorous programme, and the strain on the monarchy would become even greater.

As for the Queen, her husband has said, 'She doesn't dislike flying. For her, it's just a means of getting from A to B. I don't think it gives her any particular pleasure.' (*Captains and Kings* Neville Birch and Alan Bramson, 1972.) One cannot help wondering whether it might give her more pleasure, if she were able to travel at altitudes where there is less turbulence. After all, her subjects—snug in their jetliners—fly *over* the weather.

Owing to its limited range, the Andover is obviously unsuited to the long hauls necessary for overseas tours. On these occasions, the Queen uses a VC10 from 38 Group of RAF Strike Command, or else, as has occurred on several occasions, the host country provides one of its own airliners. But, even in these circumstances, an Andover nearly always goes along—though its journey takes very much longer. When, for example, Her Majesty went to Brazil in 1968, she made the trip in one hop, using an RAF VC10. The attendant Andover took four days to get there—travelling via Iceland and Greenland, and thence through North American airspace with plenty of landings to refuel.

The interiors of aircraft used on the longer distance flights have to be modified for their role, which means that they are out of general service for longer than the duration of the tour itself. The needs of Prince Charles in this respect are less exacting. For journeys in which the host country is one thousand miles or more away, he sometimes travels on scheduled flights. The first class accommodation is put at the disposal of HRH and his staff. The tourist compartment is occupied by ordinary, fare-paying, passengers. Prince Charles seems content with the arrangement—though he turns down the champagne that is among the perquisites of all who fly up-front in the expensive seats.

◆

The first member of the royal family to go up in an aeroplane was Edward VIII when he was Prince of Wales. It happened in 1916, when he was on a tour of the Western Front. 'It was', he recalled many years later, 'just before the Battle of the Somme. I don't think I was particularly scared. It was just a new experience.' The aircraft was a two-seater fighter that had only just come into service.

Two years later, on a tour of Italy, he was flown over the enemy lines by a Canadian pilot named Barker. Shortly afterwards, Captain Barker took part in a dog fight and was severely wounded in one arm.

Soon after the end of the war, Barker was in London, with his injured arm still in a sling. He met the Prince of Wales at a party and reminded him of their flight together over the Austrian lines. Perhaps His Royal Highness would like to go up again? The Prince said he would be delighted and suggested the following day.

Inevitably the press heard about it; and, no less inevitably, King George V read the stories that appeared on several front pages. He was less than pleased. 'He gave me absolute hell,' the Prince recalled. As the sovereign not unreasonably pointed out, if the heir to the throne was to fly, it might be as well if his pilot had the use of both arms.

The King's misgivings seemed to be confirmed shortly afterwards when Winston Churchill tried his hand at flying an aeroplane. It was not a success—he crashed. His instructor had both his legs broken; Churchill crawled out of the wreckage unharmed. But, as George V pointed out, it gave a very convincing demonstration of what *could* happen. The Prince dutifully remained on the ground until 1926, when he flew as a passenger from Paris to London in an Imperial Airways airliner.

Prince Albert (the future King George VI) met with less parental opposition. He had originally served in the Royal Navy. As a midshipman on the battleship HMS *Collingwood*, he had taken part in the Battle of Jutland. But his health was not good. After an operation, his doctors suggested that life at sea was too rigorous and that he would be better employed ashore. As a result, he was posted to the Royal Naval Air Service at Cranwell.

His duties did not include flying; nevertheless, he was persuaded to make a trip with one of the instructors of the RAF College, Cranwell, at the controls. He was not particularly eager to repeat the experience. In a letter to his mother, he wrote, 'It was a curious sensation and one which takes a lot of getting used to. I did enjoy it on the whole, but I don't think I should like flying as a pastime. I would much sooner be on the ground! ! It feels safer! !'

In 1918, Prince Albert was posted to France. He was becoming aware that there were two types of officer in the Royal Air Force and Royal Naval Air Service; those who proudly wore their 'wings' and regarded themselves as an elite, and those who were earthbound and were, a little disdainfully, known as 'quirks'. As the Prince did not wish to be a quirk he decided that he must qualify as a pilot. Strangely enough, in contrast to his attitude to the Prince of Wales, George V seems to have encouraged Prince Albert. In reply to a letter asking for permission to take lessons, the King wrote, 'I thought you told me that you had no wish to fly, therefore I questioned yr. remaining in RAF. I suppose you have changed

King Edward VIII founded the King's Flight (now the Queen's Flight) in July, 1938. Even as Prince of Wales, Edward had been enthusiastic about flying, despite his father's disapproval. This illustration, which was published in the 1932 edition of the Wonder Book of Aircraft, *shows the Prince airborne over Windsor Castle with the Thames in the background. (Opposite, top.)*

From time to time there are suggestions that the Queen's Flight should be up-dated and the Andovers replaced with BAC 111s. The suggestion is inevitably rejected as the cost would be prodigious. Consequently the turbo-prop aircraft, some of which are nearly twenty years old, soldier on. This one is taking off from London Airport in May, 1971. (Opposite, bottom.)

your mind and you can certainly do so if you wish.'

Two Avro 504Ks (the standard trainer of the RAF for more than a decade), which had just been built at Hamble, were taken to France, and the Prince gingerly embarked on the adventure. Later, when he returned to England, his lessons continued at Waddon Lane aerodrome near Croydon.

Prince Albert was a good horseman and an above-average tennis player. As this suggests, his co-ordination was good and gave him the makings of an able pilot. Before very long, he was making cross-country flights and carrying out such aerobatics as loops, stalls and *Immelmann* turns with reasonable competence.

But the doctors still had their eyes upon him. When it came to the question of his going solo, they advised that, in view of his general medical and psychological condition, it would be wise to take certain precautions. The rules were bent to allow his instructor to accompany him in the front cockpit—upon the strict understanding that the instructor did not touch the controls.

Everything proceeded satisfactorily. On 31 July, 1919, the Prince was awarded his wings by the Brigadier-General commanding the south eastern area of the RAF. Next day, the Prince was promoted to flight lieutenant, and three months later, to squadron leader.

Despite his successful performance, he never really overcame his fundamental dislike of flying, which was in contrast to his elder brother. In 1929, the Prince of Wales, with Squadron Leader David Don as his mentor, took his first flying lesson. He also bought a Gypsy Moth. It was the first of many aircraft owned by him. For some reason that he could never explain to himself, he seemed to buy them in pairs. It was expensive, 'I must have been very flush with money,' he remarked many years later.

On 17 November, 1929, after 30 hours of instruction, the Prince of Wales made his first solo flight at Northolt in Middlesex. But by this time, David Don was finding it difficult to carry out his normal duties as a full time RAF officer *and* look after HRH's flying requirements at the same time. The problem was solved when Flight Lieutenant Edward 'Mouse' Fielden was recalled from the Royal Air Force's reserve of officers. He was offered the job of overseeing the Prince's private aeroplane and acting as his personal pilot. He accepted.

When, many years later, the former Prince of Wales (by this time the Duke of Windsor) wrote *A King's Story*, he recalled that, 'I had no desire to go down in history as Edward the Reformer. Edward the Innovator—that might have been more to the point.' Among his innovations was that of using an aircraft at the conclusion of an overseas tour.

In 1930, after a trip to Africa, he flew from Malakal in the Sudan via Khartoum to Cairo, where he boarded the P & O liner *Rawalpindi* for Marseilles. From Marseilles, he flew to Le Bourget aerodrome near Paris, and thence to Windsor, where Smith's Lawn had been converted into a landing strip. The flying time for the 650 miles in the air was 6 hr 10 min— an average speed of 105mph (about 1,040km at 169km/h). The Prince wore a parachute over an old overcoat, a flying helmet and goggles. From Le Bourget to the French coast, his aircraft was escorted by nine French fighters. An RAF flying boat took over for the Channel crossing; and then, as he moved into British air space over Lympne in Kent, nine aircraft of Air Defence of Great Britain accompanied him on the last leg of the journey (the RAF was not divided into fighter and bomber commands until 1936).

He was met by Prince George (later Duke of Kent), a few friends and his dog, Cora. Later, King George V (by now, presumably, having overcome his objections to his eldest son's excursions in the sky) and Queen Mary received him at Fishing Cottage, Virginia Water. As for Smith's Lawn, the Prince began to use it as his personal airfield, and it was amazing how large an aircraft it could accommodate. In 1931, after a flight by the Prince from Bordeaux, it was even used by an Imperial Airways Argosy airliner, which was asking rather a lot of a greensward that had not been cultivated with any such role in mind.

When George V died at Sandringham in January 1936, the Prince of Wales and Prince Albert (now Duke of York) were at his bedside. The clocks at Sandringham had always been kept half-an-hour fast. The new King's first instruction was that they should be put back to conform with the other time-pieces in the realm. His second was to order his aircraft to be warmed up in readiness to take him to London for a meeting of the Accession Council. His brother accompanied him. It was, the King admitted, taking rather a chance; after all, if there had been a fatal crash, the sovereign and his successor would both have been killed. But the alternative was to go by train, and the service was 'very slow' (it would also have been possible to go by car. The Accession Council had to be held within twenty-four hours of King George V's death, which gave him plenty of time, but the King was by nature impatient).

For nearly seven years, Flight Lieutenant Fielden had been employed as his personal pilot. Having ascended to the throne, King Edward VIII saw no reason to restrict his flying; indeed, in keeping with his image of a thoroughly modern monarch, he expected to make even greater use of his aircraft. Since there was a *royal* yacht, it seemed only reasonable that some similar institution should be formed to facilitate the sovereign's journeys by air. Thus, at Edward's behest, the King's

Flight came into being on 20 July, 1936, with one de Havilland Rapide. It was based on the RAF aerodrome at Hendon in NW London. Fielden, now a wing commander, was appointed its first 'Captain' and assigned to the royal household as an equerry-in-waiting. He occupied this position until his retirement in 1962—increasing in rank and eventually being rewarded with a knighthood.

Captain of the King's (or Queen's) Flight is a civilian appointment. It is awarded to a senior RAF officer who, after a few months spent (so to speak) on probation, is quietly asked to retire from the service and accept employment as a member of the royal household.

On the abdication of Edward VIII, King George VI inherited the King's Flight, which—since the Rapide had been his brother's personal property—now had no aircraft at all! The situation was corrected in the following year by the purchase of an Airspeed Envoy. Fielden was not best pleased; it was, he thought, too small, but since nothing more suitable was available, it would have to do. In September, 1940, he acquired two larger aeroplanes (a medium-range airliner named the de Havilland Flamingo and a Lockheed Hudson), but there were other problems.

The requirements of war put a much greater strain on the aerodrome at Hendon—which, in any case, was vulnerable to enemy attack. It would, people generally agreed, be wise to move the King's Flight head-quarters to somewhere further from London. Fielden suggested that Smith's Lawn at Windsor would be suitable; it had, after all, been used for this purpose before. The Air Ministry was less enthusiastic. Instead, the Flight was removed to Benson in Oxfordshire, where it became a kind of lodger attached to No. 12 Operational Training Unit. In 1941, it was incorporated into No. 161 Squadron near Newmarket (later it moved to Tempsford near Bedford), and devoted itself to the task of dropping weapons and agents into German-occupied countries. Fielden com-manded it and, at the same time, retained the title of Captain of the King's Flight.

When, in early 1946, the King approved the revival of the Flight, Benson was again chosen for its base—not least because it was not too distant from London or Windsor and because it was sufficiently far from any of the country's main airways. Nowadays, control of it is in the hands of the Air Officer Commanding-in-Chief Strike Command, who dele-gates the responsibility to the Air Officer Commanding 38 group. He, in turn, passes on the duty to the Captain of the Flight. Although retired, the Captain has the same powers as any serving officer.

Now that aircraft have reduced the size of the globe—in time if not in distance—the Queen's frequent travels take her to distant corners, such as Whitehorse in the Yukon . . . (Top left.) . . . and Kuala Lumpur in Malaysia. The Viscount aircraft in the previous picture was provided by the Canadian Government; in this case, she is alighting from an Andover of the Queen's Flight. (Top right.) Heathrow—and the Queen, the Duke of Edinburgh and Princess Anne return to London after a trip to Canada in 1971. (Bottom left.)

Until the war, the most serious air accident involving a member of the royal family had occurred when Edward VIII was flying to Paris with the portrait painter James Gunn. It poured with rain throughout the trip, but there was no cause for alarm. On coming down at Le Bourget, however, the pilot overshot the runway. Instead of gaining altitude and trying again, he landed and attempted to turn. The propeller buckled, a wheel spun off, but nobody was hurt.

It was trifling in comparison with the tragic affair that occurred on 25 August, 1942.

King George VI's youngest brother, the Duke of Kent, was governor-general designate of Australia. He had held the honorary rank of Air Vice-Marshal in the RAF which absorbed little of his energy. When war broke out, however, he insisted that he should take a more active part in the service. He relinquished his honorary rank and became a group captain, which was appropriate to the job he had in mind. His task was to tour RAF stations as a representative of the welfare branch.

In the summer of 1942 (now an air commodore) he became the first member of the royal family to fly the Atlantic when he travelled in a Liberator bomber on a tour of RAF establishments in Canada. Before returning to England, he paid a brief visit to the United States, where he stayed with President Roosevelt. The President wrote afterwards, 'We had such a good time together at Hyde Park [the President's New York residence]. I had a great affection for him.'

Back in Britain, the Prince took three weeks' leave, and then set off on a visit to Iceland. The idea was that he should travel to the naval base at Invergordon by train. There he would embark in an RAF Sunderland flying boat from No. 228 Squadron, which was normally based on Oban.

The Duke was accompanied by his private secretary—Lieutenant J A Lowther, RNVR, by Pilot Officer the Hon. Michael Strutt—who was called in at the last moment to serve as acting air equerry and by Leading Aircraftman John Hales. The Sunderland's captain was a 25-year-old Australian pilot, Flight Lieutenant Frank Goyen. He was specially chosen for the assignment. Altogether, he had logged a thousand hours on operations over the Mediterranean and South Atlantic. He commanded a crew of nine, which included a second pilot, two radio operators, a navigator, an engineer, a fitter, and three gunners. The commanding officer of No. 228 Squadron, Wing Commander T L Mosely (also an Australian) attached himself to the Duke's party.

That morning, it rained continuously at Invergordon, though the weather was not considered sufficiently bad to delay the flight. The cloud-base over Cromarty was 800 ft (245m). Further north, over the Faroes, the forecast was that conditions would improve.

Goyen's flight plan was to fly over the sea, roughly following the coast, as far as John O'Groats, where he would turn westwards over the Pentland Firth. He would then bear to the north-west on a direct course to Reykjavik. It was a sensible idea for, in addition to the 14 men on board, the Sunderland was fully laden with depth charges in case any U-boats were sighted. With such a heavy load, the flying boat would require some time to reach its cruising altitude of about 5,000ft (1525m). To take a more direct route at the beginning would be dangerous in view of the mountains that littered Sutherland—several of them 2,000ft (610m) high, and one of them more than 3,000ft (915m).

At 1 pm on 25 August a tender carrying the Duke and his companions departed from the Invergordon jetty and, a few minutes later, came alongside the flying boat. The water was smooth. The large aircraft taxied along the Cromarty Firth and, with something of an effort, heaved itself into the sky and climbed slowly. What happened during the next 25 minutes can only be speculation. It is certain that the port wing of the flying boat hit the shoulder of a hill—that the machine turned on its back and crashed into the heather 100 yards farther on. It completely disintegrated—though there was one survivor. The tail-gunner, Sergeant Andrew Jack, encapsuled in his perspex turret, crawled out of the wreckage alive though severely injured. Having examined the Sunderland's remains for any sign of life, he hobbled away from the scene.

It was raining harder than ever.

The sound of the crash was heard by a farmer named David Morrison, who was rounding up his sheep with assistance from his son Hugh. Mr Morrison assembled a search party but the debris was not discovered until 1 pm on the following day. A 71-year-old doctor, John Kennedy, found the Duke's body lying across a rock in a natural attitude—as if he were taking a nap. Dr Kennedy noticed that the Duke was wearing a platinum wrist-watch. It had stopped 32 minutes after take-off.

What went wrong? The events that took place between take-off and the moment of impact can be only guessed at. All four engines seem to have been working when the Sunderland struck the rock. Apart from this, there was little the aeroplane's scattered remains could reveal. The question that has to be asked is—why was the flying boat put at such risk? The air accident card, on which the subsequent court of inquiry's findings are summarised, suggests that, 'accident due to the aircraft being on wrong track . . . captain changed flight plan for reasons unknown and descended through cloud without making sure he was over water and crashed . . . weather conditions should have presented no difficulties to crew of such experience.'

All of which tells us very little. The accident that caused the death of the Duke of Kent and his companions remains one of the mysteries of the sky; a mystery to which there will never be a solution.

The King and Queen were staying at Balmoral with the Duke and Duchess of Gloucester when the disaster occurred. They were in the middle of dinner when His Majesty was called to the telephone. The Secretary of State for Air, it seemed, had an urgent message for him. Later he noted in his diary:

> Archie Sinclair rang me up to say that George [the Duke of Kent] had been killed in an aeroplane accident on his way to Iceland. He had started from Invergordon in a Sunderland Flying Boat and after $\frac{1}{2}$ hour flying crashed into a mountain at Morven on the Langwell estate (Portland's). This news came as a great shock to me, and I had to break it to Elizabeth, Harry and Alice . . . He was killed on Active Service.

A disaster such as this can have done nothing to lessen George VI's dislike—or, at the very least, uneasiness—of flying. Before setting off by air to visit the troops in North Africa on 11 June 1943, he summoned his solicitor to put his affairs in order. As he noted, 'I think it is better on this occasion to leave nothing to chance.' And, to his mother, Queen Mary, 'As the time draws nearer for my departure on my journey, I wonder if I should go, but I know I shall be doing good in visiting those men who have done such wonderful deeds for this country, and will shortly be going into action again!'

The aircraft chosen for the trip was a four-engined Avro York belonging to No. 24 (communications) Squadron that, normally, was at the disposal of Winston Churchill. Fielden accompanied the royal party in his capacity of Captain of the King's Flight, but the aircraft was piloted by Group Captain Charles Slee. As Group Captain Slee recalls, 'I was a test pilot at the RAF experimental establishment at Boscombe Down. There were only three or four people who'd flown the York. I had barely finished testing it, when I had to fly Mr Churchill to North Africa.

'After I'd been home for a few days, I was told to fly the King to North Africa in the same aircraft, which was really Mr Churchill's and not the King's. The cabin was beautifully furnished. There was a lovely passenger lounge up for'ard, and a galley and toilet amidships. Then there was a long saloon with a beautiful bird's eye maple table in the middle. Aft of that, there was a small private suite. It really was small. You couldn't have swung a cat in it.'

On the evening of 11 June, the York took off from Northolt aerodrome. Soon after it had flown over Lundy Island at the entrance to the Bristol Channel, the King came up on to the flight deck. 'He certainly showed no sign of disliking flying,' Group Captain Slee said. 'It was a beautiful night, and he stayed with us chatting for about forty minutes. Then he said "Things that start well invariably end well. I'm for bed" and off he went. He was charming.'

Some hours later, it seemed to anxious members of the royal family in London that the King might have been unduly optimistic. The York was due to call at Gibraltar to refuel. Time passed and there was no report of its arrival. The Queen told her mother-in-law, 'Of course I imagined every sort of horror, and walked up and down my room staring at the telephone.' Eventually, just before noon on the next day, her mind was put at rest. Gibraltar, it seemed, had been swathed in fog, and the aircraft had been diverted to a desert air strip at Ras el Mar near Fez in Morocco.

Communications were not in very good order at Gibraltar during the early hours of 12 June. Having advised Slee to fly on to Morocco, the air traffic controllers seem to have turned their attention to something else. No message, certainly, was received at Ras el Mar. Consequently, when the York touched down and its royal occupant appeared at the door, there was nobody to greet him.

The rest of the tour—which included stop-overs at Algiers, Tunis, Tripoli, and a sea trip by the King to Malta—was uneventful. Returning to Northolt, a tailwind hurried the aircraft's progress. As a result, the flight from Ras el Mar (now more suitably prepared for royal passengers in transit) took only 8 hr 45 min. A fighter escort was due to meet the York over Lundy Island and accompany it over the final miles of the journey. When it became clear to Slee that they were about an hour ahead of schedule and that the fighters would not yet be at the rendezvous, he suggested that he should throttle back to a more leisurely speed.

Fielden, acting on the principle that the less time the York spent exposed to attack by enemy aircraft, the better it would be, urged him to press on. Winston Churchill was due to meet the King at Northolt, but he, like the fighters, was unprepared for the early arrival. Forty minutes before Churchill reached the aerodrome, His Majesty was already on his way to Buckingham Palace.

Before leaving the aeroplane, the King told members of the aircrew to present themselves at the Palace at midday. The occasion was pleasantly informal. They were introduced to the Queen. Group Captain Slee was appointed a member of the Victorian Order (he already held the Air Force Cross), while Fielden was rewarded with a CVO.

In 1944, the York was once again put at the King's disposal, this time for a flight he made to Naples. During the King's visit to Italy, he made several trips in a Dakota, which impressed him very much.

◆

On 1 May 1946, the King's Flight was re-established at RAF Benson. Fielden, now an Air Commodore, resumed his duties as its Captain.

When Edward VIII had formed the Flight, he decided that the aircraft should be decorated in red and blue—the colours of the brigade of guards. George VI believed that, since it was a unit in the RAF and had nothing to do with the Army, this was inappropriate. Instead, the four Vikings that were mustered at Benson remained in their original metal finish (polished to the nth degree) with standard Royal Air Force insignia.

Civil aviation in Britain had returned to the sky after the war with a collection of Dakotas and, to a lesser extent, Junkers 52s—three-engined aeroplanes with distinctive corrugated fuselages that had been the mainstay of the German *Luftwaffe*'s transport services (a number of them, taken over by British European Airways in 1946 by way of war reparations, were quickly renamed 'Jupiters'). The Vickers Viking was the first truly British post-war airliner designed for short and medium hauls. It was a derivative of the Wellington bomber—a twin-engined war plane that bore the brunt of bomber command's offensive before the introduction of four-engined machines such as the Lancaster (on which the York was based) and the Halifax.

Of the four Vikings in the King's Flight, two were earmarked for the King and Queen, a third was a 21-seater for members of their staff and the fourth was fitted out as a flying workshop to service the other three. A fifth was acquired for a tour of Australia in 1948.

Among their duties, when the royal family was at Balmoral, was to fly mail from London to Dyce airport near Aberdeen. From there the mail was flown along the valley of the Dee by one of the Flight's two Hoverfly helicopters (on loan from the RAF). The pilot of one of them was Flight Lieutenant Trubshaw who, years later, was to become the test pilot of Concorde.

The King's Viking and the Queen's Viking were each divided into two lounges fitted-out with adjustable armchairs. dark blue carpets and a small galley. The walls and ceilings of the cabins were decorated in beige; the doors were covered in leather. The aeroplanes were extremely comfortable—and reliable.

As time went by, the Vikings were replaced by de Havilland Herons. In the middle of 1964, the first two Andovers were delivered. For longer trips, the sovereign relied on transport command, or on one of the civil airlines—though an aeroplane from the royal flight nearly always went along too. The last of the Vikings bowed out of royal service in 1958.

When, in 1952, she set off on a tour that should have taken her via Africa to Australasia, she was a princess. When she returned hurriedly to London after the death of her father, she was Queen and her ministers were at Heathrow to meet her (Winston Churchill is on the right). The aircraft was an Argonaut chartered from BOAC.

In 1952, after the death of George VI, the King's Flight became the Queen's Flight—with Fielden still serving as Captain.

◆

The Queen's Flight, though part of the RAF, is an entirely self-contained unit—with its own workshops and staff. Tucked away in a corner, is the 'flag room', containing the collection of flags, in which a great many countries are represented.

Once a visiting royal Andover has touched down at an airport overseas, a tiny staff, flying the sovereign's personal standard and the flag of the host country, emerge through the roof of the flight deck, at a point above the navigator's seat (between the two pilots and just behind them).

All the personnel of the Queen's Flight are volunteers who have been screened by a tough selection board. Any technician or tradesman who hopes to join it, must show that his ability is above-average. The officers and men serve for a period of five years—though some extend it for longer.

It has been remarked that, 'This Flight is the most prestigious in the world. It is a rare honour for a pilot or engineer to be selected to serve in it . . . It has given value for money. . . . The problem is not how to get men to work hard, but how to make them stop work and go home.' And, 'The Queen is a prolific user of aircraft.' (Part of a question asked in the House of Commons on 18 February 1980, by Mr Cyril D Townsend, MP, Conservative member for Blackheath. Much of Mr Townsend's material was taken from an issue of *Flight International* that appeared in 1978.)

Although the unit is known as 'the Queen's Flight', the sovereign and members of her family are not its only users. During one year, it was estimated that 35% of all its journeys were made on behalf of non-royal persons—with, of course, Her Majesty's agreement. The passengers included the Prime Minister and members of the government, service chiefs and visiting heads of state. Among the list of those who, at one time or another, have fastened seat belts in a royal Andover or a Wessex helicopter are Giscard d'Estaing, Chancellor Schmidt of Germany and King Hussein of Jordan.

In the Commons, Mr Townsend, warming to his subject, pointed out that, 'If we did not have a Queen's Flight, we should have to invent one.' A remark which does not survive serious scrutiny. He was, perhaps, on safer ground, when he pointed out that it is the most cost-effective way of providing a service designed to meet a large number of public engagements with tight schedules. On this, he emphasised, governments of both parties were agreed.

The demands on the Flight are considerable. Between 1973 and 1978, its aircraft visited sixty different nations. In 1977 alone, 37 royal VIP flights flew to 22 countries. And, in 1979, the Andovers were in the air for 1,581 hours. Of these 1,033 were accounted for by training, route-proving, or positioning the aircraft for use within the host country. While 433 hours were spent carrying members of the royal family, and the remaining 115 hours were occupied by flying government ministers and other VIPs.

Except when undergoing major maintenance, all the aircraft are 100% serviceable every morning of the year—though they are over-hauled more frequently and their engines replaced more often than other

Having said goodbye to his daughter King George VI walks slowly down the steps from a chartered BOAC aircraft. If all had gone according to plan, Princess Elizabeth and Prince Philip would have travelled from West Africa to Australia and New Zealand. But the King died in his sleep less than a week later and the tour was cancelled. (Top.)

The first Hawker Siddeley Andover of the Queen's Flight. The military version of the HS748, this turbo-prop aeroplane has a cruising altitude of 15,000ft (4,572m) and, by jet standards, is slow. The first two royal Andovers were acquired in 1964. (Left.)

aeroplanes. A Dart engine on an Andover is used for about two-thirds of the life recommended by its manufacturers, Rolls-Royce. With such high standards, there is no need to provide a reserve aircraft, and the flying workshop of the Viking days is a thing of the past. Nor is there any problem with regard to spare parts. When something went wrong on a visit to Fiji, a replacement for a faulty component was delivered within 24 hours of the dispatch of a signal to England.

The Queen's Flight may be 'the most prestigious in the world', but nobody could claim that its aircraft are the most luxurious. The Queen's tastes are simple. 'Cost-effectiveness' is a word used almost as frequently within Buckingham Palace as it is in more commercial surroundings, and many an executive jet is more comfortable and certainly more flamboyant.

Nevertheless, no one could complain about the standards of the Andovers' royal accommodation. The Queen's aircraft is divided into three compartments. Her own quarters—with four armchairs and two tables—are situated at the after end. In the middle, there is a cabin for her attendants with eight armchairs and, up front, a small galley. The food, which is re-heated, is prepared by British Airways. The interior of the Duke of Edinburgh's aircraft is slightly different—not least because, like Prince Charles, he spends most of his time at the controls of the flight deck.

The interior colour scheme is a quiet blend of blue and grey, which may not be exciting, but is restful to the eye. With all the uniforms, decorations, traditional dresses and what not that greet the Queen on her tours, she probably sees enough bright colours anyway—and is glad of more subdued tints during the intervals between appearances. The general effect, to quote a member of the Queen's Flight, is 'roughly equivalent to the standard of airline first-class accommodation'.

———————————————◆———————————————

An ever recurring fear of air traffic controllers is the possibility of an 'air' miss (which is different from a 'near' miss, but is certainly to be avoided). The Queen's Flight receives the highest priority so far as clearance is concerned. The only aircraft that have precedence over it are those in distress, or a flying ambulance carrying a seriously ill patient. When operating over the UK, from the moment of take-off to the instant that its landing gear makes contact with the tarmac, it moves through a hallowed region known as 'Purple Air Space'. This invisible red carpet in the sky is a lane ten miles wide and, although it usually follows the established airways of ordinary domestic flights, the aircraft flies at a different altitude (not very difficult with Andovers; cruising at 15,000 ft [4,570m], they fly below the higher-flying jets used by most airlines).

The procedure begins in the office of the Captain of the Queen's Flight—nowadays Air Commodore Sir Archie Winskill, KCVO, CBE, DFC and bar, MRAeS and, significantly perhaps, member of the British Institute of Management. If the Queen, a member of her immediate family, or a visiting head of state is to make the trip, then 'royal flight' status is automatic—meaning that the aircraft will fly in purple airspace. Other royals, VIPs, even the prime minister, are not necessarily accorded it.

Sir Archie passes on basic data about the proposed journey to the adjutant of the Queen's Flight. Thereafter, a good many people become involved as the information goes from desk to desk. The RAF aeronautical documents section at Northolt must be informed, and likewise the aerospace utilisation section at RAF Uxbridge. The aeronautical information service at Pinner issues a NOTAM (notice to airmen) giving 48 hours warning of the flight—plus details of the aircraft's call signs (the Prince of Wales' is 'Unicorn'—his father's 'Rainbow'), a complete itinerary and the dimensions of the lane of purple airspace. This is distributed to all civil and military installations.

Purple airspace comes into being fifteen minutes before the departure of the aircraft and ends thirty minutes after its appointed time of arrival at its destination. One of the objects, however, is to disrupt air traffic as little as possible. If the royal flight lasts longer than one hour, the purple air space dissolves as the aircraft passes from one sector into another. In fact, the regulations concerning it are surprisingly reasonable. No gliders are allowed within it; down on the ground, any Ministry of Defence danger area (a military firing range, for example) must stop whatever it is doing 15 minutes before the aeroplane is due to pass overhead, and for 30 minutes afterwards. This is known as the '45-minute rule'. So far as radio is concerned, no one must practise emergency procedures on the international distress frequencies—whether civil or military. If, however, there really is an emergency, the royal aeroplane will either be diverted to the nearest available airfield or, if it is closest to the scene, the pilot will give whatever help may be possible.

Other aircraft may enter purple airspace provided they have been given prior clearance by the air-traffic-control authorities.

Beyond the United Kingdom, similar arrangements are made at diplomatic level. It works very well, though, on one occasion over Germany, something went badly wrong. In November 1960, the Queen and the Duke of Edinburgh were returning in a Comet II from a visit to Denmark. They were flying at 30,000ft (9,150m) along an airway designated 'red one'. Twenty miles north-east of Eelde, in Hanover airspace, two German fighters approached on what seemed to be a collision course. Afterwards, the Comet's co-pilot, Flight Lieutenant F J Stevens, was reported to have said, 'They had damn great Iron Crosses underneath their wings. They turned in as a pair and passed only about fifty feet above us. I do not know whether they were taking evasive action. It was a very nasty moment and I was prepared to do something drastic.'

Sir Edward Fielden was more restrained in his comment. He simply observed that, 'The two aircraft had absolutely no business to be there.' The German authorities seem to have been sluggish in their reaction. Several days later, a spokesman for the West German Defence Ministry, when asked if it was true that no action would be taken against the offending pilots, replied 'Absolutely right'.

In April 1970, Prince Charles and his father were flying over Sussex in the former's Basset, a small twin-engined aircraft in which he had learned to fly. A Piper Aztec flew dangerously close, and it is estimated that a mere three seconds separated the two aeroplanes from colliding. It is hard to know how the confusion arose, for, in all conscience, the Basset was conspicuous enough. In 1960, following a general trend, the traditional polished silver finish of the Queen's Flight aircraft had been replaced by fluorescent red paint (Prince Philip's aircraft had an Edinburgh-green line along the sides of the fuselage; the others had a royal blue line).

A series 3 Whirlwind HCC Mk 12 with Princess Anne on board, 25 April 1969. The Duke of Edinburgh, the Prince of Wales and Prince Andrew are all accomplished helicopter pilots.

The only member of the royal family not to use helicopters as a matter of course, is the Queen who, except when security demands it (for example, on a visit to Northern Ireland), confines her flights to fixed-wing aircraft. All the helicopters of the Queen's Flight are painted a distinctive shade of red. Those shown are two Westland Wessex Mk 2s converted to Mk 4 VIP transports. (Left and bottom.)

Nowadays, the helicopters are still an unmistakably bright red, though the Andovers are more subdued. Their exposed aluminium under-bodies showed signs of corrosion from constant polishing. In 1972, to overcome this problem, the Queen selected an all-white polyurethane finish. Thus the colour scheme is now predominantly red and white—with the royal blue line along either side of the fuselage.

———————————————————◆———————————————————

In late 1952, the Duke of Edinburgh was a very busy man. Not only was he acting as Chairman of the Coronation Commission, he was also learning to fly. His decision to become a pilot caused uneasy stirrings among the less-adventurous spirits in Whitehall. Once, when he had flown a light aircraft to White Waltham on a Saturday morning, members of the Reading Flying Club—whose airfield is adjacent—protested. The Duke had, they said, interrupted their activities for $2\frac{1}{2}$ hours. As one of them said, 'If the Prince wants to fly in small aircraft, why shouldn't he take the same chances that the rest of us have to take?'

Since the Duke dislikes excessive fuss, and would prefer to cause as little disruption as possible, he no doubt agreed. There was a somewhat poignant note to the letter he instructed his equerry to write to the club's secretary, 'His Royal Highness would like you to know that if you think you have difficulties getting into the air, they are nothing to what he has to go through.'

Just as, when he was still on active duty in the Royal Navy, he wanted to be treated like any other naval officer; so, in an ideal world, would he prefer to be treated as any other pilot. While the Duke is meticulous about carrying out the checks that precede take-off and landing, he is also impatient. Once, when a faulty instrument suggested (wrongly) that an engine was on fire, he was less than pleased at having to turn back and land using only one engine.

The instructor who taught Prince Philip to fly was a member of the RAF's Central Flying School, Flight Lieutenant Caryl Gordon. Later Gordon became a Group Captain and was awarded the MVO. Seldom has an honour been more richly deserved. To fit in his lessons with all his other commitments, the Duke had to observe erratic hours. He would sometimes turn up at 6.45 in the morning with a packet of sandwiches, wearing an old tweed jacket. On other occasions, such as when an engagement had been cancelled, he would telephone Gordon and bid him make ready at once. Smith's Lawn in Windsor Great Park reverted to its role as an extempore airfield—this time for Prince Philip's Chipmunk. He even used it once when snow lay thick on the ground—in defiance of the fact that the authorities had tried to prevent him from flying in winter.

But the Duke's patience was not always proof against the ways of the RAF's top brass, whom he sometimes referred to as 'their Airships'.

He was an apt pupil, and on 20 December 1952, after ten hours' instruction, Gordon judged him to be ready for his first solo. The scene was White Waltham. With a cloud base of 1000ft (304m), the weather was by no means ideal. Gordon had never been slow to criticise his pupil when he made a mistake; he had, after all, been warned on at least three occasions, 'Of course, you know the consequences if any harm comes to Prince Philip.' The Duke took it all in good part, even, on one occasion, turning up for a lesson wearing his uniform of a marshal of the Royal Air Force. When Gordon looked surprised, HRH admitted, 'I'm wearing it to shake you.'

But, on the occasion of the first solo, Gordon had nothing but praise to offer. As quoted in Basil Boothroyd's *Philip*, he said that, 'His take-off, circuit and landing were beyond reproach. The landing was a beautiful three-pointer.' He was less pleased a month later when, practising aerobatics, his pupil took rather a long time to pull out of a spin.

Prince Philip was suitably appreciative of his mentor's work and the effect it must have had on his nerves. For Christmas, 1953, he gave Gordon a silver locket. Engraved on it were the words 'A reward for diligence' and the date—20 December. 'You can use it to keep pills in,' he said.

Since then, the Duke has flown at least 40 different types of aircraft— including, for $1\frac{1}{2}$ hours over the Bay of Biscay, Concorde. He is a frequent and accomplished helicopter pilot.

The reactions of Whitehall to his learning to fly a fixed-wing aircraft were as nothing to the furore created by his determination to fly heli- copters. When the Duke's private secretary, Lieutenant-Commander Michael Parker, CVO, RN (Retd), broached the subject to Winston Churchill, who was prime minister, the old statesman nearly bit his cigar in half and growled, 'Is it your intention to wipe out the Royal Family in the shortest possible time?'

Even today the Queen confines herself to aeroplanes that have wings and do not depend upon the caprice of a rotor. She has only once flown in a helicopter, and that was for reasons of security during a visit to Northern Ireland in Jubilee year. The Queen Mother, on the other hand, frequently uses this form of transportation. On 14 October 1975, she became the first member of the royal family to land by this method on an aircraft carrier at sea. The ship, HMS *Ark Royal*, was in the Moray Firth. She made the flight from her house at Birkhall near Balmoral.

Prince Philip's tuition with Flight Lieutenant Gordon had resulted in his gaining RAF wings (they were given to him by the Chief of the Air

Staff in the drawing room at Buckingham Palace). Learning to fly a
helicopter won him wings from the Royal Navy. The Army, naturally,
was reluctant to be overlooked—especially as soldiers resented the sight of
RAF wings displayed on his khaki uniform. To satisfy the Army Air
Corps, he repaired to Middle Wallop in May 1955, and suitably established his qualifications in this respect.

In December 1967, an accident occurred that must have aroused
fear in the minds of all who had misgivings about members of the royal
family travelling in helicopters. Air Commodore Sir Edward Fielden had
been succeeded as Captain of the Queen's Flight by Group Captain
A D Mitchell, CVO, DFC, AFC, who, in his turn, had handed over to
Air Commodore John Blount. Back in 1959, two Westland Whirlwind
helicopters had been added to the Flight, and two more were delivered in
the mid 1960s. These were single-engined machines that, apart from the
seating arrangements, were identical to those used by the Royal Navy.

On 7 December 1967, Air Commodore Blount was flying from
Benson to Yeovil in a Whirlwind with three other members of the Queen's
Flight. They were due to attend a conference about future helicopter
requirements. They were over Brightwalton in Berkshire when the aircraft suddenly fell from the sky, killing everyone on board. In view of the
exceptionally high maintenance standards observed at Benson, the
disaster was described as 'baffling'. The only clue was revealed by a
photograph that suggested an entire rotor blade had been shed while the
machine was still airborne. It later became apparent that the main rotor
shaft had snapped. All the Whirlwinds throughout the services were
grounded pending the report of a court of inquiry.

At the end of the following year, the one remaining Whirlwind, was
replaced by two twin-engined Wessex helicopters. But, as the Under-
secretary of State for Defence, Merlyn Rees made clear to the House of
Commons, this was not the result of the fatal crash. The decision had been
taken some while earlier.

--------------------◆--------------------

*Chipmunk T.10 used for Prince
Charles's basic training.* (Opposite,
top.)

*Basset CC2 of Queen's Flight used by
Prince Charles for twin engine
training.* (Opposite, bottom.)

Prince Charles once told a writer that, 'My father has been flying ever
since I can remember, and then I'd always wanted to fly. It was a natural
thing to do.' During the last week of July 1968, he went to RAF Tangmere,
where Squadron Leader Philip Pinney from the Central Flying School
took him up in a Chipmunk. The object was to discover whether he had
any aptitude for aeronautics. The Prince obviously satisfied Squadron
Leader Pinney, for soon afterwards he began to take flying lessons. In
March of the following year, he qualified for his private pilot's licence
and on 2 August 1969, the Air Officer Commanding-in-Chief Flying

'Golden Eagle'. A Jet Provost T.5 in RAFC markings, with the feathers of the Prince of Wales on its air intake. (Top.)

It was snowing hard at Heathrow on a December day in 1979, but the sun was shining when Concorde touched down in the Middle East—at Kuwait. Accompanied by Prince Philip, the Queen set off on the first ever visit by a reigning monarch to the Gulf States. (Opposite.)

Training Command presented him with an RAF preliminary flying badge. Since then, he has acquired the wings of each service and, despite all his other duties, has accumulated a considerable tally of hours, flying the Andovers, helicopters and jets—pretty well anything with a pair of wings and some, such as the 'choppers', with no wings at all. He has even gone one better than his father. He and his brother, Prince Andrew, have both made parachute drops.

The Queen stifled any objections she may have entertained. It was, after all, her son's wish after completing his twelve-month course as a graduate entrant at Cranwell in five months, during 1971. To make allowances for this tight schedule, he was excused all parades.

He hurried off to the RAF parachute training school at Abingdon near Oxford, where he carried out ground simulation exercises—which is another way of saying that he learned how to land without actually breaking any bones. On 28 July 1971, he was at RAF Abingdon, ready for a flight over Studland Bay in Dorset.

The flight sergeant who was acting as a dispatcher gave him a Polo mint—presumably with the idea that it might be soothing to the nerves. And then, at 6.20 in the early evening, when the aircraft was flying over the sea at 1,200ft (365m), the Prince jumped.

The slipstream was 'terrific', he rolled over on to his back, and the next thing he knew his feet were snared in the rigging above his head.

Remarking to himself that this was 'very odd' and that 'they did not tell us anything about this', he proceeded to extricate himself. 'Fortunately,' he remembered afterwards, 'they weren't twisted around the lines, and they came out very quickly.'

Royal Marines in rubber boats snatched him from the water within ten seconds. But it had, he admitted, been 'a rather hairy experience'.

Just under seven years later, in May 1978, Prince Charles and his brother, Prince Andrew, completed a two-week course at No. 1 parachute training school, Brize Norton in Gloucestershire. Prince Charles was anxious to obtain the appropriate qualification for his role as Colonel-in-Chief of the Parachute Regiment; Prince Andrew, then at Gordonstoun, was a member of the Air Training Corps. They carried out seven jumps—from a balloon 800ft (245m) above the ground and from a Hercules transport, flying at 1,000ft (305m). Both princes found themselves in difficulties on two occasions, when their parachute lines twisted. If the episode over Studland Bay had been 'hairy', this was even hairier.

More recently, during the Falklands crisis, Prince Andrew was flying 'round the clock' as a helicopter pilot with the Task Force in the South Atlantic. A spokesman at Buckingham Palace, dismissing reports that the Prince might have been kept out of the line of fire, stated that, 'Neither operational requirements, nor indeed Prince Andrew, would tolerate him being singled out for special treatment.'

Some sixty years earlier, a King had grounded his eldest son for flying with a skilled and experienced pilot, who, admittedly, was injured in the arm. Today, the fact that the heir to the throne chooses to throw himself from the snug interior of an aeroplane—to entrust his life to the not-always-certain protection of a parachute—or that his brother flies a helicopter under active-service conditions, causes little serious comment. Even the sovereign, whilst not enthusiastic, gives her assent. This, surely, suggests something about the changing nature of British monarchy.

7
PLAIN CLOTHES AND CEREMONIAL

The executives responsible for organising the Queen's public life are known as *The Royal Household*. For many years, it was the centre of government. So long as a member remained in favour with the sovereign, he enjoyed considerable power. Nowadays, the household's duties are largely administrative. Whilst employed by the Queen, its members are paid and graded on a scale similar to that of the civil service.

Inevitably, the role and the establishment of the household have changed over the centuries. In 1844, the Prince Consort persuaded Queen Victoria to make drastic alterations to its structure; fining it down to more sensible proportions and eliminating a good deal of extravagance.

Prince Albert was, to all intents and purposes, Victoria's private secretary. After his death, in 1861, the Queen and her successors relied increasingly upon the holders of this position for advice on a variety of subjects—including the arrangements for their complex programmes of public appearances. The present incumbent, Sir Philip Moore, has held the appointment for the past 16 years. Before that, he was a civil servant working first at the Foreign Office and later at the Ministry of Defence.

King George VI increased the number of private secretaries by two—adding a deputy and an assistant. After a lapse of a good many years, he also reappointed a press secretary.

The head of the household is the Lord Chamberlain who—in addition to lesser duties such as appointing the poet laureate and deciding what are and what are not suitable souvenirs of occasions such as royal weddings and christenings—is responsible for all the ceremonials that do not concern the Earl Marshal. Although the office is no longer political (until the late eighteenth century, the Lord Chamberlain was a member of the cabinet), he must be a peer and a privy councillor. Nowadays, Lord Maclean, chief of the Clan Maclean, carries out the duties. His home is a castle on the Isle of Mull, off the west coast of Scotland. He also has a 'grace and favour' residence in Saint James's Palace, London. As his office is in the same building, it is very convenient.

One of the more confusing words that crops up in any study of the Queen's aides and councillors is *equerry*. It comes in several versions. For example, the Crown Equerry is head of the Royal Mews, and is thus the executive in charge of all the Queen's horses and carriages and cars—and the staff that rides, drives and maintains them. It is a permanent appointment. The Captain of the Queen's Flight is styled an extra equerry; like the Crown Equerry, the Captain is a member of the household. In addition to such posts as these there are the equerries who attend the Queen on her travels and who function in much the manner of aides-de-camp. Each is seconded from one or another of the armed forces for a three-year spell of duty. If, for one reason or another, the current equerry is unable to be present, the Deputy Master of the Household stands in for him.

With so many requests pouring into Buckingham Palace for the attendance of a member of the royal family at one function or another, and with so many appointments to be kept, it might seem that some sort of operations room would be necessary. The Queen, the princes and Princess Anne might each be represented by a pin stuck into a map—with, perhaps, a brief note of the date and the occasion attached to it. In fact, a palace spokesman told me that any such centralised method of royal traffic control 'would be impossible to co-ordinate. Each member of the royal family makes up his or her own programme. The Queen's is prepared ahead of the rest. It includes overseas tours and incoming state visits—both of which are scheduled well in advance. There are also regular fixtures such as trooping the colour, remembrance week and so on. The dates of these, obviously, are known in advance.

'The Queen's programme is less cut and dried than those of other members of the family. She does much bigger things. Her private secretary sets things up. If the Queen can't go to some particular event, he'll ring round the other private secretaries, to see if someone else can go. There is very little overlap.'

Prince Philip, Prince Charles and Princess Anne—each holds what is known as a 'programme meeting' twice a year. At the end of June (or at the beginning of July), they plan events for the coming autumn and winter; while at the end of November (though it may be at the start of December), they work out their programmes for the spring and summer. Every invitation is studied carefully and a schedule for the following six months is drawn up.

As with the Queen, the traditional fixtures must be included, and there are one or two organisations that receive priority. For example, each is involved with certain charities (Princess Anne's concern for the Save the Children Fund, for example, or Prince Philip's presidency of the World Wildlife Fund), and each is colonel-in-chief of at least one regiment.

Prince Philip and Prince Charles have more time to perform duties beyond the Palace walls. There are all manner of things that require Her Majesty's attention—such as the contents of the red dispatch boxes containing state documents that must be studied each day; the morning audiences accorded to newly installed ambassadors, government ministers, and other high officials; as well as the occasional investiture. When she is in residence at Buckingham Palace, the Queen normally works a four-day week—from Monday afternoon until Friday afternoon. It is a very busy time.

On one fairly typical day, she held four audiences in the morning, but found time in the afternoon to open a new hospital at Guildford. Queen Victoria had shown an interest in this particular establishment more than a century ago, and successive sovereigns followed her example. Lesser hospitals have to content themselves with lesser members of the family, or as a last resort, with the local mayor! Guildford is one of the exceptions.

Like anyone else, Queen Elizabeth suffers from 'jet lag' after a long flight, and the private secretaries allow for this in the planning of overseas tours. They realise, more than do most people, that she has been working very, very hard; talking to a great many strangers and enduring a not necessarily good climate. Consequently, they try to keep a day or two clear of engagements on her return to Britain—just as they do their best to ensure that her first day in the host country is reasonably leisurely before the round of heavy duties begins.

1981 and the newly married Prince and Princess of Wales are cheered on their way to the state opening of Parliament. They travel in the famous Glass coach bought for King George V's coronation in 1911. The Queen normally uses the Irish state coach.

Since they need not concern themselves with audiences and investitures, Prince Charles and Prince Philip can spend more time, so to speak, on the road. In planning their movements, their private secretaries depend on local knowledge, supplied by the lord lieutenants of the counties concerned. If, for example, Prince Philip has one engagement in Yorkshire, it obviously makes sense if two more can be fitted into the same day. Should they be some distance apart, a helicopter from the Queen's Flight can be used. As the palace spokesman said, 'Prince Philip and the Prince of Wales are both very strong and healthy, and they can pack a great deal into one day.'

Nevertheless, even the strong and healthy must rest occasionally. Furthermore, as with the Queen herself, it is essential that they are punctual. If they arrive half-an-hour late for the first appointment, the whole day is thrown out of sequence. For this reason, the royal train is frequently used—especially in winter, when even Andovers snug in their purple air space are at the mercy of the weather. If fog enshrouds Gatwick, the diversion of a commercial flight to Luton causes no more than great inconvenience. If an aircraft of the Queen's Flight were similarly affected, it would throw an intricately planned schedule into something not very far removed from chaos.

In this respect at least, trains are more reliable. They are also more convenient. Assume, for instance, that the Queen has an appointment in Scotland at ten in the morning: she would have to rise early to get to Heathrow in time, and, even then, her flight might be delayed by bad weather.

Clearly, then, the royal train is a better alternative. Her Majesty sets off for the station between 10 and 11 o'clock in the evening. The train moves slowly into the night, and makes its way northwards at a leisurely pace. When it reaches a point reasonably close to its destination, it is shunted into a siding. The sovereign has a restful night, can enjoy breakfast, prepare herself for the day's events, and still be at her first appointment on the dot.

A good night's sleep is important. The royal duties, begun at 10 am will doubtless continue until 5 or 6 pm—and, on some occasions, until midnight.

When they are needed, the royal cars, driven by the chauffeurs, go on ahead and will be ready waiting at the station.

Since Prince Philip and Prince Charles are not subject to the embargo on helicopter flying that restricts the Queen's use of these aircraft, they can travel from the Palace lawn by air, which makes the journey very much easier. Nevertheless, there are many occasions when they, too, prefer to use the royal train. For example, early in 1981, the

When Queen Elizabeth II opened the Victoria Line in 1969, she became the first reigning sovereign to travel on London's Underground. Eight years later, on 16 December, 1977, she again took her place in the driver's cab—for the inauguration of the Piccadilly Line extension to Heathrow Airport.

The Duchess of Kent climbs from an open-topped state landau. Grooms from the Royal Mews (situated behind Buckingham Palace) perform the function of drivers and postillions. The horses are given regular exposure to the din of city traffic.

Prince of Wales had to attend a dinner in Hampshire given by the officers of the 2nd Gurkha Rifles (the Prince is their Colonel-in-Chief). On the following morning, he had to be in Glasgow to carry out three engagements, and then return to London by way of Stafford and Derby.

It was obviously easier to travel overnight by train. Apart from its other virtues, it provided him with accommodation for the trip.

When the royal family goes to Balmoral for what—in theory, at any rate—is its summer holiday, the royal yacht is used. On these occasions, as indeed whenever the Queen is travelling from one of her homes to another, 20 Squadron of the Royal Transport Corps is responsible for providing what is known as the 'royal baggage train'. This is made up of six 25 cwt vans. The vehicles are normally employed on military duties, but they are at Her Majesty's disposal whenever she requires them.

This unit is housed in an old barracks near Regents Park in London. The buildings date back to the Crimean war, and some of the sequences of the most recent version of *The Charge of the Light Brigade* were filmed there. Among the unit's other duties is the provision of cars for the chiefs of staff and defence ministers.

Usually, the Queen spends January at Sandringham, April at Windsor, and from mid-August to mid-October at Balmoral. But even these interludes are liable to be interrupted—as in 1981, when she had to cut short her stay in Scotland to travel to Australia (a trip that also included visits to New Zealand and Sri Lanka) to meet the heads of Commonwealth governments.

As the palace spokesman said, 'The Queen is never 100 per cent on holiday. Life goes on and the red boxes go on—wherever she may be.' The contents of the boxes take up an hour or more of each morning. At Balmoral and Sandringham, however, she does manage to avoid public occasions, though she may well put in an appearance at some local function—the Women's Institute at Sandringham, for example, or something to do with the little church at Craithie, where the royal family worships during its annual sojourn in the Highlands. 'The Queen', we were told, 'likes to be involved with some local affairs.'

Since the word 'yacht' suggests a craft used for pleasure, the royal yacht is, perhaps, ill-styled. It is essentially a ship of state—as far removed in purpose as in size and design, from the delights of 'messing about in boats'. The Duke of Edinburgh may invite sailing companions aboard during Cowes week in early August. But, even at this event, the presence of *Britannia* is as obligatory as anything to do with royalty can be. Without it, the ramparts of the Royal Yacht Squadron would be blown apart by its members' rage, and, no doubt, by disappointment on the part of the local public.

The British and Russian royal families, united by blood and a love of yachts, at Cowes in 1909. King Edward VII (centre) preferred the Tsar's company on these occasions to that of his nephew, the Kaiser, who had the tiresome habit of trying to re-write the rules of yacht racing to suit himself.

Even the strictest protocol can be disturbed by a sudden gust. The Queen clearly saw the funny side of a situation that occurred when she was visiting New Zealand in 1963. Her host was less certain.

About the nearest *Britannia* ever gets to pleasure cruising is the annual journey up the coast to Aberdeen *en route* for Balmoral, and the cruise to the Western Isles that is an almost ritualistic part of the royal holiday. Even on these occasions the Queen tries to fit in a public engagement or two, thus combining business with the delight of a sea voyage. The inhabitants of the islands have no cause to feel overlooked, and she nearly always visits one of the North Sea ports on the trip up the coast.

On all these occasions, which are informal compared to the magnificence of more ceremonial affairs, the Queen is accompanied by one of her private secretaries, by a lady-in-waiting, and by her equerry. All the private secretaries are employed on working out her programme, the deputy (or the assistant) attends to the details of specific engagements. So far as overseas tours are concerned, one (or the other) makes a reconnaissance in advance—to liaise with the embassy in the host country, and with the officials responsible for on-the-spot arrangements.

Among the duties of the lady-in-waiting is that of carrying a supply of cash in case the Queen wishes to buy anything (by tradition the sovereign seldom carries any money).

In some instances, there will also be a specialist present. If, for example, horses are involved, the Crown Equerry will accompany Her Majesty. Government ministers attend when it is appropriate. A visit to a military establishment will probably involve the Defence Services Secretary; the Foreign Secretary is frequently present on overseas tours, and so on. The Queen insists upon being well-informed, not least, so that she can ask relevant questions.

◆

The Lord Chamberlain is responsible for all the royal ceremonial apart from those occasions that fall to the Earl Marshal. Royal weddings, for example, are among the events that he has to organise. That of Prince Charles to Lady Diana Spencer, which took place in July, 1981, was unique in at least one respect: it was the first to be held in Saint Paul's Cathedral.

Royal weddings seem to have grown in complexity over the years. Despite the fact that she was the sovereign, Queen Victoria's marriage to Prince Albert was a comparatively quiet affair held in the Chapel Royal at Saint James's Palace. From a travel point of view, the most dramatic thing about it was the Channel crossing that brought the future Prince Consort to Dover two days before the event. The weather was so bad that the packet boat took five hours to accomplish it. The Prince was horribly seasick and required a day in which to recover. Four days earlier, Victoria had gone down with a severe cold, which alarmists in the Palace mistook

for the first symptoms of measles. Fortunately, they were both in good health by their wedding day on 10 February 1840.

Edward VII (as Prince of Wales) was married in Saint George's Chapel at Windsor. After that (with the exception of the future King George V and Queen Mary, who followed Queen Victoria's example by using the Chapel Royal for their wedding in 1893), the scene moved to Westminster Abbey.

The present pattern came about in 1858, when Victoria's eldest daughter, Princess Victoria, married Prince Frederick of Prussia. The Abbey was used for the ceremony. Afterwards the couple drove in state to Buckingham Palace—where, very much to the delight of the crowd, they set a precedent by appearing on the balcony.

By choosing Saint Paul's Cathedral for what was widely referred to as 'the marriage of the century', the royal family might have seemed to have set the Lord Chamberlain a problem. After all, the Queen (when she married Prince Philip in 1947), and Princess Anne (when she married

Although most royal weddings have taken place in Westminster Abbey, when the Prince of Wales married Lady Diana Spencer in 1981 Saint Paul's Cathedral was chosen for the ceremony, which was broadcast to fifty countries.

Captain Mark Phillips in 1973) both travelled a familiar route to a familiar church. They also used a familiar vehicle—the Glass Coach, which George V had purchased in 1911. (It had been built by a London firm in 1910 as a sheriff's town coach.)

Now, however, the church, the route—even, possibly, the conveyance—were different. Furthermore, as a spectacle, a great deal was demanded of it. Princess Anne had wanted her wedding to be as simple as possible. Since she was the only daughter of a sovereign, this, obviously, was going to stretch the concept of simplicity. There was, admittedly, only one head of state on the guest list, Prince Rainier of Monaco; but there were intruders in the shape of 50 television cameras ready to transmit every detail to a public that, in the midst of a gloomy winter made worse by power cuts, was hungry for colour and glamour.

If Princess Anne's was kept relatively simple, quite clearly there would be nothing simple about Prince Charles's marriage. There was, however, enough time in which to make preparations, and the prospect of Saint Paul's Cathedral did nothing to daunt Lord Maclean and his assistants. It had, after all, been used for the Queen's Jubilee celebrations in 1977, and for the thanksgiving service to mark the 80th birthday of the Queen Mother in 1980. A lot was known about it; not least, how to arrange a seating plan for the guests.

The route, too, had been well trodden by past royal ceremonial processions so there was no cause for anxiety.

It is tempting to imagine a library of volumes, rather like a collection of music scores or choreographs of ballets, in the Lord Chamberlain's office. Whenever a royal ceremonial is scheduled, the appropriate manual might be taken down and consulted on matters of procedure, logistics and so on.

In fact, things are not quite like that. What the Lord Chamberlain's establishment does have is a great deal of experience. Some of it takes the form of reports stored in its capacious filing system; each a careful account of what happened on a particular occasion—and how it was made to happen. More exists in the minds of the people employed there. Rather as, before the days of printing, stories were passed by word of mouth from one generation to the next, so is the lore of ceremonial passed on. There is always somebody who will *know*.

Naturally the Lord Chamberlain depends upon many people beyond his office to produce a satisfactory royal ceremonial. The soldiers are nearly all supplied by the Household Division, which has its headquarters in the Horse Guards and is commanded by a major-general who is also GOC London District. It is made up of the five regiments of footguards and three cavalry regiments—the Life Guards, the Blues and the Royals.

The Kaiser and King George V in 1913, somewhere in Germany. Since they used to swap ranks in each other's armies, it is not all that surprising to see the British sovereign in a German field-marshal's uniform. A year later, of course, such a thing would have been unthinkable.

The assistant adjutant general, a lieutenant-colonel, is responsible for liaison with the Lord Chamberlain's office. Its contributions range from providing a sovereign's escort of cavalry, to arranging 'trooping the colour'. All the men in it are combat troops; a soldier may be patrolling a street in Northern Ireland one week then marching along the Mall, wearing a bearskin and a scarlet tunic, the next.

It is, perhaps, indicative of the general insecurity of past sovereigns that so much of present day ceremonial has to do with the monarch's safety. The Life Guards, as their name implies, were formed for this very purpose. Most regiments of footguards owe their origins to a similar role: in addition to these full-time soldiers, there are three royal bodyguards who turn out in the glory of their beautiful uniforms when the need arises.

The most ancient of the ceremonial bodyguards, the Yeomen of the Guard, date back to Henry VII, who gave them their name. Because their uniforms are so much alike, they are frequently mistaken for the so-called 'Beefeaters' at the Tower of London. W S Gilbert was guilty of this error when he entitled his operetta *The Yeoman of the Guard*. What he really meant was *The Yeoman Warders of the Tower of London* (though one sympathises with him; as titles go it would not have been nearly so good).

The Yeomen Warders are responsible for the safe keeping of the crown jewels, the ravens and the tourists. As employees of the Department of the Environment, they have actually gone on strike—something a Yeoman of the Guard would never do.

Although the Yeomen of the Guard used to be recruited wholly from the Army, they have latterly included some ex-Royal Marines plus, on George VI's insistence, a few former members of the RAF. There are 87 of them and there is a long list of aspiring members. To stand a chance of being accepted for one of the rare vacancies, a man must be at least 42 years old. He must have attained the rank of sergeant or above in the service, and he must have been awarded the long service and good conduct medal. It helps if he has distinguished himself in action. The present Yeomen include a publican from Worcester, a businessman from Bournemouth, and the director of a steel firm. The one full-time member who is known as the Sergeant-Major of the Queen's Body Guard, has an office in Saint James's Palace. He is a former member of the Welsh Guards who, before taking up this appointment, was RSM at the Royal Military College, Sandhurst.

Strangely, perhaps, the Captain of the Yeoman of the Guard is a political appointment. It is held by the Government Deputy Chief Whip in the House of Lords.

The Honourable Corps of Gentlemen at Arms was created by Henry VIII in 1509, and went on parade beside the Yeomen of the Guard at the Field of the Cloth of Gold. Originally, it was conceived as a mounted body guard: and its uniforms nowadays reflect this. A Yeoman of the Guard, with his partisan in his hand (the half-initiated might mistake it for a halberd, the uninitiated for a spear), is unmistakably Tudor. Indeed, until Edward VIII abolished the practice in 1936, the yeoman was even required to grow a Tudor-style beard.

A gentleman at arms, on the other hand, wears a uniform that replaced the original version in 1840 and was based upon that of an officer in the dragoons. Queen Victoria seems to have taken a particular interest in this corps—possibly because, in 1848, its members were mobilised to defend Saint James's Palace during the Chartist Riots. Prudently, no doubt, the chartists did not attack the Palace and the Gentlemen at Arms were dismissed without having fired a shot. But it must have been comforting for the Queen to know they were *there*.

To join the corps, it is necessary to be a retired officer from either the Army or the Royal Marines. Queen Victoria stipulated that no member should be 'connected with trade'—though this restriction does not apply nowadays. In any case, it is difficult to become a gentleman at arms: with a strength of only five officers and 27 gentlemen, there are few vacancies. As with the Yeomen of the Guard, command of the corps is political. The Captain is the Government Chief Whip in the House of Lords. From 1974 to 1979, to some people's dismay and to others delight, the appointment was held by a woman, the Baroness Llewelyn-Davies of Hastoe.

In Scotland, the sovereign's safety—ceremonially if not in actuality —is a matter for the Royal Company of Archers, which is much larger than its English counterparts: there are 450 members. The bodyguard originated in 1704 at the behest of Queen Anne. George IV, after a visit to Scotland in 1842, was so satisfied with their performance, that he appointed them 'The Royal Body Guard for Scotland', meaning that they should occupy 'the position immediately next to the sovereign's person'. In 1842, this matter of proximity caused the company one of the few setbacks in its illustrious career. Queen Victoria was on her way north in the royal yacht to pay a state visit to Scotland. The voyage was abominably rough, and *Victoria and Albert* was twenty-four hours late in docking at Leith. The Queen then threw everything into greater confusion by coming ashore earlier than anyone had expected. No doubt she did it with the praise-worthy intention of trying to catch up lost time. Unfortunately the men of the Royal Company of Archers were not there.

Since she had to have some sort of escort, a squadron of dragoons was used. The little procession set off at a brisk trot. Somewhere down the road, they were joined by the proper body guard, which was on foot. It does not seem to have occurred to anyone that the archers might have found it easier to be 'immediately next to the sovereign's person', if the horses were persuaded to amend their trot to a walk. Jogging for all they were worth, the archers tried to keep up, but eventually ran out of breath and had to retire. As the Queen noted in her journal, 'The Body Guard were . . . dreadfully pushed about.'

To qualify for this establishment, a Scotsman must (among other things) actually be an archer. King George VI was particularly interested in their marksmanship. After watching a demonstration of their skill, he decided he would like to take lessons. Two of the company tutored him and by all accounts he became a very fair shot.

All three groups of body guards are employed on various ceremonial occasions. Before the annual state opening of parliament, the Yeomen of the Guard enact a charade of searching the cellars for gunpowder. The actual business is carried out very much less flamboyantly by members of the Special Branch assisted by labradors—whose noses are particularly sensitive to the scent of high explosives.

————————————◆————————————

Nowadays, a bow and an arrow, or even a sword such as the Gentlemen at Arms wear in addition to the long-handled battleaxes they carry, would be of little avail against a determined would-be assassin. The guardsmen, who line the ceremonial routes, have no live ammunition in their rifles; whilst the police, who stand with their backs to the passing show, the better to watch the crowd, are not armed with revolvers. The sharp end of the security operation is carried out by plain-clothes officers belonging to the Metropolitan Police's royalty protection branch. At events outside London, they are reinforced by members of the local Special Branch departments.

The officers, who are armed, have undergone special training. On occasions such as trooping the colour or the state opening of parliament, they must fit into the overall security pattern handled by *A Division* of the Metropolitan Police—a unit that has its headquarters in Cannon Row off Whitehall. As one of its officers told a leading newspaper, its awareness of the neighbourhood is essential to such work—not least when checking the route and searching buildings. 'Special squads brought in from outside the district,' he said, 'could not be expected to have the local knowledge which will ensure that no nook or cranny is overlooked.'

During Queen Victoria's reign, there were six attempts on the sovereign's life. All of them took place on informal occasions in the streets of London. None was carried out with competence and, almost without exception, they can be regarded as gestures rather than as serious bids to kill.

In one of them, the would-be assassin actually forgot to load his pistol. Before that, in 1842, 'a swarthy ill-looking rascal' named John Francis made two attempts. On the first, his pistol misfired and he escaped into the crowds lining the Mall. Next day, he tried again. He pressed the trigger at a range of five paces; the shot went wide of its mark, and he was arrested.

Francis was condemned to death. On 1 July of that year, however, he was reprieved. The Queen said that she was 'glad'. But this was not the end of the matter. Unhappily only two days after Francis's delivery from the shadow of the gallows, a deformed boy of very low intelligence named John Bean discharged a pistol in the general direction of Her Majesty. Since the weapon was loaded with a mixture of paper and tobacco and no more than a minute quantity of gunpowder, the effect was not very dramatic.

He, too, was arrested. As a result of these incidents, Section 2 of the Treason Act was passed later that year. It was intended to deal with cases in which harmless weapons were brandished in the face of royalty.

The last attempt on Queen Victoria's life occurred on 27 February 1872, when a Fenian (a forerunner of the IRA) named Arthur O'Connor was overpowered by the joint efforts of John Brown and Prince Arthur, Duke of Connaught. John Brown was rewarded with a gold medal and an annuity of £25; Prince Arthur received a gold pin. O'Connor was transported overseas after one year in jail. It was difficult to take him very seriously as a terrorist; he was the one who overlooked the basic requirement of murder by pistol—that the weapon should be loaded. No doubt the judge bore this in mind when passing sentence.

Apart from an episode at the 1936 trooping the colour, when another Irishman, 32-year-old George McMahon, threw a revolver in the general direction of King Edward VIII (McMahon denied that he had intended to harm the King and was jailed for a year), there were no more threats to the safety of the royal family until 1974. On this occasion, a 26-year-old young man named Ian Ball attempted to kidnap Princess Anne.

It was evening. The Princess and Captain Mark Phillips were driving along the Mall to Buckingham Palace. After ramming the royal car, Ball opened fire and wounded the couple's police bodyguard. Ball's motive, apparently, was to hold HRH to ransom. The court that tried him decided that he should be detained under the Mental Health Act.

The climate of potential political violence has become more pronounced. Despite it, however, the royal family does not seem to be under any greater threat. It is significant that, when the Queen's Jubilee procession traversed the centre of London on 7 July 1977, the number of police officers on duty was less than required for a street brawl between the far right and its opponents.

But nothing can be taken for granted when the sovereign's safety is at stake. In 1981 President Sadat of Egypt was murdered and there were attempts on the lives of President Reagan and the Pope. In the United Kingdom, the violence generated by the deaths of H-block hunger strikers in Northern Ireland caused the police to double the number of guards responsible for the security of the Queen and other prominent people (including the Prime Minister). When Her Majesty opened the oil terminal at Sullom Voe on Shetland in May of that year, a bomb exploded in a power house. Fortunately, it was some distance away and nobody was hurt.

Princess Anne and her husband, Mark Phillips, were returning to Buckingham Palace one night in 1974, when a gunman attacked the car. The royal couple escaped unharmed, but a police officer and three other people were injured.

And then, at trooping the colour on 13 June, a 17-year-old youth from Kent discharged six blank cartridges as the Queen rode by. His weapon was a replica hand gun, modelled on the Colt Python, which he had bought from a shop less than half a mile from the incident. Thanks mainly to Corporal Galloway of the Scots Guards, who was on duty lining the route, the lad was quickly overpowered. The police dragged him to a nearby first-aid tent *en route* to Cannon Row police station, where he was charged under Section 2 of the Treason Act. His quick removal from the crowd was no doubt as well for him. There had been shouts of 'hang the b—!', and an American tourist observed afterwards, 'For a moment, it looked like a lynch mob was in the making.'

The Queen's mount, a 19-year-old veteran of the trooping named Burmese understandably shied at the noise of the blanks. But, with a neat display of horsemanship, Her Majesty rapidly brought the situation under control and the ceremony passed off without further incident.

As her behaviour at Ascot during the following week made clear, the Queen had no intention of allowing such threats to place a barrier between herself and her people. As a senior police officer told *The Sunday Times*, 'It would be a victory for terrorism if we had to mothball the state coaches and replace them with bullet-proof limousines. The Queen won't contemplate that and so we have to work accordingly.'

———————————◆———————————

The state opening of parliament, in which the sovereign travels in the Irish state coach preceded by Queen Alexandra's state coach in which the regalia is carried, is an annual event. So, too, is the trooping the colour that takes place every year on the Queen's official birthday (which has nothing to do with her actual birthday; the custom began in the reign of Edward VII, who was born in November—a month when the weather is not suitable for displays of martial excellence. Queen Elizabeth II was born on 21 April, when the weather, although uncertain, might promise better than Edward's dark and often foggy month but, by this time, a tradition had been established). The even more elaborate ceremonial occasions are much fewer and farther between. In the present century, there have been the funerals of four monarchs, four coronations, two weddings of heirs to the throne (George VI was not the heir to the throne when he married Lady Elizabeth Bowes-Lyon at Westminster Abbey on 26 April 1923), and two silver jubilee processions. Spread over a period of 82 years, it does not amount to very much.

But in matters of ceremonial, no matter how short the journey nor how infrequently it takes place, it is a certainty that horses will be involved.

The titular head of the Royal Mews at Buckingham Palace is the Master of the Horse—nowadays the Earl of Westmorland. In practice, since 1920, the day-to-day running of this department has been the responsibility of the Crown Equerry. It is he who fits the Queen's horses and conveyances into the overall picture devised by the Lord Chamberlain or, when appropriate, the Earl Marshal.

The Royal Mews used to be in Charing Cross. It was moved to its present location when George III bought Buckingham House in 1764 and transformed it into Buckingham Palace. There is a riding school,

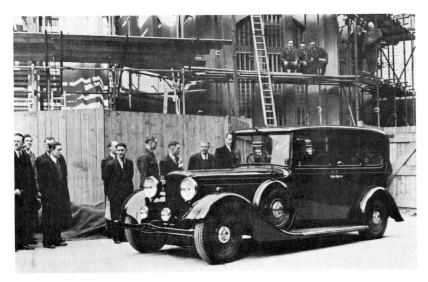

In April, 1937, King George VI and Queen Elizabeth—plus the inevitable royal Daimler—went to Westminster Abbey to inspect preparations for their forthcoming coronation.

where members of the royal family practise before an event, and where the horses are conditioned to the not necessarily pleasant experience of performing in public. Recordings of the alarming noises they will hear are played *fortissimo* (the cheering of crowds, the blare of bands and so on).

If there are any stars among the beasts that inhabit the stables, they are probably the Windsor Greys who always draw the Queen's carriage or coach. Each must be at least 16.1 hands tall, and many are named after places that have been visited by the Queen on one of her overseas tours (Canberra, Philadelphia, Rio, etc).

Normally a horse is four years old when it enters royal service. Its useful life is about fifteen years, after which it is pensioned off to a less exacting existence. Tuition in the riding school is all very well, but the experience necessary to perform faultlessly on a state occasion can only be gained by actually tramping the streets of London, and learning that there is nothing to fear from the flash of photographers' equipment, the waving of flags and all the other determinations to applaud or record.

A fairly familiar sight in the streets of London SW1 is a black brougham, hauled by two horses, which mingles with the traffic like a ghost from the nineteenth century. Twice daily, it makes its journeys—running an errand here and another there. Within its dark interior you will find no red boxes, no state documents that might arouse the interest of an unfriendly power. After all, to stop and rob such a defenceless vehicle would not tax the talents of any reasonably competent thief or special agent.

No: the missions of the brougham are of a domestic nature—tasks for which, it might seem, a small van or even a motorcycle would be more appropriate. However, there is another purpose behind these trips. They give the thirty horses of the Royal Mews weekly experience of an outside world populated by cars and made horrible by hubbub, and serve also to allow the younger coachmen to practise their art regularly.

The rehearsals for a ceremonial occasion take place very early in the morning, when the streets have yet to be polluted by the noise and stink of traffic, and when a procession can be simulated without fear of being frustrated by a traffic jam. Rehearsals for the Queen's Silver Jubilee procession to Saint Paul's began in October 1976—eight months before it took place. The Windsor Greys were harnessed to the state coach; the grooms assumed their role of postillions; the Crown Equerry, armed with a stopwatch, timed it very carefully. At a steady three miles an hour, the horses clattered through the empty streets—and then went back to the Mews. This was the first of many such outings made by the light of dawn to ensure that all would be all right on the day.

The royal progress at Ascot (another annual event) is a great deal less elaborate. The carriages, which are landaus, are kept at Windsor. The Queen's is hauled by four horses with a postillion to each pair. The postillions' jackets are scarlet, purple and gold, and appropriately enough match Her Majesty's racing colours.

◆

On certain occasions, the Lord Chamberlain carries a white staff of office. At the funeral of a sovereign, he snaps it in two and drops the pieces into the grave. The gesture, like so much of all ceremony, is symbolic: it signifies the end of his service to the departed monarch—and the successor's freedom to appoint a new household. Seldom is an act of resignation and re-appointment more quickly accomplished.

The Earl Marshal is responsible for the state opening of parliament, though the Lord Chamberlain is also involved. He does not travel in the small procession from Buckingham Palace to the House of Lords: instead, he remains behind at the Palace. The purpose of this is to see that, during the sovereign's absence, nobody tries to usurp the throne. Since this is an unlikely eventuality, it, too, must be placed in the file labelled 'tradition'.

His other duties include the arrangement of investitures and royal garden parties, and, accompanied by the Lord Steward, greeting visiting heads of state when they arrive at the Palace.

◆

Henry VIII was doubtless convinced that, when he produced that lavish spectacle known as the Field of the Cloth of Gold, nobody would be able to better it. He was not entirely wrong. There were certainly no similar excursions abroad until more modern times, and then never on quite the same scale. In 1814, with Napoleon defeated and expelled to Elba, the Prince Regent decided that a meeting in London with the sovereigns of the Grand Alliance might be a pleasant celebration of their feats of arms.

The Emperor of Russia (Alexander I) and King Frederick-William III of Prussia, landed at Dover at noon on 6 June. They spent the night at hotels in the town. Next morning, they set out for London. Communication does not seem to have been very good. The Lord Chamberlain waited at Saint James's Palace to greet the Russian Emperor; Alexander, however, had gone quietly to his hotel, where he was waiting to be met. Eventually matters were sorted out. A military parade in Hyde Park and a review of the fleet at Spithead meant that the rest of the three-week visit was rather more successful.

In 1843, Queen Victoria made the first visit to France by a reigning British monarch since Henry VIII's extravagant excursion. She and

Prince Albert stayed with Louis Philippe at his Chateau d'Eu, having crossed the Channel in the royal yacht. Later, the Queen entertained the French sovereign and his wife at Buckingham Palace. The visit was remarkable mainly for Louis Philippe's gift to Victoria. It was an open-sided horse carriage with a row of seats, one behind the other. As he proudly explained, it was called a *charabanc*. While it may have not had much significance so far as royalty was concerned, it was the ancestor of the now familiar motor coach which, packed with trippers, is a familiar sight in summer.

When the Great Exhibition was held in Hyde Park in 1851, Queen Victoria made no fewer than 34 visits to it, to admire, and then to admire again, what was really Prince Albert's handiwork. Any foreign king or prince who wished to be assured of Her Majesty's approval felt bound to visit it; the Shah of Persia went twice. No doubt foreign royalty was the better informed for having seen the exhibits, though a more significant discovery was made by the Queen and Prince Albert, almost by accident and quite informally, seven years later.

The royal couple were returning to Britain after a cruise in the royal yacht. Coming up the Channel, they called at Cherbourg, where the alert eye of the Prince Consort noted that, 'The war preparations of the French are immense, ours are despicable. Our Ministers use fine phrases, but they do nothing. My blood boils within me!' The Queen contented herself with refusing to kiss the French Foreign Minister's wife who, as she very well knew, was her host's (Napoleon III) mistress. Her husband's mind, however, was concentrated upon more important matters. The thought process, which had begun as the barge from *Victoria and Albert* crossed the waters of Cherbourg harbour, became evident two years later, when a new warship, HMS *Warrior*, was commissioned. She was Britain's first battleship.

◆

State visits during the nineteenth century and in the early part of the twentieth tended to be between Britain and Europe; not least because a journey to another continent took a long time, and the sovereign had to attend to business at home. In 1875, the Prince of Wales extended the horizon by travelling to India; and in 1911 King George V became the first British monarch to visit that sub-continent, when he appeared at the Durbar held to celebrate his coronation. More significant than this was a journey made by King George VI and Queen Elizabeth in June 1939. On the eve of World War 2, they set off across the Atlantic to Canada and the USA. The trip George III ought to have made was accomplished at last. But, of course, by then the world had become rather smaller.

8
BEYOND THE HORIZON

Just after ten o'clock on the night of 9 June 1939, a royal train carrying King George VI and Queen Elizabeth crossed the frontier between Canada and the United States of America at Niagara Falls. And thus, for the first time in history, a British sovereign entered the USA. One of the King's first actions was to confer a knighthood on his private secretary, Alan Lascelles, and to invest him with the KCVO. Their Majesties' tour of Canada had been sufficiently triumphant; the events of the next seven days were to produce even greater acclaim. As one newspaperman wrote, 'No American has ever received such an ovation from his own countrymen.'

King George VI, though the first British monarch to visit the USA, was by no means the first member of the royal family to make the trip. During the War of Independence, when the future William IV was serving with Admiral Digby's staff on the Hudson River, there had been a plan to kidnap him and the Admiral, and to bring them before the Continental Congress in Philadelphia. George Washington agreed to the commando-style operation, upon the assurance that it would be 'unnecessary to caution you against offering insult or indignity to the person of the Prince or the Admiral'.

The raid never took place, and Prince William Henry was left in peace to carry out his not very rigorous duties with the fleet.

In 1860, the future Edward VII, then the Prince of Wales, was a 19-year-old undergraduate at Oxford. Faced with the prospect of the long summer vacation, his parents decided that he might do worse than to practice the art of royalty by carrying out his first overseas tour. It should be to Canada, though, inevitably, he would visit the USA as well (a matter that required some tact: it was all very well to tour Canada as the Prince of Wales; within the United States it might be better if he assumed the less ostentatious title of Lord Renfrew).

The Prince sailed from Plymouth on 12 July 1860, in the screw-driven battleship, HMS *Hero*. Twelve days later, the warship arrived at

Edward VII—who, as Prince of Wales, travelled further afield than any previous member of the royal family—made a trip to Egypt in 1869. A luxury barge named **Dahabieh** *was provided for his journeys up and down the Nile.*

The opulent interior of the Dahabieh. *The vessel was accompanied by six blue and gold steamers. Each towed a barge filled with supplies: including three thousand bottles of champagne, four thousand bottles of claret, and four horses. Four French chefs were responsible for the cuisine.*

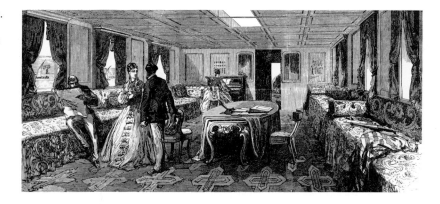

Saint John's, Newfoundland, which was then little more than a small fishing station. On 30 July, *Hero* docked at Halifax. Caught up in the general enthusiasm, the shopkeepers closed their premises for two days. Unfortunately, the newspapers followed the retailers' example and also shut down the better to celebrate. Consequently, the royal coming (and the royal going) received less than adequate local coverage.

It would, perhaps, be an overstatement to describe the royal visit as a complete success—though this was not the Prince's fault. The cause was that recurring flaw in British and Irish politics, that dreaded word 'Orange'. In Quebec, which is a largely Roman Catholic city, the Prince had been properly polite to the heads of the church who, in their turn, had found no fault with the Prince. However, the Orangemen, of whom there were more than enough on the royal route westwards to Niagara, were less than pleased. Such courtesies, to what they clearly regarded as the enemy, were not to be tolerated. They erected arches based upon the design of *the* arch in Londonderry and insisted, as factions are apt to insist, upon parading in the streets.

At Kingston, Ontario, the Prince was compelled to remain in the steamer that was taking him westwards, while his companion, the Duke of Newcastle, lodged a protest with the mayor. That night, the mayor discussed matters with the corporation. The talks went on for a long time, during which they all drank rather too much. The outcome of their deliberations was to decide that the Prince should come ashore and be festooned with the Orange colours. If he refused he could, in the words of one councillor, 'go to hell'.

This was obviously out of the question. The steamer departed for its next port of call; while on the quayside the stubbornly loyal supporters of the long dead William III stood and jeered—not a very happy initiation into the business of royal tourism.

By the time the ship reached Niagara, the Prince's popularity had increased considerably. The Duke of Newcastle, on the other hand, was virtually a nervous wreck. Nor was his condition improved by what should have been a pleasant diversion beside the waterfalls. That maestro of the delicate art of balancing upon a tightrope, Charles Blondin, had arranged to take one of his strolls across the cascading waters—a feat described by *The Times*, in one of its more petulant moods, as fitting 'the performer for the highest place in the lunatic asylum.'

The Prince watched with delight as Mr Blondin delicately trod his straight but awesomely narrow path from the United States to Canada. Blondin assured him that, if one had a talent for this sort of thing, it was not unreasonably dangerous. Indeed, he would be happy to return whence he had come—taking HRH with him in a wheelbarrow. The Prince said yes, but the Duke, who had visions of the heir to the British throne being wiped out by one false step, had the unhappy task of dissuading his charge from such folly. After a brief argument, he succeeded. As if to show the Duke how unnecessary the fuss had been, Blondin made the return journey on a pair of stilts.

In his *persona* as 'Lord Renfrew' (which fooled nobody), the Prince of Wales travelled to Washington in a luxurious directors' car attached to a train put at his disposal by the US Government. He stayed with President James Buchanan at the White House; paid visits to West Point and Harvard, and planted a chestnut sapling beside George Washington's grave at Mount Vernon. It did not do very well. When, many years later, the Prince heard of its early demise, he sent a young oak as a replacement, which fared better. (During a visit to Australia in 1981, the present Prince of Wales explained that trees planted by his father did less well than those installed by the Queen. The conclusion to be drawn from this, he suggested, was that 'trees are snobs'.)

On his way to Portland, Maine, to rejoin HMS *Hero* for the return journey to Britain, 'Lord Renfrew' called at New York, where he was accommodated in considerable comfort at an hotel on 5th Avenue (he compared the rooms to his apartments at Windsor and Buckingham Palace, and remarked that they were very much better). The highlight of the visit was a ball given at the Academy of Music. Three thousand invitations were issued to those New York citizens who were regarded as socially acceptable. In the event, another 2,000 managed to intrude, which was more than the dance floor could stand. Just before the Prince's entrance was heralded by a fanfare of trumpets at 10.30 pm, the wretched thing collapsed under the strain and sank three feet.

A team of carpenters worked on it for the next two hours; by half-past-midnight, the floor was sufficiently repaired for the ball to proceed. The Prince did not enjoy himself. He was compelled to dance with diamond-encrusted New York matrons, while their more comely daughters eluded him.

Nor was the voyage back to Britain anything less than a nightmare. For 26 days, the battleship struggled against high seas and adverse winds before, at last, arriving at Plymouth on 15 November. Three days later, the Prince was back at Oxford.

◆

That the future Edward VII was one of nature's travellers is beyond dispute. In 1875, he decided that it would be good for India and for himself if he were to visit the sub-continent. Nothing was simple. Parliament was hesitant to pay for the trip. The Queen had misgivings about any journey her son might undertake with his friends—whom not without some justification, she described as 'the fast set'. His wife, Alexandra, wanted to accompany him, but this was considered unsuitable —she had, after all, five children who merited her attention.

Eventually the first two objections were cleared up, though the Princess of Wales was harder to placate. She was bitter about being excluded and, to judge from the Prince's unusually sombre mood when he arrived in Paris on an early stage of the journey, she had made her feelings very clear to him. Perhaps the most noteworthy aspect of the tour at this stage was the dress worn by the royal suite at dinner. The all-male

When the future Edward VII visited India in 1876, it was decided to keep expenditure to a reasonable minimum. But, despite the viceroy's warnings, the rajahs insited upon greeting the Prince of Wales with their customary extravagance.

entourage wore short dark blue jackets, black trousers and black ties. By giving his approval to it, the Prince had become a party to the invention of the dinner jacket (or 'tuxedo').

The sea voyage was made in HM Troopship *Serapis* which was escorted by three frigates. When she docked at Bombay on 8 November, two more officers were attached to the royal party. Each, by a coincidence, had only one arm. Major-General Sam Browne VC had lost his in the Indian Mutiny; Major Edward Bradford had sacrificed his to an understandably angry tiger he was about to shoot. The former was head of the secret police, and was in charge of the Prince's safety. He performed his duties diligently, if not altogether to the liking of the other members of the suite. They must, he insisted, surround their royal master at all times; and they must take turns at sitting up all night outside whatever room or tent he might be sleeping in.

No doubt prompted by the financial objections that had been the House of Commons' initial reaction to the royal tour, the Viceroy of India insisted that, whilst presents must obviously be exchanged between the visitor and his hosts, the business should be kept within reason. Specimens of the products manufactured in the various regions were deemed in order; anything more extravagant was excluded. Nor was there to be any *durbar* (a public levee held either by the Viceroy or by an Indian prince) to celebrate the occasion. Fairly early on in the arrangements, reports reached Britain that the Nizam of Hyderabad had actually

The Prince of Wales on the quarter-deck of the troopship Serapis, *bound for India. The deckhouse between the mainmast and the mizzen was built especially for the trip. Afterwards, the wives of army officers used to squabble about the right to use it during the sweltering passage through the Red Sea.* (Top left.)

The Prince's bedroom in Serapis *was a study in comfort. To lessen the motion when the ship was rolling, the bed was constructed in the manner of a swing. Whether or not it worked is not recorded.* (Top right.)

refused to meet the Prince. The very idea was intolerable—until somebody pointed out that the Nizam was only eight years old, and that his hesitation (for it was no more than that) had nothing to do with convictions about the Raj. He was a delicate child, and there was rather a lot of cholera about.

There was nothing parsimonious about the train that was assembled for the Prince of Wales. There were 17 carriages, including two saloons decorated with crimson-silk hangings, cords and tassels. Each had two full-length mirrors, and all the mouldings and metal fastenings were finished in gilt. As *The Times* man telegraphed to his editor, 'The accommodation for the lavatory and other purposes will be in strict keeping with the furniture of the state apartments, and nothing is omitted in the way both of luxury and convenience which can be missed by the most fastidious.'

During his travels, the Prince met all the right Indian princes—including the 12-year-old Gaekwar of Baroda, who was decked out with diamonds worth £600,000 and who offered his guest six gold cannons valued at £40,000 apiece (since they could not be regarded as products of the region, they had to be discreetly returned). In Poona, the Prince stuck pigs and hunted cheetahs; elsewhere, he diminished the population of elephants, tigers and other wild life. However, on a more significant note, he gave a number of British officers severe dressing-downs for referring to Indians as 'niggers'. He visited the jail at Lahore, where he had an interesting interview with a veteran *thug* who had escaped the executioner by turning Queen's evidence. Not without relish, this elderly fanatic gave brief details of the 250 assassinations he claimed to have carried out.

On another matter of Indian tradition, the Prince put his foot down and said that, on no account must the daughter of one ruler be allowed to commit suttee (an act of immolation in which a man's widow throws herself upon his funeral pyre) when her dying husband passed away. The ruler agreed; though, when he himself died at the hands of a murderer not long afterwards, his final testament did not excuse his own three wives from committing their bodies to the ashes.

The Prince returned to England in May of the following year—just as his mother was about to be declared Empress of India. Her Majesty's Customs and Excise had agreed that he need pay no duty on the gifts he brought back with him, which was just as well. Despite the restrictions, there were a great many. But the present that pleased Queen Victoria the most was an edition of her book *Leaves from the Journal of my Life in the Highlands,* which had been translated into Hindustani and bound with covers of inlaid marble.

Queen Victoria was impressed by her eldest son's success in India. Despite her misgivings about the 'fast set', he had behaved himself well. On his return, she gave a dinner in his honour. On board the *Serapis,* however, there was a less happy result. One modification for the Prince of Wales's voyage had been the construction of a cabin on deck. Unlike the rest of the accommodation, the cabin remained cool while the troopship negotiated the sweltering waters of the Red Sea. It was afterwards reserved for officers' wives and their children; each family to be housed in it for one night at a time according to a roster. This was all very well until a titled matron decided that her delicate offspring required special treatment, and insisted upon occupying the cabin for the entire trip. A row of such spectacular proportions erupted, that the ship's officers decided they would happily have settled instead for an all-male mutiny.

◆

In its own way, the placing of steam-engines inside ships, to provide a more predictable form of propulsion than the wind, was as significant as the installation, a good many years later, of jet-engines in aeroplanes. It substantially reduced the time required for a journey and thus, in terms of time if not of distance, made the world smaller. Among other things, it extended the ability of royalty to travel; and indeed, with the large number of nineteenth century additions to the British empire, the need for such excursions had been increased. The British sovereign was, after all, sovereign of a great many other places as well, and it was only right that, if not the actual monarch, then at least some closely connected representative should be seen by these faraway subjects.

As Duke and Duchess of Cornwall, the future King George V and Queen Mary set off from Portsmouth in 1901 on a prodigious journey in the Orient liner *Ophir* (6,900 tons), which had been taken over by the Admiralty, repainted in white, and re-classified as a royal yacht. The itinerary included Australia, New Zealand, Tasmania, South Africa (despite the fact that it was still in a state of war), and Canada. One of the royal duties was to inaugurate the Australian Parliament at Melbourne on 9 May (Canberra did not assume the role of capital until 1927; indeed, in 1901, the city did not even exist). As part of the proceedings, the Duchess was to press a button that would cause a Union Jack to be hauled to the masthead at every school throughout the land—*simultaneously*. Unfortunately, nice idea though it was, something went wrong.

The Duchess applied the necessary pressure to the button, but no Union Jacks ran up any masts. When the procedure was repeated two days later, it was more successful.

People in these distant lands said that they liked their royal visitor because he seemed to be so *interested* in whatever they told him. His stamina in this respect must have been considerable. During a journey that lasted eight months and covered 45,000 miles (72,000 km), the royal couple laid 21 foundation stones, listened to 544 addresses, presented 4,329 medals, and shook 24,855 hands at receptions alone.

Although she had been proclaimed Empress of India, Queen Victoria was never able to visit the sub-continent. The best she could do when her thoughts travelled East of Suez was to repair to the so-called Durbar Room at Osborne. Its Indian atmosphere was contrived by John Lockwood Kipling (father of Rudyard), formerly keeper of the museum at Lahore. Victoria's son went to India as Prince of Wales, but never as Emperor. In his coronation year of 1911, George V resolved that the celebrations should not be confined to Britain. They should be followed on 12 December by a massive durbar at Delhi.

By this time, a new species of locomotion, the motor car, had reached India. The Indian princes, determined that the new Emperor should not find them backward in this respect, bought motor cars at a rate that would have astounded lesser mortals. It was the beginning of a craze that reached its peak some years later, when a rough estimate suggested that one rajah owned no fewer than 150—including 18 Rolls-Royces.

George V at the gate to Delhi on the occasion of his coronation durbar in 1911. Such was his passion for hunting that the King insisted upon time being found to allow for this, prompting Lord Crewe, the Secretary of State for India to write, 'It is a misfortune for a public personage to have any taste so strongly developed as the craze for shooting is in our beloved Ruler.'

On the day of the durbar, an industrious official, who took the trouble to count the vehicles, reported that 2,000 motor cars, plus 200 motor cycles were assembled within an area of ten square miles. Had there been a competition for the top scorer, the winner would have been a prince who brought along no fewer than 36 vehicles.

For the King Emperor's convenience, two vehicles were set aside; a six-cylinder 50hp Wolsley and a 38hp Daimler.

The King and Queen had sailed from Southampton on 11 November in the ss *Medina*, the latest P & O liner, which had been chartered for the occasion. She was larger than the *Ophir*, registering 13,000 tons. But then she needed to be. All told, there were 733 people on board—including the Gentlemen at Arms and (their first excursion abroad) a contingent of the Royal Company of Archers.

When George V (as Prince of Wales) had previously been to India in 1905, he had allowed himself some leisure for a hunting foray. This was a more hurried occasion. The durbar itself was held in a huge arena in the centre of which, and mounted on a platform, was a pavilion capped by a large golden dome. The King and Queen, wearing their crowns and their coronation robes were escorted by members of the 10th Hussars and the Imperial Cadet Corps. As their carriage approached the arena, 101 guns discharged a salute. The royal couple then walked the short distance to the pavilion and sat down on two thrones. Thereafter an apparently endless stream of rajahs and other Indian elite filed past to pay homage. Next day, King George laid the foundation stone of a new capital for the British Raj —which, appropriately enough, if not with very much imagination, was to be called New Delhi. The seat of power was transferred to it in the following year.

On 5 February, the *Medina*, her moment of glory over, returned to Southampton and the King and Queen disembarked to find snow on the ground.

---◆---

At the end of 1918, the world picked itself up and shuddered, then tried to face up to the reality of peace. Among Britain's assets, the Prince of Wales (later Edward VIII and still later Duke of Windsor) had to be accounted extremely valuable. He had shown himself to be courageous during the war—and would willingly have been even more so if it had been permitted. He was good-looking, had considerable charm and, although his father may not always have approved, his style was original. During the next six years the Prince was to spend much of his time in the battle-cruiser HMS *Renown* (latterly HMS *Repulse*, when *Renown* was in dock) touring the world on royal business. No matter whether it was a matter of showing the flag in a dominion, or creating a presence in the Argentine—where Britain had £400 million invested but from which trade appeared sluggish—the Prince was there. All told, he made four official voyages between 1919 and 1925, travelled 150,000 miles (*c*240,000 km) and visited 45 countries. He also made a number of unofficial voyages in passenger liners.

Like his grandfather, Edward VII, the Prince of Wales made his debut with a journey to Canada. (Also like his grandfather, he took the title 'Lord Renfrew' out of the cupboard, and used it when he judged it best to travel incognito—a ruse that never worked). The trip was noteworthy for two reasons. One was that it gave him an abiding love for North America; the other was its demonstration of a very much less formal approach to the appearance of royalty.

He believed in getting in among the people; of actually allowing them to *touch* him if they chose. As he recalled in *A King's Story*, the Prime Minister, David Lloyd George, had suggested that 'the Dominions wanted, if not a vaudeville show, then a first class carnival in which the Prince of Wales should play a gay, many-sided and natural role.'

The Prince played it to perfection. The Canadians responded by giving him the treatment that, nowadays, is accorded to a pop star. In Quebec, for example, the crowd broke through the police cordon; somebody stole his handkerchief, others tried to pull the buttons from his

jacket. The Prince was undismayed. 'In fact,' he remembered afterwards, 'I rather liked it.'

Nor was he averse to shaking hands. He would stand on a small
platform, and shake away, much to the delight of his future subjects.
Once he overdid it and his right hand became so bruised by this seemingly
endless exercise, that he had to use his left.

Although he was as fond of horses as the next man, he believed that
there was a time and place for everything. His visit to Toronto was timed
to coincide with Warriors Day, an occasion that would be attended by at
least 27,000 veterans. His advisers insisted that he should make his
entrance on a horse.

When the Prince suggested that the sight and sound of all the
enthusiastic ex-servicemen might be rather daunting for the unfortunate
animal, he was assured that it had been 'specially trained'. In any case, all
that was required of it was that it should walk up and down the ranks,
allowing him to inspect what would be a quiet gathering. Once this had
been accomplished, the horse would convey him to a small platform,
where he would dismount and make a speech.

This may have been all very well in theory, but the assembly of onetime warriors was far from quiet. The moment he rode into the arena,
the veterans broke ranks. The horse may have been 'specially trained'
but, under the circumstances, there was nothing it could do. It was
virtually smothered by the crowd, as the Prince was snatched from the
saddle and passed from one pair of hands to another until he reached the
rostrum.

Thereafter, his opinions were taken more seriously, and there were
no more attempts to place him on horseback.

From Toronto, the Prince travelled onwards towards Vancouver in a
train supplied by the Canadian Pacific Railway. His accommodation was
in the rearmost coach, which was fitted with an observation platform,
giving him an excellent view of the tremendous landscape; but which also
added to his labours. Whenever the train stopped, a crowd gathered and,
as crowds will on such occasions, demanded an impromptu speech. The
Prince did his best to oblige, but there were difficulties. Politicians are
practised in the art of the 'whistle-stop tour'; the Prince of Wales had less
experience. 'On more than one occasion,' he wrote, 'disconcerting bursts
of laughter instead of the customary applause informed me that I had
made the lamentable blunder of confusing my audience with a rival
community some distance down the track.'

But he was enchanted by almost everything he saw. Forty miles
south of Calgary in Alberta, he bought himself a 4,000-acre ranch. The
object was, 'to immerse myself, if only momentarily, in the simple life of

the western prairies. There, I was sure, I would find occasional escape
from the sometimes too-confining, too-well-ordered, island life of Britain.'

His father was less happy about it. He had, King George V insisted,
set a precedent. The Australians would now expect him to purchase a
sheep station; the South Africans, an ostrich farm.

Before returning in *Renown* to Britain, he visited Washington, where
he was a guest at the White House. As President Woodrow Wilson had
been stricken with paralysis, the Prince's entertainment was entrusted to
the Vice-President, The USA was in the grip of that fearful post-war
epidemic: prohibition. The Prince, who was by no means a heavy drinker
but enjoyed a cocktail, seems to have favoured a version of bootleg gin
known as 'White Rock'. He suffered no ill effects; though, after a visit to
the Naval Academy at Annapolis, his police motorcycle escort found
themselves in trouble. The officers had fallen in with a squad of revenue
agents, who had recently captured a quantity of illicit liquor. The officers
were invited to share it—with the result that, when they headed the
motorcade back to the capital, they were seen to wobble. Eventually, the
two leading riders veered off into the gutter, fell off their machines, and
quietly passed out.

In New York, the Prince went to the theatre, visited Grant's tomb,
and behaved much like a tourist. The show was the *Ziegfeld Follies*.
Though its message may not have been very profound, it remained
firmly fixed in his memory. Recalling the trip, he wrote, 'Curiously what
lingered in my mind was not so much the grand things that happened to
me . . . rather it was a haunting little song I heard at the *Ziegfeld Follies*:

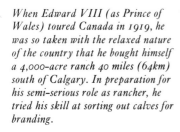

*When Edward VIII (as Prince of
Wales) toured Canada in 1919, he
was so taken with the relaxed nature
of the country that he bought himself
a 4,000-acre ranch 40 miles (64km)
south of Calgary. In preparation for
his semi-serious role as rancher, he
tried his skill at sorting out calves for
branding.*

"A Pretty Girl is Like a Melody." '

Three and a half months after his return to Britain, he set off again in *Renown*: this time to Australia and New Zealand. And so it went on. As he remarked, the battle-cruiser became 'my floating home for the next few years'. Not that he disliked it; the Prince was restless and, when there were no official tours to be undertaken, he made journeys of his own— several of them to the ranch in Alberta. On these occasions, he travelled by passenger liner.

In 1924, he crossed the Atlantic to New York in the Cunard liner *Berengaria*. This fine ship, which was one of the most prestigious vessels on the North Atlantic run until she was scrapped in early 1939, had been built to the order of a German shipping company and named *Imperator*. After the war, she had been handed over to Britain as part of the payment exacted as the price of defeat. The Prince was quartered in the Imperial Suite—possibly the most luxurious accommodation afloat. Ironically, the previous occupant had been his distant cousin the Kaiser—who was now languishing in exile in Holland.

Since he professed to be travelling incognito, the Prince once again used the title 'Lord Renfrew' (a perfectly legitimate ploy—the Prince of Wales is also Earl of Chester, Duke of Cornwall and Duke of Rothesay, Earl of Carrick and Baron Renfrew, Lord of the Isles and Great Steward of Scotland. As this information was available in the appropriate reference books, it is not surprising that it never afforded him anonymity).

Once it was realised that the Prince would be travelling, a great many Americans cut short their holidays in Europe to return home in the same ship. Cunard was determined to treat its royal passenger in the manner to which its directors assumed he was accustomed. The liner's officers were ordered to wear swords and frock coats, and there was an attempt to provide a guard of honour at Southampton. But, when the Prince of Wales stressed that such ceremonial would come amiss and that he wished to travel as quietly as possible, the instructions were cancelled. Even the press, which gathered in force on the quayside to see him off, was frustrated. He boarded the liner from a launch off the Isle of Wight at four o'clock in the morning.

The purpose of his visit was to attend some polo matches in the United States and then to visit his ranch in Alberta. In New York, he decided that a little night life would not be out of place. Nothing to do with the heir to the British throne ever escapes attention. One New York newspaper told its readers, '*Prince Gets In With Milkman*', another, 'Here he is, girls—the most eligible bachelor yet uncaught. Oh! Who'll ask HRH what he wears asleep? Prince of Wales has 'em guessing in the wee hours!'

Inevitably, the cuttings reached Buckingham Palace and did little for King George V's comfort. Thankfully, the Prince's most significant and prophetic remark went unreported. Shortly after landing in New York, a swarm of newsmen gathered around him. Among them was a woman journalist who asked, 'Would you marry an American girl if you fell in love with one.' The Prince replied 'Yes' but his answer was drowned by the clamour of other reporters.

◆

The Prince of Wales became Edward VIII in 1936 and, in that same year, abdicated. True to his unheard answer on that day in 1924, he had married an American woman.

His brother, George VI, had a less flamboyant style, but it was very effective. A British sovereign had yet to visit the USA, and the time had clearly come when this should be put right. Any such tour would, of course, include Canada within its scope.

Mackenzie King, the Canadian premier, was partly responsible. When he discussed the idea with his friend President Roosevelt, the latter was enthusiastic. Yes, he said, if the King were to visit Canada, of course he should come to the United States as well. The project was first mooted at Buckingham Palace in 1937, when Mackenzie King came to London

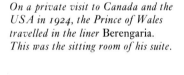

On a private visit to Canada and the USA in 1924, the Prince of Wales travelled in the liner Berengaria. *This was the sitting room of his suite.*

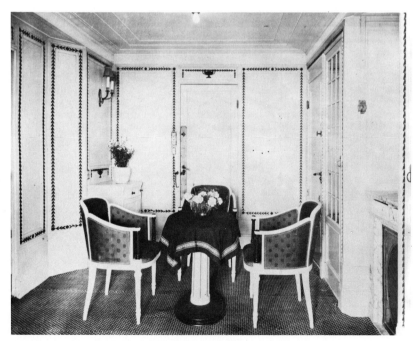

Many of the Prince of Wales's overseas tours were made in the battle-cruiser Renown. *However, in 1926, the Duke and Duchess of York (later King George VI and Queen Elizabeth) also used the* Renown. *Their well-appointed quarters included this beautifully decorated dining room.*

Not the least of the Prince of Wales's gifts as a roving ambassador for George V was the interest he took in local customs—such as the display put on by these usutu dancers in Zululand in 1925.

for the coronation. But already there were signs that another war with Germany was a possibility, if not yet a certainty. In fact, President Roosevelt's invitation for the King and Queen to pay a state visit to the USA arrived during the last week of September 1938, when Britain was in a state of partial mobilisation over the 'Munich Crisis'.

By 1939, there were many doubts about whether, in the prevailing state of tension, it would be wise for the King and Queen to be out of the country for several weeks. Among those who urged that the trip should go ahead despite the international situation was Lord Tweedsmuir, Governor General of Canada (the novelist John Buchan). Eventually this school of opinion prevailed—though Lord Tweedsmuir was later to remark that when he persuaded the King to go, 'I did not realize I was pulling the string of such a shower bath!'

Originally it had been intended that the royal couple should travel in HMS *Repulse,* which, in 1925, had taken the former Prince of Wales on his last official overseas tour (to South and West Africa and thence to South America). On 3 May 1939, however, the Admiralty advised that it would be wrong to remove a capital ship from the fleet when she might be required for more warlike duties. Instead, the liner *Empress of Australia* was hurriedly chartered from the Canadian Pacific line and classified as a 'royal yacht'. With the white ensign at her stern and the royal standard flying from the foremast, she sailed from Southampton on 5 May. *Repulse* accompanied her half way across the Atlantic, and then returned to her base.

As the liner edged away from the quayside, somebody in the crowd was heard to cry, 'For God's sake bring them safely back to us.' The anonymous person spoke for a great many people.

The voyage was not an easy one. The icebergs had strayed unusually far south that year, and, to make matters worse, there was thick fog for three days. As the Queen wrote to her mother-in-law, Queen Mary, '. . . the foghorn blew incessantly. Its melancholy blasts were echoed back by the icebergs like the twang of a piece of wire. Incredibly eerie, and really very alarming, knowing that we were surrounded by ice, & unable to see a foot either way.

'We very nearly hit a berg the day before yesterday, and the poor Captain was nearly demented because some kind cheerful people kept on reminding him that the *Titanic* was struck, & *just* about the same date!'

However, the King was grateful for the rest that the extra days at sea allowed him, and the chief purser's canary seemed unperturbed. For the first time in its life, it laid an egg.

The result of the bad weather was that the liner was off Newfoundland when it should have been at Quebec. Once the royal party was ashore, every day was filled with engagements and most of the nights were spent on the royal train. Just as King George VI was soon to be the first sovereign to enter the USA, so was he the first to visit Canada. As some critics pointed out, it was about time. King of Great Britain he might be; Emperor of India he might still be; but he was also *King of Canada.* Their message was given added point by rumours that, if Europe went to war again, the dominion would stay out of the conflict. The royal visit quickly put an end to any such notion. As the premier of one province told the monarch, 'You can go home and tell the Old Country that any talk they may hear about Canada being isolationist is just nonsense.'

On a day in early May, 1939, King George VI and Queen Elizabeth sailed away from Britain in the CPR liner Empress of Australia. *It was the first visit of a British king to America, and the royal couple's charm influenced the American President's attitude to Britain during the war that was only four months away from starting.*

Prepared at Southampton, the royal drawing room aboard the Empress of Australia *was palatial in both size and decoration.*

The battle-cruiser Repulse *escorted the extempore royal yacht halfway across the Atlantic—and then turned and headed back to her base. The King (with advice, apparently, from the Queen) took shots of the escorting warship with his cine-camera.*

It would be understatement to describe the visit as a success; it was far more than that. The Canadians took to *their* King immediately, and *their* Queen excelled herself by her determination (later shared by her daughter) to mix with the ordinary people. When she laid the foundation stone of the new judicative building in Ottawa before a crowd estimated at 70,000, she overheard some masons speaking with Scottish accents. She strolled over to them, and spent ten minutes chatting about Scotland. Similarly, when she unveiled a memorial to the dead of World War 1, she mingled with a crowd of 10,000 veterans. Even her escort of police officers was alarmed; as a member of the Royal Canadian Mounted Police helpfully informed one of the men from Scotland Yard, this was something that no President of the United States would ever dare to have done.

The King and Queen travelled as far west as Niagara Falls and
thence to Washington. There were reports that representatives of the IRA
were active in Detroit and Buffalo, which did not seem to bode well for
the visit. Nobody need have worried. In the USA as in Canada, the
reception was little short of ecstatic. The route from Union Station,
Washington, to the White House was lined by so many people that the
President's wife, Mrs Eleanor Roosevelt, felt bound to confess that she
had never seen such a crowd. A local newspaper headline announced that
'*The British Retake Washington*'; a senator told the King that he was 'a
great Queen-picker', a boy belonging to the Civilian Conservation Corps,
who suddenly found his hand being shaken by the King of Great Britain,
became slightly muddled, and said, 'Gee, I never ever shook hands with
a congressman before.' And Mrs Roosevelt observed that, 'They have a
way of making friends, these young people.'

Because the sun shone hard from an unblemished sky making it
unpleasantly hot in the capital, the Queen went about much of her
business carrying a parasol. This immediately started a craze that inspired
the magazine *Life* to remark, 'To makers of parasols . . . the reign of
King George VI of England will be memorable not for the Munich Pact
nor for the first North American trip of Their Britannic Majesties. To
them the reign of George and Elizabeth will ever be the period when a
Queen . . . raised the parasol . . . to unprecedented pinnacles of international significance and chic.'

The most important result of the trip was the friendship that sprang
up between the King and the President. After a visit to New York by
train, as far as Red Bank New Jersey, and thence in the US destroyer
Warrington, the King and Queen spent a couple of nights at the Roosevelt
family home, Hyde Park, NY. It was here that Roosevelt first discussed a
plan he had in mind for use in the event of war. It included the trading of
British bases in the Caribbean for US destroyers, and the ingredients of
what eventually became known as the 'lease lend agreement'.

As for the King, he wondered, 'Why don't my Ministers talk to me
as the President did tonight? I feel exactly as though a father were giving
me his most careful and wise advice.'

◆

When King George VI flew to North Africa in an Avro York in 1943, he
unknowingly created a new precedent as far as royal travel was concerned.
It happened to be the first inter-continental flight by a reigning sovereign
of Great Britain. There was already a King's Flight, but its aircraft were
small and it was certainly not equipped for ventures such as this. For such
purposes, the Captain of the Flight had to look elsewhere.

Nearly ten years were to pass before long-haul aeroplanes became anything like a commonplace of such journeys. When, in the winter of 1946-1947, the King, Queen and the two princesses visited South Africa, they made the voyage in the last of the great British battleships, HMS *Vanguard*. She had been laid down in 1941 at Clydeside, though, even then, her armament was hopelessly out-of-date. The eight 15-in. guns were relics of two World War 1 battle-cruisers, HMS *Glorious* and HMS *Courageous*, that, in the latter part of the 1920s, had been converted into aircraft carriers. Since they had no more need for heavy armament, these giant weapons (four on each) were placed in store and eventually mounted on what, otherwise, was Britain's last word in capital-ship technology.

Princess Elizabeth named *Vanguard* at the launching ceremony in 1944. By the time the battleship was completed in 1946, the war was over; and, in any case, the development of aircraft as instruments of sea-warfare had rendered her as obsolete as the proverbial dodo. Carrying the royal family to Capetown and Durban was about the only useful thing *Vanguard* did in her short life (she was scrapped in 1960).

Just as the trip to North America had been made despite doubts about its advisability in view of the international situation, so was the King uncertain about the wisdom of this tour. Britain was in the thrall of one of the coldest winters on record. There was a serious shortage of coal; it seemed to him wrong that the sovereign should leave his subjects to their chilly ordeal, while he enjoyed the sunshine of South Africa. However, he was persuaded that it was necessary and, after some argument, he agreed.

Travelling in cars, a royal train and the Vikings of the King's Flight, they journeyed from Capetown up into the Rhodesias. A thousand veterans of the Boer War amply demonstrated their loyalty. The King gave to the Premier, Jan Smuts, President Kruger's bible—which had been captured with other of the Boer leader's effects during the South African war. He even quoted Kruger, when he advised South Africans to, 'Take from the past all that is good and beautiful; shape your ideals therewith and build your future on this ideal.'

In Capetown on 21 April, Princess Elizabeth celebrated her coming of age by broadcasting from a room in Government House. Her audience was estimated at 500 million people residing in various parts of the UK, the Commonwealth and the Empire.

This was the last occasion on which a large warship was used for a royal tour. When, in 1951, Princess Elizabeth and the Duke of Edinburgh visited Canada, they made the journey in a BOAC (British Airways) Stratocruiser. There were undoubted advantages: in 35 days, they twice crossed the continent, travelled 10,000 miles (*c*16,000km), and visited every province including Newfoundland.

On 31 January 1952, Princess Elizabeth and the Duke of Edinburgh boarded a chartered BOAC aircraft at London Airport. The aircraft was to take them to Nairobi on the first leg of a tour scheduled to last five months. Since the new royal yacht *Britannia* was not yet complete, the Shaw Saville and Albion liner *Gothic* was to pick them up at Mombasa at the end of their visit to Kenya. The *Gothic* would convey them to Australia and, later, New Zealand.

The King was at the airport to see them off. Many people remarked on how tired he looked, but this was not surprising. His Majesty had been ill for some time; although, so far as is generally known, he never realised it, he had been suffering from cancer of the lung. He had undergone

During the 1947 tour of South Africa and Rhodesia (now Zimbabwe), King George VI and the royal party travelled in Viking aircraft of the King's Flight and by train. The latter was made up of twelve coaches built in the record time of eleven months. For their ceremonial journeys, the car—as nearly always—was a Daimler.

All manner of vehicles are used to transport the Queen during her journeys abroad—such as this ornate carriage used when she came to Katmandu in 1961. Showing her the sights is that country's monarch, King Mahendra. (Top.)

1965, and a visit by the Queen and the Duke of Edinburgh to Berlin. Commenting on the Wall, the Queen said, 'Nowhere is the tragedy of a divided world more evident than in this city'. (Right.)

surgery for it on 23 September of the previous year. The bulletin making the matter public described it as 'an operation for lung resection'.

Whilst it was successful, the doctors were bound to admit that a coronary thrombosis might develop at any moment—probably with fatal consequences.

On 5 February, the King and Queen were staying at Sandringham. The King spent most of the day out of doors, shooting hares. The sport was good and when he retired to his room at 10.30, he seemed in good spirits. He went to bed at about midnight. When, next morning, his valet brought him his tea, he discovered that his royal master was dead. The coronary the doctors had feared occurred at about 2 am. The sovereign had died in his sleep.

Princess Elizabeth (Queen Elizabeth II, as she now was) had known for some time about the seriousness of her father's condition. When she and Prince Philip had visited Canada and the USA in the previous autumn, her papers included a sealed envelope to be opened only in the event of the King's death. Among its contents was a draft of the Accession Declaration and a message to both Houses of Parliament. Now, after four days of hard work in Kenya, she and her husband were resting at Tree-tops—a hunting lodge in the shadow of Mount Kenya on the banks of the Sagana river. Their staff were staying in an hotel nearby. The time was 11.45 in the morning.

It is difficult to unravel the situation at the hotel. There was a telephone call; a word from a reporter from the *East African Standard*, who had received a story about the King's death from one of the news agencies; and, apparently, an attempt by Princess Elizabeth's private secretary, Martin Charteris (now Lord Charteris of Amisfield) to pick up a BBC news bulletin on the wireless. He was unable to tune into any news, but discovered that the scheduled programmes had all been replaced by recordings of solemn music. This, in itself, was sufficiently eloquent: there could be no doubt that the King was dead.

Prince Philip's private secretary, Lieutenant-Commander Michael Parker, had the unenviable task of telling the Prince. He afterwards recalled that, 'I never felt so sorry for anyone in all my life. He looked as if you'd dropped half the world on him.'

Within an hour, the royal party was on the move. A short-haul aircraft provided transportation to Entebbe, where a BOAC Argonaut was waiting to take Queen Elizabeth II and her husband back to London. The rest of the tour was cancelled.

Had anyone been wondering what kind of sovereign was about to wear the crown, this sad episode provided a more than adequate answer. Prince Philip's reaction has been described. The grief of Elizabeth was

Polo was invented by the Persians over 2,500 years ago and introduced into Britain by Army officers in the late nineteenth century. The game is much the same wherever it is played, but circumstances vary and when the Queen went to watch a match at Delhi in 1961, she arrived in an unusually exotic vehicle. (Following page, top left.)

The trappings of the mysterious orient might have been missing when the Queen drove through Karachi with President Ayub Khan in 1962 (indeed, to judge by the cavalcade of cars, a downpour of ticker-tape would not have seemed surprising), but they were certainly not missing during the Queens tour of Brunei in 1972. (Following page, top right and bottom.)

obviously as great; probably greater. But, as on all occasions in front of the public, her composure was complete. Not by an expression, not by a word did she betray her emotions. Like an actor on the stage, she had a role to play. She played it faultlessly. Her distress was her's alone. It was fitting that Elizabeth the private person should be sorrowful; but Queen Elizabeth II was a different matter. The two had to be kept apart. Her coolness under stress, her imperturbability; they were both apparent on those sorry February days of 1952.

Harold MacMillan observed shortly after her accession, 'She means to be a Queen and not a puppet.' Monarchy is a profession; the Queen is very professional.

—————————————◆—————————————

Not long after the Queen's accession, a plan was put forward that the Queen's Flight—still composed of Vikings—should be disbanded. It was not, its critics suggested, under sufficient pressure of work. Instead, BEA and BOAC (both forerunners of British Airways) and the RAF should take over its duties, co-ordinated by an air equerry with a small staff.

Before a radically-inclined government robbed them of their power in 1970, the Indian rajahs bought Rolls-Royces by the dozen. The Queen travelled in this particularly superb example of the coach-builder's art, when she was entertained by the Governor of Rajasthan during a royal tour of India in 1961.

The topic was debated by a committee on which the royal household, the Treasury, the Air Ministry and the Ministry of Civil Aviation were represented. Its conclusions were that the Flight should continue; but that the Ministry of Civil Aviation should provide aircraft for journeys beyond the capability of the Flight's own aeroplanes. Significantly, by December of the following year, the Queen had agreed that certain VIPs might also make use of the Flight.

Between June 1960 and March 1979, British Airways carried members of the royal family on 118 flights. The Queen has travelled exclusively in chartered aircraft arranged by the Department of Trade. All the others—including the Queen Mother, the Prince of Wales and Prince Philip—have, at one time or another, been accommodated in first class compartments on scheduled services. Pretty well every type of aircraft owned by British Airways has been used with the exception of Jumbo Jets, which are rather larger than necessary for such purposes.

The Queen has flown three times in Concorde. In November 1977, she used it on her return from Barbados to London, following a three-week Silver Jubilee tour of Canada and the Caribbean. In February 1979, outward bound for a visit to the Middle East, she flew faster-than-sound from Heathrow to Bahrain (travelling time: 4 hours, 10 minutes); and, afterwards made hops in this elite airliner to Riyadh in Saudi Arabia and Dhahran (the Suadis' oilfield headquarters), where she was met by the royal yacht. The flight back to England, however, was made in a more leisurely fashion in a VC10.

According to a representative of British Airways, 'We receive months and months notice of these flights; usually a minimum of three months. Preparing and refurbishing an aircraft takes less than a week—sometimes the work is begun only three days before departure. After that, it is sealed and put under guard. Normally, the changes involve the

The Shaw Savill & Albion liner Gothic, *which did duty as a royal yacht during the coronation tour of the Commonwealth in 1953–1954. The royal party left the liner at Aden, having travelled more than one-third of the distance round the world in her.*

seating: the single first class seats are used, or else the swivel chairs fitted in the upstairs first-class lounge of a Jumbo. Settees are sometimes used, too. But, whatever it is, it must have had Air Registration Board approval, and must be fastened to rails on the floor. Sometimes, they may be re-covered, though they are not changed structurally. The decor is usually the same, spruced up, of course, for the occasion.'

The cost of a charter is about £6,000. When the aircraft is provided by an airline belonging to the host country (for example Quantas or Air Canada), that country pays the bill. In Britain, the Foreign Office 'sorts it out'—not least because the Queen's visits are usually made on the Government's recommendation.

On 23 November 1953, the Queen and the Duke of Edinburgh boarded an aircraft at London Airport *en route* for the West Indies. The journey that began in this unassuming manner was a coronation year tour of the Commonwealth. By the time it was done, the royal couple had travelled once round the world.

At Bermuda, they embarked in the liner *Gothic*. The new royal yacht *Britannia* was still being fitted-out on the Clyde; the Shaw Saville and Albion ship was already equipped for such a project. She had, after all, been standing-by less than two years earlier, for the proposed visit to Australia and New Zealand, which was cancelled due to the death of George VI.

The *Gothic* made her way through the Panama canal and then headed westwards for the long haul across the Pacific. The liner's officers knew the route well enough; it was more or less the same course that they followed on more normal journeys between the UK and New Zealand. Among those who greeted the Queen when she landed at Suva in the Fiji Islands was a gentleman named John Christian, a descendant of the *Bounty* mutineer, Fletcher Christian. He and his wife had made the journey all the way from Pitcairn Island, which was 3,500 miles (c5,600km) away.

At Tonga, Queen Salote, the sovereign, provided a London taxi for her royal guest's journeys on shore. She had bought it when she came to Britain for the coronation six months earlier. In Auckland, New Zealand, it rained as the Queen approached the town hall. The deputy mayor handed a plastic raincoat to the New Zealand Prime Minister, who draped it over Her Majesty's shoulders—thereby being rewarded with, 'Thank you very much, Sir Walter Raleigh.'

The latterday royal progress continued via Australia and Ceylon and across the Indian Ocean to Aden. At this point, the *Gothic* was relieved of her responsibilities, and aircraft took over again. Eventually, the Queen and the Duke arrived at Tobruk, where Prince Charles and Princess Anne were reunited with them. The children (for such they then were) had sailed from Portsmouth in the now-completed *Britannia* and had been staying on Malta with Lord and Lady Mountbatten. Lord Mountbatten was in command of the Mediterranean Fleet.

But an epoch was coming to an end. At Aden, Prince Philip showed considerable interest in a recently completed oil refinery. It seemed to augur well for the colony's future. He cannot have suspected that, within five years, Aden would be in a state of emergency, and that British soldiers would be locked in battle with terrorists.

Similarly, in Uganda, the Queen opened the sluices of a new dam across the Nile at Entebbe. This, too, might have been regarded as an act of faith in the future. There was nothing to suggest the tyranny that independence would eventually produce; the starvation and the massacres.

Even Malta has changed. From the deck of *Britannia*, the Queen watched with delight as the Mediterranean Fleet steamed past in review order. Whilst the island is still popular with tourists, several years have passed since Valletta harbour was last thronged with the grey shapes of British warships.

The sun had not yet set on the British Empire, but it was close to the horizon.

9
RULE *BRITANNIA*

Since Her Majesty's yacht *Britannia* was completed in 1954, she has steamed more than ½ million miles (800,000km). She has circumnavigated the globe six times; during one 5-year period she covered 100,000 miles (161,000km); and, playing her part in the Silver Jubilee celebrations of 1977, she exceeded 40,000 miles (64,000km) in twelve months. Her ports of call have ranged from Helsinki to the New Hebrides, from New York City to Fremantle, from Western Samoa to Yucatan, from Stockholm to Rio de Janeiro. She has even visited the Galapagos—a cluster of islands on the equator, 600 miles (960km) west of Ecuador,

The royal yacht Britannia *carrying out speed trials off the Isle of Arran. (Bottom right.) She was designed so that in time of war she could be converted into a hospital ship. However, a problem of fuel supply prevented her carrying out this role during the Falkland Islands crisis, although the liner* Uganda *which was used was larger and therefore more suitable.* (Bottom left.)

where the reptile population exceeds the number of human inhabitants.

If the sum of her ports of call were marked on a map of the world, the dots would produce a speckled effect, causing observers to remark on the places that *Britannia* had *not* visited—rather than on those at which she had called.

The cost of building her amounted to £2,098,000, which is less than one year's running costs at today's prices. Subsequent refits have consumed a great deal more money (the most recent, according to Treasury figures, worked out at £5 million). But any accountant who tried to assess the royal yacht in terms of profit and loss would be doomed to failure. It is an equation that simply cannot be calculated.

How, for example, do you estimate the effect on morale that a visit from the sovereign produces? How do you work out the effect on Britain's export trade of an overseas tour by the Queen? (No-one disputes the fact that it *does* have a beneficial effect.) How do you express the value of monarchy itself in financial terms? No matter how hard a critic of the royal yacht might try, the mathematics are impossible.

In any case, the alternative uses to which the royal yacht is put, or can be put, should be taken into consideration. For example, there was George VI's insistence that she must be a dual-purpose ship; in the event of a conventional war, it is theoretically possible to convert her into a hospital ship. There is evidence of this in her laundry, which is larger

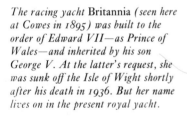

The racing yacht Britannia *(seen here at Cowes in 1895) was built to the order of Edward VII—as Prince of Wales—and inherited by his son George V. At the latter's request, she was sunk off the Isle of Wight shortly after his death in 1936. But her name lives on in the present royal yacht.*

than even a vessel of her status would require; but no bigger than a hospital ship would need. The after part, which is occupied by the royal household can, in fact, be quite quickly turned into a complex of wards and operating theatres able to accommodate 200 patients and 60 medical staff. Part of the verandah deck near the stern has been specially reinforced to serve as a landing platform for helicopters (though it has never been used for this purpose).

About one-third of *Britannia*'s year is spent on what is known as 'royal duty'. For the remainder, at the Queen's request, she is put at the disposal of the Admiralty for use in national and NATO exercises. She usually plays the role of a 'high value target', in other words, she represents the convoy-commodore's ship on which the enemy concentrates its attack.

Even when she is on royal duty, she sometimes fulfils yet another function known as 'sea days'. These take place when Her Majesty is on shore. Since they are arranged by the Department of Trade, they clearly have some commercial significance, subtle though it is. On these occasions, prominent businessmen are treated to a day at sea—usually attending a seminar during the morning, and watching a demonstration by the escorting warship in the afternoon.

During the Queen's visit to Italy and North Africa in 1980, *Britannia* carried out all three roles. On her way through the Mediterranean to Naples (the Queen and the Duke of Edinburgh flew to Italy), she took part in a NATO exercise code-named DISPLAY DETERMINATION. There was all the glamour of a state visit, and, while the royal couple was in Rome, Italian businessmen were treated to a sea day. The subject of the seminar was finance. During the naval demonstration in the afternoon, the more intrepid spirits were allowed to make the high-wire journey by breeches-buoy to the escorting warship and back. Afterwards the frigate's helicopter flew past, trailing the Italian flag.

The occasion was obviously a success. Some months later, it was reported that the City of London had gained business worth more than £260 million as a result of it. Among the deals was the financing of a £55 million hydro-electric project for Colombia.

A similar event took place at New York, when the Queen and Prince Philip visited the USA for the bicentennial celebrations in 1976. The then president, Giscard d'Estaing, of France may have felt that he was going one better than anyone else by making his arrival in Concorde. As things turned out, *Britannia* stole the show. This 23-year-old grande dame of the ocean, representing a form of passenger transport that had become outmoded by the jet age, delighted the Americans. There were, moreover, certain practical advantages. You cannot, after all, properly entertain 56 people to dinner within the slim fuselage of Concorde; nor can you possibly accommodate 250 at a reception.

Moreover, no aeroplane—no matter how well appointed—can ever be regarded as home. The duties of an overseas tour are extremely exhausting and the Queen, excellent though her health may be, is human. When the day is over, the babble of conversation hushed and the final words of polite admiration uttered, Her Majesty can retire to her apartment and relax. No hotel, no official residency, could provide such a facility. In a world that is alien despite its friendliness, *Britannia* supplies familiar surroundings—the peace only to be found in a place of one's own.

But this is not quite all. An airliner landing or taking off, supersonic though it be, is unremarkable. It has none of the magic of a fine ship coming into view and eventually edging her way gracefully alongside the quay. But even this palls before the spectacle of what has become the royal yacht's almost traditional method of departure when the Queen is on board.

The evening begins at about 8.30 pm, when the Queen returns her host's hospitality with a dinner party at which 56 people sit down at three tables in the yacht's dining room. Most of the guests are familiar with similar functions held at the British Embassy. It is the setting that makes an exciting change; just as the hostess has a kind of magic to which not even the most imposing ambassador can aspire. The menu, supervised by a chef from Buckingham Palace, will have received the sovereign's approval. Though written in French, the emphasis tends to be on English dishes, which are deceptively simple and depend upon the best quality raw ingredients. The music, provided by string orchestra (one of the several roles of the versatile 26 members of the Royal Marines band) will be undemanding; tuneful enough, but not likely to set up a barrier against conversation.

Afterwards, more guests arrive for a reception held either in the ante-room or, on a fine night, the verandah deck. Each is photographed as he or she comes aboard. The films are developed in the ship's dark room and everyone takes away a picture as a souvenir.

Towards the end of the evening, the band of the Royal Marines beats retreat—either on the quarter deck, or else on the quayside. Then, at about 11.30 pm, when all the guests have gone ashore, a floodlit *Britannia* moves gently from her berth and heads away into the night. Nobody who has seen it can ever forget the magnificence of the sight.

Such a spectacle cannot, by its nature last for long. Nevertheless, it might be accounted one of *Britannia*'s most important roles. The Queen and her family like to mix with ordinary people and to be seen by them.

The Silver Jubilee review of the fleet in 1977. Britannia, *an elegant splash of colour amid an assembly of warships, is followed in line astern by* HMS Birmingham *and the Royal Fleet Auxiliaries* Engadine *and* Lyoness. *On the foremast, the royal yacht flies the Queen's flag as Lord High Admiral and, on the main, she flies the royal standard.*

Before a visit to Australia the official in Canberra who was responsible for the arrangements, received a little tactful advice on the compilation of guest lists. Whilst he obviously had to include the appropriate local dignitaries, less illustrious Australians should also be invited.

In Nigeria, the Queen's concern for the wellbeing of the less privileged went to what some regarded as an extreme but others saw as an important gesture. During her travels, she visited a leper colony and gave encouragement to its inhabitants. As the settlement's supervisor said, 'The Queen's visit will do more to conquer man's fear and hate of the disease than any other single act I can think of.'

So far as the royal yacht is concerned, no more than 300 or so can go on board and enjoy the Queen's hospitality, but thousands can experience the magnificent showmanship (for that is what it really is) that attends her departure.

There is, of course, some small deception about it. Her Majesty is not really sailing for home. Unless the port is reasonably close to the UK (as in the case of the state visit to Norway that took place in the summer of 1981), she will eventually be taken to an airport for the return journey. *Britannia*, bereft of her owner, will steam back to home waters in her own time. The voyage is not always comfortable; after the state visit to Italy and North Africa in 1980, the journey took five days, each one of them attended by gale force winds.

'Considering her size,' one of her officers said, 'she is a very good seaboat. But she is only about 5,000 tons and you cannot expect her to be as steady as, say, a 50,000-ton merchant ship.' She is, of course, fitted with stabilisers, but they are of small avail against the worst excesses of a tempest.

◆

Britannia is a twin-screw, steam turbine-driven ship displacing 4,961 tons (5,769 tons gross). She is larger than a frigate; smaller than a guided missile destroyer. Her fuel capacity gives her a range of 1,776 miles (c2,850km) at a cruising speed of 20 knots. At 18 knots, she can travel 2,452 miles (c3,950km) without the need to replenish her bunkers. When on royal duty, she never exceeds 12 knots at night. To travel faster would be to create unacceptable vibrations in the area where the royal bedrooms are situated. This is no discredit to her; most ships are similarly affected. It is a problem to which neither naval architects nor marine engineers have been able to discover a solution.

The accommodation for the sovereign, her family, members of the household, and the staff from Buckingham Palace occupies about one third of the ship—roughly the space between the main and mizzen masts. Deep down, level with the engine room, there is a wine cellar and a strong room in which the royal jewels are safeguarded. Moving upwards, the lower and main decks are occupied by cabins and sitting-rooms for guests and for the thirty or so members of her staff that accompany the Queen on a royal tour. The royal apartments were decorated by Sir Hugh Casson, now President of the Royal Academy, who based his ideas on 'a restrained English country-house style'.

Understandably the Queen took a considerable interest in his work. Moving forward from the verandah deck, which overlooks the stern, there is a sun lounge with enormous windows, the ante-room (which might also be described as the drawing-room), and the royal dining room. The last of these also serves as a cinema; two 35 mm projectors are installed in the adjacent servery.

The rooms are comfortable, and Sir Hugh carried out his brief very well. If one were suddenly deposited in one of the world's more expensive hotels, that hotel's decor would give few clues to what country, let alone what town, one had arrived at: the colours, the pictures, the furnishings would be too cosmopolitan. In the royal yacht, there would be no such confusion. It is unmistakably British; slightly old fashioned—possibly— though, like good clothes, created in a style that never really dates. The many relics of *Victoria and Albert* that survive in the ship seem unremarkable, for one loses all sense of time. Even a small gimbal table in the ante-room, designed goodness how many years ago by Prince Albert in the not-altogether-sound belief that he could create a surface un-affected by a vessel's movement, does not appear out of place.

Now and then, however, one's eye catches sight of something that might seem to come from a museum: such as the tiny white ensign that Captain R F Scott flew from his sledge on his journey to the south pole, or two remarkably ornate silver-gilt vases, each shaped like an urn. One of them commemorates the victories of Admiral Collingwood, the other commemorates Trafalgar. Both were paid for by public subscription. As time went by, the vases passed into obscurity until, in the early days of the present century, one was discovered in a sale room, and the other turned up in a watchmaker's shop at Portsea. King Edward VII purchased them and restored them to more appropriate surroundings.

Another silver-gilt masterpiece in the ante-room portrays a camel standing in perpetual patience beneath two palm trees. A closer inspection shows that, with a praiseworthy attention to detail, the craftsman has placed dates on the trees—whilst an even closer look identifies the fruit as clusters of small rubies. It was a gift to the Queen during her tour of the Gulf States in 1979.

Two rugs, a large Persian carpet and various ornate daggers also recall this trip.

Her Majesty's sitting room, on the starboard side, is a small room decorated in quiet, pastel shades. The furnishings are nearly all relics of the voyage to South Africa in HMS *Vanguard*, though the light brackets and the ornate mirror above the fireplace are from the liner *Gothic*. The Queen's desk is in front of a window looking out across the deck.

Prince Philip's study is on the port side and has a more masculine style to it. 'Tobacco' might be a suitable word for the predominating colour scheme. His desk is set against a bulkhead on which a glass case containing a model of the frigate HMS *Magpie* (his last command) is mounted. When working, he can see a small head-and-shoulders colour photograph of the Queen wearing her crown. It was, presumably, taken on some state occasion. Next to it, and more functional, there is an un-pretentious calendar of a type to be found on a great many office desks, and an anglepoise lamp.

The Queen's interest in her yacht is not confined to matters of interior decoration. Ever since the first *Victoria and Albert* steamed on to the pages of history, the hulls of the royal yachts had always been black. The Board of Admiralty had proposed that *Britannia* should continue this custom. But Her Majesty had other ideas, and she eventually settled on a shade of blue that is, literally, unique. No other ship in the world is painted in an identical shade. She also insisted on the gold strip, which really is gold, that runs along either side.

Whilst the Queen is concerned with the aesthetics of her ship, Prince Philip takes a considerable interest in the technical details. Although *Britannia* was built according to merchant ship practice (her only weapon system was two saluting guns, which have since been removed), it was intended to use davits of the type employed by the Royal Navy for lowering boats. Prince Philip pointed out that they had to be swung outboard, and that those used by the merchant navy would suit the purpose better.

Like his uncle, the late Earl Mountbatten, the Duke of Edinburgh is fascinated by technical innovations. By no means infrequently, a cutting from some professional or technical journal is delivered to *Britannia* from the Palace with a note from Prince Philip's private secretary attached to it, asking 'Does the royal yacht have this facility? Is it worth investigating?'

The royal barge is now sixteen years old. In four—possibly five—years' time, it will be due for retirement. The Duke is already studying options for a replacement.

Britannia must be the easiest ship in the world to identify. There is not only her buff funnel but also her blue hull and her very distinctive shape. Another clue is provided by the fact that, unlike any other vessel, she does not display her name. There is no need: the royal crest on her bow and the royal cipher on her stern provide all the information that is needed.

There is also the matter of her masts. *Victoria and Albert* (II and III), had three of them and the practice is maintained. They certainly add to her elegance, though this is not the reason for them. They are needed to fly the appropriate flags. When the Queen is on board, her flag as Lord High Admiral (a yellow anchor on its side set against a red background) is worn on the foremast; her personal standard flies at the main; and the union flag on the mizzen. The White Ensign, in the manner of any other ship owned or administered by the Royal Navy (the Queen owns *Britannia;* the navy mans and moves her from place to place) is flown at her stern.

When the occasion demands it, the masts are also used for dressing ship. It is a matter of some pride that, at least once, 48 flags and pennants, reaching from her stem to her stern via the three mastheads, were arrayed in the incredibly short time of three seconds.

In 1959, *Britannia* took the Queen to Canada for the opening of the Saint Lawrence Seaway. Since on this and subsequent trips, it was necessary for the royal yacht to pass beneath a number of bridges, the top twenty feet (6m) of the main mast and the radio aerial on the foremast were hinged. These can now be lowered (*scandalised* is the Navy's way of

putting it). It is a device that served her well in 1976 when, after attending the bicentennial celebrations in the USA, *Britannia* steamed up the coast of Canada and up river to Montreal, where the Queen opened the XXI Olympics. She then travelled one thousand miles (1,600km) inland along the seaway to Lake Ontario, where the sailing events took place.

On the funnel deck, opposite the davits that hold the royal barge, there is a garage big enough to contain one of the Rolls-Royces. In fact, the garage is mostly used as a store; on the rare occasions when one of these cars is needed, it is usually flown to its destination overseas in an RAF Hercules transport.

———————————————◆———————————————

The Duke of Edinburgh is now the senior Admiral of the Fleet. As Lord High Admiral, however, the Queen outranks everyone else. When, for example, a review of the fleet takes place, she—in theory at any rate—is in command. To enable the proceedings to take place, the Flag Officer Royal Yachts must send a signal on her behalf to the fleet commander. The text of it is: 'Please continue to administer the Fleet.'

On a rather less elaborate level, the Queen is the only person who is piped aboard the royal yacht. At sea, she is the only member of the royal family entitled to an escort warship, usually a frigate or a destroyer. This is basically a fail-safe measure to provide a back-up in the unlikely event of *Britannia* breaking down, running aground or falling victim to some other disaster to which any vessel is vulnerable. In addition to this, however, the warship's helicopter assists communications (for example, by collecting the red dispatch boxes, which are then transferred by a line and pulleys). Her guns are used for firing any salutes that may be appropriate.

In fact, the Queen Mother is nearly always provided with an escort— though on a somewhat smaller scale (quite often a couple of inshore minesweepers). But this, one understands, is really a measure of the service's affection for her. Significantly when, during the week before the thanksgiving service to commemorate her 80th birthday, she visited the Cinque Ports, *Britannia* was on hand and, afterwards, brought her to the Pool of London. On the day of the service, officers from the royal yacht were among those who performed the duties of ushers.

Britannia is the only ship flying the white ensign to be commanded by an admiral. The Flag Officer Royal Yachts (as he is known) is still an active member of the service, though, during his term of duty, he is also a member of the household. Consequently, when the Queen is aboard, he spends most of his time at the after end, and, in common with other members of the household, takes his luncheon and dinner at the Queen's table. For this reason, and unlike any other vessel, the royal yacht numbers five commanders among her 21 officers. There is *the* Commander, who is in charge of administration, ceremonial and the ship's appearance, and who is the link between the yacht and the Queen's private secretary. The Navigating Commander is responsible for planning the ship's movements and making sure that *Britannia* and her escort arrive at the correct place on the correct day. There are also the Admiral's secretary—who carries out the duties of the supply officer as well; the Engineer Commander (whose engine room is so immaculately scrubbed and polished that it is hard to believe that, far from being a show place, it is the source of power upon which everything depends); and the medical officer. The last of these is a qualified anaesthetist. The Queen's personal doctor accompanies her as a member of the household.

Britannia preparing to dock at Prince George's wharf in Nassau, Bahamas. Since she came into service in 1964 she has circumnavigated the globe six times.

All the officers, with the exception of the Admiral and a lieutenant who is known as 'the Keeper and Steward' (assisted by 14 RN stewards, he is responsible to the Master of the Household for the royal apartments), serve on board for a period of two years—after which, they return to normal duties. The Flag Officer and the Keeper and Steward usually serve for five years, though, in the latter's case, it could be for longer. Since she was built, *Britannia* has had six commanding officers.

The 254 ratings on board when *Britannia* is employed on royal duty are known as 'yachtsmen'. They can easily be identified by the fact that they wear white arm-flashes on their uniforms instead of the usual red. They tuck their jumpers inside their trousers instead of wearing them outside; and, to perpetuate the mourning for Prince Albert, each has a small black silk bow stitched to the back of the waistband.

No orders are transmitted by loudspeaker when the Queen is on board; they are passed by word of mouth, or else pinned up on what is known as a 'red hot notice board'. Indeed, to make everything as quiet as possible, the yachtsmen go about their duties in white gymshoes. To reach the quarterdeck (the aftermost part of the ship that becomes active when entering or leaving harbour), they travel by an 'underground' route—thus avoiding the royal apartments. When one or another has to carry out some task on the verandah deck, the yachtsman concerned never wears his cap. This, technically, means that he is out of uniform. The idea is that, if the Queen is on deck, he will not have to salute her—and she will be spared the necessity of acknowledging it.

Yachtsmen serve on board for a probationary period of two years. About two-thirds of them remain permanently with the ship; some of them have been on the strength for a very long time. The present coxswain, for example, joined her as an AB when she was still under construction at John Brown's. Now he is a chief petty officer.

The snag about serving permanently on board is that promotion is apt to be slower than elsewhere in the service. Despite the importance of her role and the glamour of the ship, the crew receives no extra pay or leave; indeed, until the royal yacht underwent a refit in 1972, the yachtsmen might have been regarded as rather less privileged members of the Navy, for they still slept in hammocks. Nowadays, they are more comfortably accommodated—four to a cabin equipped with folding bunks.

At no time, however, are they allowed to forget the importance of good appearances. Outside every mess, there is a full-length mirror attached to the bulkhead. Before returning to duty, each must make a quick appraisal of his turn-out to make sure that it is smart.

This is not to suggest that life as a crewman on board the royal yacht is rigid to the point of never being able to relax. In the preface to a booklet about *Britannia*, Prince Philip referred to the longer serving yachtsmen as 'trusted friends'. He pointed out that, 'Life on board is not all polish and scrubbing and official entertainment, although it may well seem like it sometimes. There are times for sports and games, concert parties and crossing the line ceremonies to relieve the tension and to refresh the spirit.'

Since each Flag Officer Royal Yachts is an admiral, it might be imagined that he has become more accustomed to controlling the movements and tactics of large formations, rather than commanding a single ship. It may have been some time since he last practised the precise art of entering or leaving harbour and the more basic aspects of ship-handling. There are, of course, the five commanders to assist him; and, as somebody remarked, 'It's rather like riding a bicycle; you never really forget how to do it.' Nevertheless, after any long spell in harbour, *Britannia* puts in a couple of weeks at the Sea Training establishment at Portland. The crew are not only exercised in their more routine duties; a lot of time is spent on such matters as fire fighting, damage control, and other emergency work which reminds one that *Britannia* is no less vulnerable to the hazards of the sea than any other ship.

At sea, the Duke of Edinburgh and his two eldest sons appear fairly frequently on the bridge—showing the kind of interest one might expect

When the Queen visited the Scilly Islands, Lieutenant Commander T Dorrien Smith, owner of Tresco, acted as her host. The transport was modest, as becomes a small island. The horse's name was Socks.

from men who are, themselves, naval officers. The Queen seems to be less concerned about the finer points of navigation. Nor, in any case, can she spare it much time: she is too busy attending to the business of monarchy that follows her wherever she goes.

Planning an overseas tour usually begins at least one year in advance—more probably, two. The idea is that *Britannia* shall arrive at her destination five days ahead of the sovereign, who will no doubt make the journey by air. This gives time in which to spruce up the ship after her sea voyage and make preparations for the ceremonial. It also enables the yachtsmen to enjoy a little shore leave and go sight-seeing.

As, like any other ship, *Britannia* has her limitation, the Navigating Commander has to take this into consideration when planning her movements. For example, when making arrangements for the royal visit to Australia in 1981, he had to advise on whether to travel eastwards via Suez or westwards through the Panama Canal and across the Pacific. Prevailing climates (political as well as meteorological) obviously had some say in the matter. But there was, to a no lesser extent, the question of fuel. If *Britannia* were to cross the Pacific, she would have to rendezvous with a fleet auxiliary tanker and replenish her bunkers in mid-ocean.

On one of these occasions, in the area of Pitcairn Island, a fire broke out in the tanker's engine room. As a result, she was immobilised, and the royal yacht had to take her in tow to Tahiti—1,300 miles (2,100km) away.

Britannia has performed two other rescue missions, though neither of them quite so spectacular. When crossing the Atlantic, one of the radio operators picked up a distress call from a merchant ship. The master, he was told, had suffered a stroke. The patient was brought on board and accommodated in the hospital for the remainder of the voyage.

The other occasion was on a journey in the Far East, when a seaman from a container ship was treated for an acute appendicitis.

So far as food is concerned, the Palace attends to the finer details (which include a supply of Earl Grey's tea to which Her Majesty is partial), but *Britannia*'s supply officer is responsible for the bulk purchasing of the more basic requirements. The ship has a very large cold store, which makes it possible to lay in sufficient food to last for several weeks. It also assists in the floral decorations in the royal apartments. Although they are sometimes augmented by blooms from the host country, the majority of the flowers come from the royal gardens at Windsor.

Another essential for royal duty is a large stock of Malvern water. A palace press officer has remarked that, 'The Queen is a remarkably unpernickety person. There are very few things she doesn't like.' She does, however, refuse shell fish on these trips—just as she relies on the Malvern water rather than on local supplies. This is for the sensible reason that, though it may be permissible, if regrettable, for a tourist to succumb to 'gippy tummy' on holiday, for the Queen to fall ill on an overseas tour would be a major disaster, causing a great deal of disappointment to others, and wrecking intricate and carefully devised arrangements.

Unlike any of her subjects—and this includes her immediate family —the Queen does not require a passport when she goes abroad. She does, however, have to pay duty on any purchases she has made, though official gifts are exempted. Predictably, she receives a great many. Since she has four houses and the royal yacht—which is almost a fifth house—there is no problem about accommodating them. Occasionally an item of particular ethnic interest is loaned to a museum—for example, a dug-out canoe to the National Maritime Museum at Greenwich.

The presents received on her tour of the Gulf States have been described as 'fabulous'. 'On the whole,' said the palace spokesman, 'the gifts the Queen receives are rather nice things. People take enormous trouble to find out what she'd like. Sometimes they are marvellous examples of a country's specialist crafts.'

◆

Her Majesty does not give interviews to the press. The role of a constitutional monarch would, in any case, make the business of answering pointed questions almost impossible. Inevitably, there is immense curiosity about her life, even to the most trivial details. Magazines, in particular, have an insatiable appetite for such things, and 'a friend of the Queen told me' has become a common-place of journalism.

No matter how industrious a journalist may be in her or his research, mistakes are bound to occur in reportage that owes a good deal to hearsay. There was, for example, one story that gained popular currency that, if you were a woman who did not wish to arouse the Queen's displeasure, you would never wear magenta in her presence. In fact, a more accurate source has described Queen Elizabeth II as 'a remarkably down-to-earth, unfaddy, person'. She usually wears lightish, brightish colours for the sensible reason that she can be seen more easily in them. She hardly ever wears black except when in mourning, though she sometimes wears navy blue; and, in Paris, she created a sensation by appearing in a brown coat and hat (why this should have created a sensation is not easily apparent). She, herself, does not favour magenta, and would not commend it to her dressmaker. But this is no reason why anyone else need eschew it.

A writer once remarked that King George V's racing cutter Britannia *was 'the undisputed Queen of Cowes Roads'. Something similar may be said of her magnificently-arrayed namesake, whose presence at Cowes Week is as near obligatory as anything to do with royalty can be.*

Similarly, it has been written that 'The Queen is a bad sailor'. In fact, she fares no worse than most people at the hands of a rough sea. During at least two of the annual cruises to the Western Isles, the weather was abominable. On one of them, the string orchestra from the band of the Royal Marines was so ill, that it seemed doubtful whether its members would be fit enough to play at dinner that night. The Queen was aware of their discomfort—to the point of congratulating them on their recoveries when, albeit still a little green about the gills, they rendered the evening's repertoire with adequate gusto.

In fact, and despite the climatic snags, the royal family thoroughly enjoys these trips and so, too, do the islanders. How, otherwise, would the inhabitants of such remote places as Stornoway, or that minute particle of land named Islay (dedicated though it is to the praiseworthy cause of producing fine single-malt whisky) be able to catch a glimpse of their sovereign?

At the conclusion of these holiday voyages, it is customary for *Britannia*'s officers to invite members of the royal party to dine with them in the wardroom. It is also customary for their guests to present signed photographs which are framed and hung on the walls. The collection includes what is probably the best picture ever taken of Princess Anne (by Lord Snowdon) and one of Princess Margaret who, on her last visit, felt that it might well be replaced by a better likeness.

Relics of *Victoria and Albert* abound in the officers' quarters. Much of the wardroom's silver comes from previous royal yachts. The lamp fittings are from *Victoria and Albert* (III), and there is a silver gilt Russian punch bowl that was presented by a grateful czarina of Russia after a Mediterranean cruise in 1909.

But perhaps the nicest touch is more modern: a small wooden monkey that can usually be found hanging from a bracket. It was acquired during a state visit to Copenhagen in 1957. According to a small guide book that assists the officers when they show visitors round the ship, or when (as they often do) they act as hosts at official receptions, 'He is moved daily and gets cross if he is neglected.' Sure enough, he is never to be found in the same place two days running.

◆

A critic of *Britannia* has asserted that 'the Royal Yacht is an anachronism'. If this is true, then the same must be said of monarchy, for the ship is an essential part of it. It might even be argued that the sovereign would be diminished without her. What, precisely, it all amounts to can no more be defined than it can be equated in cash value. A stranger to this planet might find it strange that so much effort and equipment is devoted to the conveyance of a middle-aged woman, who cannot make laws nor dispense justice, and who has no special skills except that of being royal (which would be incomprehensible to the visitor).

When the stranger knew more about the matter, and discovered that this . . . this whatever-it-is can somehow be appreciated and indeed is applauded—not only by the Queen's own subjects, but also by people all over the world—then mystification would be complete.

The stranger's only hope would be to learn the meaning of the word 'magic'. Magic takes many forms, and by no means the least is the sight of the floodlit *Britannia* departing into the night, with the small figure of the Queen waving from the verandah deck, and the cheering of goodness knows how many people ashore. Then, simply by being there, the stranger would understand; and yet still be unable to rationalise it, any more than I can explain it here. The ingredients are obvious enough; the strange chemistry they produce when put together defies explanation.

The first chapter of this book described some royal progresses that took place before Queen Victoria came to the throne. They showed a fawning, venal, often devious collection of subjects—ready to give their sovereign more or less anything that he or she wanted. There was only one thing that, in many cases, they withheld: love.

Similarly, the monarch accepted as a kind of divine right all that was given, and sometimes took more than anyone wanted to give. The miracle, perhaps, is that the throne survived.

Certainly in the nineteenth century, there were several sovereigns whose crowns sat insecurely upon their heads, and some who had good reason for such misgivings. But the crunch came after World War 1. The Kaiser of Germany departed in haste for exile in Holland; the Tsar of Russia and his family had been murdered by the revolutionaries; Franz Joseph had been fortunate enough to pass away without having to witness the dismemberment of the Austro-Hungarian empire. Britain was one of the few European powers that still had a monarch; a king who, far from being reduced by the years of war, was now more popular than ever.

Somehow—subtly, perhaps—British royalty has managed to adapt its style to the times. By travelling more widely, the Queen has come closer to her people, though the barrier remains. She will never, one suspects, step across it. It is, conceivably, just as well. Familiarity, apart from anything else, destroys magic; or, to put it another way, without an element of mystery, magic cannot exist. In *Delight*, J B Priestley wrote (of actors), 'They did not belong to our world and never for a moment pretended to belong to it.' That was what was so fascinating about them.

Queen Elizabeth II is more evidently part of our world, and yet not too much a part of it. *Britannia* is one substantial item of the evidence in this respect. The popularity of royal tours is immense. One has only to see all those cheering people to know that—certainly so far as Britain and the Commonwealth are concerned—royalty cannot be an anachronism. And nor, come to that, can the royal yacht.

SELECT BIBLIOGRAPHY

Balfour, Michael, *The Kaiser and His Times*, Cresset Press, London, 1964.

Barker, Ralph, *Great Mysteries of the Air*, Chatto & Windus, London, 1966.

Birch, Neville and Bramson, Alan, *Captains and Kings*, Pitman, London, 1972.

Boothroyd, John Basil, *Philip—An Informal Biography*, Longman, London, 1971.

Brooke, John, *King George III*, Constable, London, 1972.

Brooke-Little, John, *The British Monarchy*, Blandford Press, Poole, 1976.

Cookridge, E H, *The Orient Express*, Allen Lane, London, 1979.

Crabtree, Reginald, *Royal Yachts of Europe*, David & Charles, Newton Abbot, 1975.

Edward VIII, King, *see* Windsor, Duke of.

Ellis, Cuthbert Hamilton, *The Royal Trains*, Routledge & Kegan Paul, London, 1975.

Eyton, R W, *Court, Household and Itinerary of King Henry II*, London, 1878.

Fraser, Antonia, *King Charles II*, Weidenfeld & Nicolson, London, 1979.

Garrett, Richard, *Motoring and the Mighty*, Stanley Paul, London, 1971.

Gavin, Charles Murray, *Royal Yachts*, Rich & Cowan, London, 1932.

Grigsby, Joan Evelyn, *Annals of our Royal Yachts, 1604–1953*, Adlard Coles; Harrap, London, 1953.

Hatton, Ragnhild, *George I*, Thames & Hudson, London, 1978

Holden, Anthony, *Charles, Prince of Wales*, Weidenfeld & Nicolson, London, 1979.

Hough, Richard, *First Sea Lord*, Allen & Unwin, London, 1969.

Lacey, Robert, *Majesty*, Hutchinson, London, 1977.

Longford, Elizabeth, *Victoria RI*, Weidenfeld & Nicolson, London, 1964.

Magnus, Sir Philip Montefiore, *King Edward the Seventh*, John Murray, London, 1964.

Massie, Robert K, *Nicholas and Alexandra*, Victor Gollancz, London, 1968.

Maxtone-Graham, John, *The North Atlantic Run*, Cassell, London, 1972.

Montagu of Beaulieu, Lord, *Royalty on the Road*, Collins, London, 1980.

Morris, James Humphrey, *Pax Britannica*, Faber & Faber, London, 1968.

Nichols, John, *The Progresses and Public Processions of Queen Elizabeth* Vols I, II and III, London, 1823.

Nichols, John, *The Progresses, Processions & Magnificent Festivities of King James I* (4 Vols), London, 1828.

Nicolson, Harold, *King George V*, Constable, London, 1952.

Ollard, Richard, *The Escape of Charles II*, Hodder & Stoughton, London, 1966.

Page, Martin, *The Lost Treasures of the Great Trains*, Weidenfeld & Nicolson, London, 1975.
Paget, Sir Julian, *The Pageantry of Britain*, Michael Joseph, London, 1979.
Quennell, Peter (ed), *Memoirs of William Hickey*, Hutchinson, London, 1960.
Rogers, Colonel Hugh CB, *Troopships and their History*, Seeley Service, London, 1963.
Smith, Cecil Woodham, *Queen Victoria*, Hamilton, London, 1972.
Turner, Ernest Sackville, *The Court of St. James's*, Michael Joseph, London, 1959.
Wheeler-Bennett, Sir John Wheeler, *King George VI*, Macmillan, London; St Martin's Press N.Y. 1958.
Windsor, Duke of, *A King's Story*, Cassell, London, 1951.

INDEX